Technological Competition
in
Global Industries

TECHNOLOGICAL COMPETITION
IN
GLOBAL INDUSTRIES

Marketing and Planning Strategies for American Industry

David T. Methé

QUORUM BOOKS
New York • Westport, Connecticut • London

Library of Congress Cataloging-in-Publication Data

Methé, David T.
   Technological competition in global industries : marketing and
planning strategies for American industry / David T. Methé.
    p. cm.
   Includes bibliographical references and index.
   ISBN 0-89930-480-X (lib. bdg. : alk. paper)
   1. International business enterprises—Management.
2. Corporations, American—Management. 3. High technology
industries—Management. 4. Technological innovations.
5. Competition, International.   I. Title.
HD62.37.M48 1991
620'.0068—dc20   90-8908

British Library Cataloguing in Publication Data is available.

Library of Congress Catalog Card Number: 90-8908
ISBN: 0-89930-480-X

First published in 1991

Quorum Books, 88 Post Road West, Westport, CT 06881
An imprint of Greenwood Publishing Group, Inc.

Printed in the United States of America

The paper used in this book complies with the
Permanent Paper Standard issued by the National
Information Standards Organization (Z39.48-1984).

10 9 8 7 6 5 4 3 2 1

To my parents,
Paul and Wanda;
my brothers and sisters
Mark, Brian, Janice and Barbara
for their unwavering encouragement.
And for Tai and Mya
who continue to enrich my life.

Contents

Tables and Figures

Tables

Figures

Preface

A combination of record trade deficits, slumping productivity, and increasing awareness of the innovative capabilities of our economic partners has fueled concern over the international competitiveness of industry in the United States. Widespread debate has arisen about the causes of and remedies for these trends. The focus of this book is upon the interaction between the diffusion of technological innovations, firm strategy, and public policy. The central thesis is that there are reciprocal relationships between the characteristics of technological innovations, a firm's strategic approach to technology, and public policy. Technology, the firm's technology strategy, and public policy are linked to one another through their influence on the informational and financial resources needed for innovation.

Four research lessons are derived from previous work on the technology-strategy-environment interaction. These lessons are reviewed in the context of the Japanese and U.S. DRAM integrated circuit industries. Information on these industries and the firms' strategies and public policies has been gathered through interviews with key people in the Japanese and U.S. governments and industries. This information is used to provide insights into the lessons.

The central thesis is supported: reciprocal relationships exist between technological innovations, firm technology strategy, and public policy. The four research lessons also receive support. Technological innovations in the DRAM industry are shown to develop along defined paths, called technology innovation envelopes. To progress along these innovation envelopes requires more informational and financial resources in order to maintain the innovation process. This innovation imperative alters the competitive conditions of the industry. Changes in market structures result that affect the supply and demand of these required resources. The strategic approaches that firms adopt when confronting this technological innovation imperative affect their ability to continue to innovate and therefore remain viable competitors in the industry. Firms in the United States and Japan which adopt strategic approaches that are innovative, broad-based and vertically integrated are better able to acquire the resources necessary to continue the innovation process. Public policy instruments that alter both the informational and financial resources are found to affect the innovation process while policies that affect only one of the resources are found to have no effect. Various public policies are examined, including the VLSI Cooperative Research Project for Japan, and the Sematech initiative and changes in the capital gains tax for the United States.

The research for this book was begun in 1985. I would like to gratefully acknowledge Mr. J. Warren McClure for his support, provided through a research fellowship, during a two-year period from 1987 to 1989. I am deeply appreciative of the support given to me during my field stays in Japan by the Nomura Research Institute. Their help not only made my research in Japan successful, but also pleasant. I would also like to thank the Rochester Institute of Technology for providing me the opportunity to work on this project. While each of these organizations, and numerous people in them were of immeasurable assistance in the research and writing of this book, I alone am responsible for the opinions expressed in it.

I would also like to add a personal note of thanks to Don Wilson, who as a colleague provided insights and guidance and who as a friend helped me to keep my sense of humor and perspective on this task. Also to Mrs. Ock Hee Hale and her husband Robert and their children Michael and Yvette for allowing me to intrude upon their family life. These intrusions allowed me the time to recuperate, regroup and complete this task.

Technological Competition
in
Global Industries

1

Japan, Strategic Management and Technological Innovation

OVERVIEW

Japan's status as an economic superpower is undisputed. It ranks second only to the United States in terms of Gross National Product. It is first in terms of GNP per capita and wealth. Japan's position in the world financial and banking communities is in transition from being an important participant to being the dominant player. It is becoming a cliché to cite the litany of industries which were once dominated by U.S. firms and are now dominated by the Japanese. It is not a cliché, however, to note that the dominance of Japanese firms is increasing in the very industries which were supposed to be immune to Japan: our high technology industries. This increasing dominance is calling into question the notion of the unchallengable supremacy of American business's creativity and innovation.

Why have Japan and Japanese companies become so successful? Are the Japanese going to dominate the high technology industries in the same way they now dominate other industries? Are the Japanese more original and innovative in their approach to product development and meeting market needs? Where are Japanese companies going in the future and by what means? How these questions are answered is critical to determining the response by American companies.

Many explanations have been offered for Japan's economic ascendence. These explanations relied first upon wage differentials, then upon the fact that the Japanese worked longer hours. During the early 1970s the Japanese were termed "economic animals." Another explanation relies on the role of the Japanese government, especially the Ministry of International Trade and Industry (MITI). MITI is seen by some scholars as the mastermind behind the increasing dominance of Japanese companies. Differences in culture have also been used to explain Japan's rise. Somehow the Japanese were more attuned to cooperation and this combined with MITI guidance resulted in "Japan, Inc."

Recent research has been aimed at examining the systemic and structural differences in Japan's economic, social, and political make-up to explain the nation's success. The multilayered and complex distribution system, hiring practices and the *keiretsu* or business groups have now become the focal point of scholars and government trade negotiators alike. All of these explanations have merits and drawbacks. Most likely, some subtle interplay of many cultural, governmental, and systemic factors is at work in contributing to Japan's economic rise. What is a fact is that Japan's economy is a dynamic, evolving one, and Japanese companies must compete in it. It is also a fact that Japanese companies are becoming the leaders in many industries.

All of these explanations offer little help to us in understanding how Japan is making the transition from being a technological follower to a technological leader, especially in high technology industries. This is particularly the case if our perspective shifts from Japan, the nation, to the role of Japanese companies. It is the purpose of this book to examine Japan's rise from that perspective. In the process, some of the previous explanations may be examined indirectly. However, it is not the purpose of this book to examine or evaluate these explanations. Although such an undertaking is needed, the purpose of this book is much less ambitious. It is to focus attention on an area that should receive more scholarly interest: the strategic use of technology by Japanese firms in their rise to market dominance. By examining this area, it is hoped that the role one important set of actors, the companies, are playing in Japan's transition from technological follower to leader can be better understood. This new understanding will then be used to shed light on where Japanese companies are going in terms of their technological development.

The focus of this book will be on technological strategy and how it can be used by companies to compete effectively. In examining this area, it will be important to also define technology, technological change and the interaction of this change with an industry's evolution. In order to set us on this path let us begin by examining the importance of technology to the United States and some of the problems that current management and economic theories have with explaining technological change.

IMPORTANCE OF TECHNOLOGICAL INNOVATION

Technological innovation as a wellspring of economic growth is well-documented by scholars (Mensch, 1979; Rosenberg, 1976; Solow, 1954;

Schumpeter, 1936). It is held as particularly important in the United States, where innovation is seen by some economists as the only way to maintain economic vitality. It is argued by many scholars that since the United States is a high labor cost and a high capital cost economy, it will begin to lose its comparative advantage in an industry as the technology of that industry matures. In order to maintain both its high standard of living and its position in the world economy, the United States must continue to innovate (Lundstedt and Colglazier, 1982; Abernathy, Clark, Kantrow, 1983).

While the importance of innovation is recognized, the process of innovation and the factors which affect it are little understood. Many current economic and management theories were developed to explore and explain issues of allocational efficiency for labor and capital in a static and comparative static approach. These approaches to economics and management have tended to shift the focus of attention away from technology and technological change. This has resulted in deficiencies in how we view technology.

The inadequacies of the current economic and management framework for the study of innovation are threefold. First, the research done on innovation using this framework fails to recognize that innovation is not a single activity, but an intricate process which occurs at many different technological levels. Second, many current approaches work well in explaining competition based on static allocational efficiency criteria, but are less effective in explaining competition based on dynamic efficiency emanating from technological innovation. As a result, research undertaken often is cross-sectional and technological change is viewed as exogenous. Finally, notions of technology used by previous studies have been inadequate in capturing all the dimensions of technology. Technology has been seen mainly as changes in machinery and capital equipment which result in the substitution of capital for labor. It has not been seen as a knowledge base from which new products and manufacturing processes spring. Changes in the knowledge base have not been viewed as both the source of creation and the source of destruction of industries.

The impact of technology and more importantly of technological change on the management of organizations has also been, until recently, largely ignored. Technological change has been seen as flowing orderly from corporate laboratories or fostered by pathsetting entrepreneurs. Balancing the quixotic elements in the innovation process with the need for sustained and ordered approaches to finance the manufacture and marketing of new products has not been well understood (Betz, 1987). This lack of understanding has been singled out as one of the most important reasons for our waning competitiveness in international markets (Hayes and Abernathy, 1980).

This lack of understanding is also acutely felt by policymakers now that the United States is faced with challenges from abroad. Many reports have been written on the innovation process and the effects of both business and government policies upon it (U.S. Congressional Budget Office, 1983; U.S. General Accounting Office, 1982; Defense Science Board, 1987). They raise questions of not only what policy instruments, tax credits, procurement systems and the like are appropriate, but where in the innovation process they should be applied. Does the United States lead in the generation of ideas, but falter in their development? Is the United States efficient in diffusing an idea throughout an industry while maintaining competition within that industry? These questions are doubly critical because of the implications they hold for the United States as it confronts the major economic transition now occurring. Answers to these questions are doubly confounded by the use of inadequate analytical frameworks. We require a more sophisticated definition of technology, and a more sophisticated understanding of technological innovation and the stages of the innovation process.

It is evident that technology plays a vital role in the growth of a nation's economy. It is also evident that our understanding of technology and the frameworks used to analyze it is lacking. The frameworks that will be used in this book will offer a better understanding of technology. Before describing these frameworks, however, the definition of technology utilized by them will be discussed.

DEFINITION OF TECHNOLOGY

Technology may be defined as the process by which a stock of knowledge is used to reduce the uncertainty in achieving some desired end. It represents what is often called the "state-of-the-art" in a particular field—the set of commonly accepted rules, procedures and theories concerning some subject area that can be invoked to solve a specific set of problems for a particular group of people. Technology, then, is a process for creating solutions to problems. No distinction is made at this time between "high technology" and "low" or "mature" technology. This distinction will become important, however, in discussing knowledge generation.

Often associated with the concept of technology is the idea of tool use and toolmaking. The knowledge base is what is drawn upon to make the tools. It also provides the rules and procedures for the proper use of the tools. The more complete the knowledge base, the greater the probability that a proper tool will be developed and used in the most effective manner to meet a need. Technology is most properly and most simply thought of as a set of tools, and rules to make and use these tools to solve problems. This follows closely the thinking of Rogers (1983) in discussing the composition of a technology as both physical/material and knowledge/concept. It extends Roger's thoughts, though, in that technology is viewed as two stocks, one being a stock of knowledge, and the other a stock of tools. These tools can be viewed, from an economic perspective, as a stock of capital. The stock of knowledge, from that same economic perspective, can be viewed as a stock of scientists and engineers.

Knowledge Generation: The Importance of Scientific Technology

Beginning in the early 1900s, with the establishment of the first research and development centers associated with business companies, a process has been put into motion which has changed the development of technology. Prior to that time, technological knowledge bases were often generated and expanded through the "trial and error" efforts of class of people called "inventors." This method of "know-how" development still goes on today. But the generation of modern technological knowledge bases relies on something more.

The generation of modern technological knowledge bases has become closely intertwined with another activity carried on by contemporary societies, that of science (Betz, 1987). Science is concerned with establishing and expanding knowledge bases. As it is carried out today, particularly in Western societies, it is not concerned with whether the knowledge it adds has any immediate practical value. That it adds knowledge is value enough.

Science has given to modern technology two elements of immense importance. The first is expanded knowledge bases from which to draw upon for answers to practical problems. The second is methodology for solving problems, the process of theory-guided hypothesis testing known as the scientific method. This has resulted in a new form of technology, unique to the modern age, which has been called "scientific technology" (Betz, 1987).

This phenomenon has been related by Phillips (1971) to the degree of technological opportunity that exists in an industry. Technological opportunity is described as the extent to which the industry is science-driven: the more sensitive the industry technology is to developments in science, the higher the industry's technological opportunity (Phillips, 1971; Nelson and Winter, 1982). It is the degree of technological opportunity, that is, how scientific the technology is, that draws the distinction between "high technology" and "low technology."

This distinction lies fundamentally in the knowledge bases. High technology industries are tightly coupled to their scientific knowledge base. Changes in the knowledge base are rapidly transmitted to the industry, thus increasing the degree of technological opportunity. This important relationship between science and technology is critical to understanding the manner in which technological knowledge bases change. Industries with high technological opportunity require some form of systematic mining of the knowledge base. In modern organizations this systematic approach to developing and exploring the scientific knowledge base of a technology is commonly referred to as research and development.

Technology has been defined as composed of a stock of knowledge and a stock of capital. It has been shown that the stock of knowledge is becoming increasingly important because the technical know-how base has become more closely coupled to the scientific knowledge base, resulting in what has been called "scientific technology." In order to understand how scientific technology can be used by companies to compete, the way that technology changes must be described.

TECHNOLOGICAL CHANGE: THE INVENTION-INNOVATION INTERLINK

Changes in a technology knowledge base are often embodied in a probabilistic event called an invention. Changes in a scientific knowledge base occur with the discovery of new fundamental relationships or laws of nature. All discoveries enhance the probability of invention, however, not all of these discoveries result in inventions, and there can often be a long lag between the new discovery and its embodiment in an invention. It is the discoveries which do become embodied in inventions that are important to business, because a portion of these will become products. Invention can spring from research, but it need not necessarily do so. Sources of invention will be discussed in another section of this chapter. First, the difference between invention and innovation must be examined.

Joseph Schumpeter has distinguished between invention and innovation (Schumpeter, 1936). Invention is characterized as the creation of a new concept or machine. Innovation is the putting to use of that invention in society. When an invention is commercialized, then it is called an innovation. This distinction implies a process by which an invention becomes an innovation. While the relationship between these two phenomena will be described in greater detail in another section, it is important to note two issues here. First, the process by which an invention becomes an innovation is characterized by a series of states or stages. The probability that the invention will progress from one state to the next is dependent upon the stock of knowledge and capital available. Second, inventions embody potential for changing the technology. These potentials for change actually exist on a continuum ranging from small to large. For ease of discussion, this continuum will be categorized into three types of potential change. These will be examined here.

There are three types of invention. These correspond to the potential for change they present to a knowledge base. The first is a radical change in a technology. This holds the greatest potential for change because it can fundamentally alter the knowledge base used to design, manufacture, and use a set of tools. Recent examples of this were the development of the transistor in the late 1940s and recombinant DNA in the mid-1970s. This is the type of change that results in a new technology supplanting an existing technology (Foster, 1989). The corresponding radical innovation will often result in the emergence of a new industry.

The second type of invention occurs within an established knowledge base, but brings about a major improvement through the introduction of a new tool or the substantial improvement in the processing technology of an existing one—for example, the replacement of the 16-bit microprocessor with the 32-bit microprocessor or the replacement of the open hearth furnace by the basic oxygen furnace. This type of potential change may be recognized as a progression within a technological knowledge base, rather than a replacement of it. The resulting major innovations are new classes of products which may help to launch new firms in an already established industry.

The third type of invention corresponds to improvement in an existing product through minor or incremental changes in the processing or design technologies. An example is a 32-bit microprocessor which can process its information faster or uses less power than another 32-bit microprocessor model. This results in the type of incremental innovation which improves one company's product to such an extent that it can over take other company's products in terms of market share. This is also the type of innovation most closely associated with the learning curve phenomenon.

One more distinction must be noted. There is a difference recognized by many scholars between the invention and innovation of a product and the invention and innovation of a process. Quite simply, inventions in products result in either improvements in existing products or new products. These improvements are usually seen in the functions that the existing product can do that it could not do before or in the new applications that a new product may fulfill. Process inventions are improvements in the way existing products are being produced or the development of new ways of producing new products. Consequently, inventions in products and processes are often interrelated. The importance of this relationship has been discussed elsewhere (Abernathy and Utterback, 1982). The various qualities of this relationship need to be explored further.

The primary focus of this book will be on the innovation portion of the invention-innovation link. Emphasis will be placed more on how inventions become innovations, rather than on how and why inventions are stimulated and brought into existence. Further, the second type of innovation, the major innovation, will be examined. While the description offered below is applicable to all three types of inventions-innovations, it fits most closely the major invention-innovation type. Also, invention-innovation in both products and process will be examined.

From the above, it should be clear that it is through invention that technology knowledge base changes can effect industrial environments.

The impact of inventions can be large or small, depending on how much they change the knowledge base of a technology. For a company, however, invention is only part of the process. The invention must be brought to market. This is called innovation. It is to this process that our attention must now focus.

DESCRIPTION OF THE INNOVATION PROCESS

Innovation resulting in a major product change is a complicated activity which begins with the recognition of a problem and the conception of an idea as a possible solution to that problem, continues through the actual utilization of the idea in the solution of the problem, and finalizes with the adoption of that idea as the predominant mode of solution to that problem (Lundstedt and Colglazier, 1982). As noted above, the process by which an invention becomes an innovation can be characterized by a series of stages, each with a probability associated with it and each incorporating a variety of activities which are designed to combine the stocks of knowledge and capital in such a way as to maximize the probability of innovation.

Many of these activities, such as research and development, have become synonymous with innovation, but they are different. In many cases they make up essential activities in the innovation process and in others, such as invention and diffusion, they are conceptually different from the act of innovating, but are still a part of the innovation process. It should be remembered that innovation, the act of commercializing the invention, is only one stage in the innovation process.

The Innovation Process and Research and Development

The innovation process can be likened to a flow, but it is a complicated flow with many sources, eddies, and backwaters. Invention is the starting point of the innovation process. The research and development process can play an important role in invention since research provides a source of knowledge for the invention. When this type of invention occurs, it is often referred to as a technology push invention, which results in a technology push innovation. Many sources of invention lay outside the formal research process. These arise out of some need in the market. When these types of invention occur, they are called market pull inventions. But even in this type of invention, research is crucial for converting the invention into a commercially successful innovation. Research is also important because it is an attempt by organizations to rationalize and systematize the innovation process in order to make it more predictable; that is, to make known the probabilities of moving from one stage to the next.

In a study of the research and development process, the National Science

Foundation has provided a concise set of definitions for the stages of re search. It defines the stages as basic research, applied research, and development (U.S. National Science Foundation, 1972, p. 19). Basic research is described as original investigations for the advancement of scientific knowledge which do not have specific commercial objectives. Applied research consists of investigations directed to the discovery of new scientific knowledge having commercial objectives. Development relates to the technical activities of a non-routine nature concerned with translating research findings or other scientific knowledge in products or processes. While these definitions are adequate, one modification is made for this book. Applied research is not only concerned with the discovery of new knowledge for commercial use, but also the application for commercial use of knowledge already discovered in the basic research stage. As such, applied research is concerned with invention and the early portion of the innovation process.

Applied and developmental research, because of the commercial objectives related to them, are affected by the market pull forces of invention. Applied and especially developmental research may be initiated and guided by these market pull forces. This extends the research and development process beyond the stages described above by incorporating stages concerned with the commercial application of products and processes. The commercial application stage has been further refined by the more recent work of Abernathy and Utterback (1982). They have divided the stage into the commercial introduction of a new product or process, and the diffusion of the new product or process throughout an industry.

A graphic representation of the innovation process is presented in Figure 1.1. This representation combines the notions of invention, innovation and diffusion of the economists and management theorists with the definitions of the research stages and compares them against the broader concept of the difference between science and technology and production. All three activities are concerned with some aspect of knowledge. Science is the process most generally concerned with generating new knowledge through the discovery of fundamental laws of nature. Technology is the process most generally concerned with the application of knowledge to meet certain needs or solve specific problems. Production is most generally concerned with refining the solutions generated in technology so that the knowledge can be applied most efficiently.

Relationship Between Knowledge and Research

This model may appear complex, but it is actually simplified in that it ignores feedback loops which are more characteristic of the actual innovation process. Beyond this, the point of demarcation between science,

Figure 1.1
Comparison of Research/Development/Invention/Innovation Continuum with Management Challenges and Research Strategy Foci in the Innovation Process

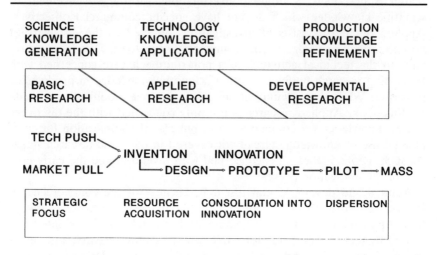

technology and production in the model, and the relationship between these and the research activities, need to be discussed. Some science is carried out in the applied research stage and some production is commenced in the development stage, especially with the use of prototype facilities. Still, the demarcation is important, since this is a study of changes in technology, not science.

Many concepts are thought out in scientific form long before they can take physical form. Consequently, a crucial boundary is drawn between what is conceived of conceptually and what can be worked on materially. An example from history is the work of Leonardo da Vinci. Many of his machines were theoretically possible, that is, the science and mathematics existed to support them; but the engineering or technological component necessary to materialize them did not. His design for a helicopter is a case in point. Thus, the crucial difference between the initial conditions necessary for the introduction of a radically new technology and the conditions necessary for innovation within that technology must be recognized. The case of da Vinci also illustrates that not only are there lags between invention and innovation, but also between the discovery of fundamental aeronautical principles and their embodiment in an invention.

The model also recognizes that the research focus of firms differs. In industrial areas where the basic understanding of physical phenomena is necessary before commercial products can be brought about, the research focus is on science. Biotechnology is such an area. As the knowledge of the industrial area increases, the research focus shifts towards technology and finally into production engineering.

Transitions in the Innovation Process

It should also be noted that the act of innovation has been distinguished from both science and invention, which are seen as its sources, and from the diffusion stage. This distinction is in line with those made by Schumpeter and other economists. As noted above, this model goes beyond prior observations and makes a distinction between the act of innovating and the innovation process itself. The act of innovating may spring from market pull invention or it may use scientific discovery, but it is neither of these. It is the process by which the invention is designed to meet some anticipated need, and is developed through a working prototype, pilot manufacturing, and, finally, mass manufacturing.

Hence, an invention may be seen as generalized solution to some set of problems. During the design activity, this generalized solution is narrowed according to a set of criteria which must relate market needs to manufacturing constraints. This set of criteria is used to determine which variant of the generalized solution has the greatest probability of meeting both the marketing and manufacturing needs. This results in a prototype of what will eventually become the product. The ability to manufacture this prototype is tested at a pilot facility before investments are made to mass-manufacture it.

Once the prototype product is released to the market, usually during the pilot phase of manufacture, the diffusion process begins. Diffusion of innovations is the means by which an innovation is spread throughout an industry and thus replaces an older technology (Lundstedt and Colglazier, 1982). Consequently, diffusion is part of the innovation process, but it cannot be called innovation. The diffusion process is extremely important because it is at this time that the decisions made early on in the innovation process are determined to be correct or not—that is, does the innovated product sell in the market? It is also during the diffusion process that the stage is set for other firms to react and for further innovation to occur. Hence, the diffusion stage will provide a focal point for much of the discussion on strategy which will occur in this book. It is the issue of strategy, and the strategic management of technology, which now must be addressed. In doing so, the approach that his book will take towards strategy will be discussed. Finally, the activities of strategy process presented in Figure 1.1 will be examined.

APPROACHES TO STRATEGY

It is important to discuss what is meant by strategy in order to clarify how it will be viewed in this book. There are two issues that are often discussed in considering strategy. First, broadly, what is strategy—how is strategy formulated and carried out? Approaches to this question of strategy abound. Strategy can be formulated according to a set of well-studied and specified goals established to meet thoroughly examined conditions in an environment, or it can develop according to some very vague goals, and in response to environmental changes. In the first case, strategy formulation can be viewed as a highly formal, centralized activity, implemented from the top of the organization down. In the second case, strategy formulation can be viewed as informal and decentralized, with implementation occurring concurrently with formulation at whatever level of the organization is involved (Methé and Perry, 1989). In essence, these two cases form the extremes of a continuum with one end viewing strategy as a synoptic activity and the other regarding it as an incremental activity. The key issue common to all these approaches is that strategy must relate to an environment and match the resources of the organization to environmentally imposed needs.

The second issue examines the specific manifestations of the above process. This issue is more concerned with how a firm will compete in a given environment. Which specific strategies or plans will be successful? In this book, the issue will not be whether the activities are carried out synoptically or incrementally, but rather, which activities are most successful in matching the organization's resources to the needs of the environment. One of the most important environmental conditions is the degree of technological change that exists. How the organization manages technology is critical.

As the model illustrates, management is challenged by many factors which change throughout the innovation process. The strategic challenge that confronts management is illustrated by the strategic focus, generation, consolidation and dispersion segment of the model. This segment of the model represents the core activities of the strategic management process. At each stage, this process must be linked with the activities occurring at the research and development and invention-innovation-diffusion levels. Successfully linking these levels of activity is the aim of strategic management of technology. In his way management increases the probability of converting a scientific discovery into an invention and, in turn, increases the probability of converting the invention into an innovation. The goal of management is to foster innovation. The role of managers is to increase the probability of innovation through the adroit use of resources and the removal of obstacles to their most effective use. Their actions must be guided by the company's strategic approach to technology.

The initial strategic action of the firm is to identify its strategic focus. It must decide what industries it will participate in, what products it will produce and for which customers, and how it will produce them. An important element of these decisions is technological. A product may be made up of a number of different technologies, or knowledge bases, which the firm will have to be cognizant of if it is to produce the product. It is the role of management to identify which knowledge bases offer the greatest probability of successfully innovating a product. Once it has decided its strategic focus, its main strategic activities will relate to generating or acquiring resources for innovation, consolidating them into innovations, and dispersing innovations in markets as new products. This entails developing the capabilities of understanding the selected knowledge bases and further, being able to utilize these to make products that will sell in the market. This means adding to existing stocks of knowledge and capital and diversifying these into the newer technologies determined to be crucial for future product development.

Each stage has its own unique challenges in the strategic management of technology. Initially, generating the knowledge bases for creating the innovation is crucial. Knowledge of a technology is a critical resource for the firm in carrying out innovation. The strategic management of technology challenge in this stage is to be open to internally and externally generated knowledge. Organizations must foster supportive structure and systems that continually encourage either the generation or acquisition of new knowledge.

During the consolidation stage, many of the ideas must be weeded out and the most technically and economically feasible supported. The types of reward, communication and staffing needed to carry out these activities are different from the ones necessary for creativity. Strategically, the challenge is to select and implement the most promising invention generated and to bring these to fruition as commercial products.

Further, once the ideas are developed into products these must be dispersed in the market. Timing of the introduction of the innovation is critical at this stage. Not only are products selected, but the successful ones are likely to be copied by competitors. Strategically, the firm must decide when to introduce the new innovation, to what potential customer groups, at what price and level of follow-up service. It must further prepare itself for the actions of its competitors, by continuing to foster invention and redesign of existing innovations.

It is important to note that the challenges presented in strategically managing technology have both an internal to the firm and an external to the firm component. Thus a new set of managerial challenges presents itself internally to the firm. Each of the challenges, taken in isolation from the others, can be handled. Taken together, however, these challenges present strategic problems of internal consistency for a firm's reward, communication, decision system. Consequently, the firm must be sensitive to the different internal needs of each stage.

The strategist must also be concerned with the different needs which arise externally. This book will focus on this external component. While there are a number of external issues relating to firm size, market structure and inter-firm relationships, the primary focus will be on the ability of the firm to continue innovating. In order to do this, it must acquire the resources necessary to carry out the innovation process. In order to do this strategically, it must identify the necessary resources.

It has been shown that innovation is a complex, multi-stage process involving change in a number of technologies, that, when carried out in an organizational setting, must be linked together with several activities. Important among these is the research and development activity and the strategic management activity. If it is to be the guiding force behind innovation, the strategic management activity must be able to acquire and organize the resources needed for continued innovation. To do this, these resources must be identified.

RESOURCES NEEDED FOR INNOVATION

As noted above, technology is composed of two stocks: knowledge and capital. Innovation is a probabilistic event resulting from a change in either or both of these stocks. Whether a firm is generating an innovation internally or acquiring it from an external source, it requires capital and knowledge. Consequently, these stocks can be viewed as required resources for innovation. These resources can be divided into "hard" resources such as laboratories and equipment and "soft" resources such as people and procedures. The "soft" resources are often embodiments of new information on technology. In this book, the first set will be called financial resources and the second set will be called informational resources. Proper combination and matching of these resources is what results in a successful innovation.

Financial and informational resources are the flow variables which bring about changes in the stock variables of technology. Thus, adding informational resources changes the stock of knowledge, and adding financial resources changes the stock of capital. Consequently, within each stage a particular set of matchings of financial and informational resources is necessary before advancement is possible.

Further, the initial conditions for innovation, that is, the initial combination of financial and informational resources that generated the innovation, may not be sufficient to sustain it. Thus at each stage, the combination of resources must change in order for innovation to continue to supplant current technology and become the new dominant technology. This book, then, will be concerned with major innovations in a technology that has already established itself, and not with a technology which has yet to be economically proven.

Environmental Conditions Affecting Innovation

Since the primary focus of this book will be on the external strategic issues of resource acquisition for innovation, environmental factors which effect these resources must be examined. Innovation resources are sensitive to changes in factors which affect both the capital and knowledge side of technology. Many environmental conditions have been noted as having an effect on technology and, consequently, an effect on the innovation process (Tushman and Moore, 1982, pp. 29–33). These environmental conditions are shaped by both business and government.

There are two major environmental factors that have been identified from previous empirical research which will be important for our purposes. The first is that the effect of firm characteristics and market structure may differentially affect the innovation process. In the earlier stages of research and development a somewhat curvilinear relationship exits. This presents the notion that both competitive pressure and market opportunity are at work. Intermediate values in concentration ratios and firm size may induce the most research effort, with these being modified by the degree of technological opportunity for an industry.

In the latter stages of innovation, the commercial introduction and diffusion stages, the larger firms and more concentrated industries may be slightly favored. In any case, it is important to realize that these industry characteristics are essential and that in any study of innovation, they must be accounted for in order to clearly determine the dimensions of the innovation.

Factors such as firm size, industry concentration, and capital intensity have been studied by many researchers (Kitti and Trozzo, 1976; Noll, et al., 1974; Kamien and Schwartz, 1982). These and other factors comprise the industrial setting for the innovation process. There is growing recognition that managerial practices play a direct role in the successful combination of innovation resources (Tushman and Moore, 1982). This is particularly so in both strategy formulation and implementation by the firm (Gruber, 1981). Firm strategies must be sensitive to both resources. Further, the organizational arrangements between firms in supplier and customer markets and the stability of a firm's work force should affect the firm's ability to efficiently combine these resources.

The second finding was the inter-industry effect. While the causes of it are not fully determined, the phenomenon has been related to the degree of technological opportunity that exists in an industry (Phillips, 1971). Technological opportunity was described in an earlier section. It should be noted that technological opportunity can be viewed as placing a high need for the resources of innovation, especially the informational resource. Consequently, the innovation process will vary by industry in terms of resource need, depending on the degree of technological opportunity that exists.

This differential effect is also found in studies conducted on another major factor in the innovation environment: government policy (Kitti and Trozzo, 1976; Nelson, 1982). It is related to and at the same time independent of the inter-industry effect. Thus, a government policy's effect will vary across industries because of the inter-industry effect and will also vary within an industry because of differential effects on the innovation process.

As has been seen, the resources needed for the innovation process to be carried out are linked to changes in the technology stocks, knowledge, and capital. With the flow of new information or money, these stocks change. Consequently, for firms to continue to innovate, they must constantly acquire these informational and financial resources. Environmental conditions, particularly market structure and governmental actions, can effect the pool of these resources available to firms. As already indicated, the study of the innovation process presents difficulties for researchers using the current economic and management approaches. New approaches must be utilized.

RESEARCH APPROACH UTILIZED

New Approaches to Technological Innovation

Two major theoretical streams have emerged which offer better understanding of the dynamics of technological innovation. The first is work on technology-driven market evolution, which shows that the prime mover of the development of an industry is change in its underlying technology. The second is the work currently being done on the management of technology, especially the work related to the strategic management of technology.

While these two approaches focus on different aspects of industrial development and innovation, they offer advantages over the framework used in other studies. The approach taken in this study is to combine work done by strategic management theorists with that done by evolutionary economists. A brief explanation is provided below. The two schools are described in greater detail, along with the combined framework and its advantages, in chapter two.

Both are concerned with industry structural change, but from different perspectives. Evolutionary economists posit that the prime mover in industrial change and development is innovation in technology (Schumpeter, 1954; Solow, 1957; Nelson and Winter, 1982; Klein, 1984; Mensch, 1979).

Competition through innovation is what maintains efficiency and the potential for future growth. Changes in industrial structure toward monopoly will only be temporary because of the irresistible pressure for innovation.

Nelson and Winter have advanced the notion that a technology develops along definable paths or trajectories. The successive waves of innovation or technological change that occur as a technology moves along its trajectory are reflected in changes in market structure and firm characteristics. Firms compete to bring about the next innovation, and those that are successful are able to capture a share of the market from other firms. This increases the firm's chances of survival and growth in the market and alters the opportunities for entry of other firms. Thus, Nelson and Winter affirm that market evolution is powered by technological change or innovation (Nelson and Winter, 1982).

Strategic management theory attempts to develop a framework from which methods can be created that systematically enhance the chances of a firm's survival in changing market and industrial settings. Much recent work done by these management theorists has been aimed at developing an understanding of how to strategically manage the technological innovation process (Clark, 1985; Tushman and Moore, 1980; Abernathy and Utterback 1978; Foster, 1986). Technological change is not some exogenous phenomenon that inexorably destroys a firm. It is a weapon that can be used in the strategic attack or defense of an industry.

While these two approaches differ in their perspectives as to the prime mover for industrial change, the common meeting point for these two theories is in the definition of technology presented earlier. According to Nelson and Winter a firm alters its market power through technological innovation. This provides an incentive for all firms in an industry to invest in innovation. The supply and demand of the resources necessary for innovation, if carried out in a market setting, are subject to strategic manipulation as discussed by the strategic management theorists. From this general framework, several theoretical assertions are derived concerning the innovation process. These assertions are then applied to firms operating in a technologically turbulent environment.

SUMMARY

The framework for this book has been presented in general terms. The technological competition between the Japanese and the United States has been introduced as the underlying theme of the work. This chapter has meshed this theme with terminologies, definitions and the research approach used to present the points of the study.

Distinctions have been drawn between technology, which is viewed as an existing stock of knowledge and capital, and innovation, viewed as changes in these stocks. Innovation is comprised of informational and financial resources, the supply and demand for which is affected by the current technology, the market structure, firm strategy, and public policy environment.

The works of strategic management theorists such as Kim Clark, Richard Foster, and William Abernathy, and evolutionary economists such as Richard Nelson and Sidney Winter, have been chosen to provide a theoretical structure for the development of a base to explore the process of innovation. The importance of this problem is conceptual and practical terms has been set forth.

The following chapters will build upon this base established in this chapter. In the next chapter, the conceptual foundations discussed here will be expanded. The elements of this discussion will focus on the development of both the evolutionary economic framework and the management of technology framework. The meeting ground for these two streams of work is in the emerging strategic management of technology field. From this discussion several theoretical assertions will be derived which will guide the discussion in the remaining chapters.

In chapter three, the conceptual framework of the book will be focused on a particular technological setting in an industry. The importance of this technology and industry will be established, and the framework applied. The impact of technological innovations on the level of resources needed to continue to innovate will then be assessed. This will lay the groundwork necessary to understand the changes in environmental conditions described in the next chapter. The conditions generated by this technology's innovation imperative create the environment that firms must compete in.

This environment and competitive activity of firms is described in chapter four. The impact of changes in the level of required resources for innovation is analyzed for both the firm and the market. The strategies that firms use to compete in these conditions and the result from these changes in industrial structure are then described. Which strategies have been successful, and the impact of this success on the competitive environment, is then investigated.

This discussion is continued in chapter five. The process by which diffusion takes place in this industry and the impact on the survival rate of firms is judged. How firms have coped with the changes in the technological and market environment is also assessed.

In chapter six, the role of government is elucidated. The impact of various government policy on the resource pool needed for innovation by firms is examined. Areas where attention must be paid by government are also described.

In the final chapter, the important trends discussed in the preceding text are integrated into a view of what competition in the 1990s and beyond will be like for firms. Suggestions of how firms can better compete, and what the proper role of government should be, are also put forth.

2

Theoretical Foundations and Research Questions

OVERVIEW

This chapter will present some of the most relevant contemporary thought of scholars concerning the role of technological innovation in an industry's development, and the importance of understanding that relationship for the strategic management of technology. Since the purpose of this chapter is to present the reader with the most salient thinking concerning these issues, the model of the innovation process presented in Figure 1.1 will here be configured into a model of the strategy-environment-technology (SET) interaction presented below to highlight these most important issues. Therefore, the following review will not be comprehensive in its scope but focused to our present needs.

The lens for that focus has been presented in the previous chapter. As noted, an essential activity for the firm is to link strategy with technology. This description will now be further refined by examining how the interaction of technology and strategy can play out in the development of an industry. This viewpoint will then be employed to guide the reader to a deeper understanding of the differences between American and Japanese firms' approaches to the strategic management of technology presented in later chapters.

STRATEGY-ENVIRONMENT-TECHNOLOGY INTERACTION

One way of envisioning the diverse research streams concerned with strategy and technology is presented in the ven diagram in Figure 2.1. The three circles represent the content knowledge derived from studies of strat-

Figure 2.1
General Representation of Content Knowledge Derived from Studies of Strategy, Technology, and Environment of Firms

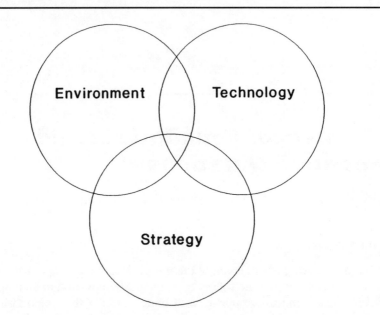

egy, technology and the environment of firms. This is a rather wide-ranging literature. Studies of the firm's environment range over topics that include political, social, ecological, and economic. Studies of technology range from pure engineering to debates about technology's role in the advancement of mankind. Studies of strategy range from discussions on whether strategy formulation is a synoptic or incremental activity, to how best to compete in a given market, to how best to implement strategies in organizations. The focus of this book is located at the intersection of these three circles; that is, the area of strategy-environment-technology (SET) overlap.

In order to fully understand the focus of this book, the other areas of overlap in our diagram will be discussed briefly. One area that has received much attention is the strategy-environment interface. The most relevant question asked in this area of overlap concerns how a firm competes in its environment. What are the most effective and general environmental conditions that exist? Issues of implementation of strategy are not covered. Much of the work on strategy done by Porter (1980, 1985) and Schendel and Hofer (1979) would fit into this area of overlap.

The next area of overlap is the technology-environment section. The most relevant research question asked here concerns how changes in technology effect the environment of firms. To a lesser extent, questions concerning the influence of environmental conditions on changes in technology are also relevant. This particular area of overlap has been dominated by economists. The work of Mansfield (1971), and Scherer (1980), represent one approach to these issues, empirical studies derived from standard neoclassical economic theory. The works of Schumpeter, Nelson and Winter and Sahal represent another approach, evolutionary economic theory. This book borrows predominantly from this latter group.

The third area of overlap is the strategy-technology area. This area is just recently emerging, although a number of antecedents concerned with issues of management and technology have existed. Much of the earlier work has related to the management of research and development, and more recently, to the management of technology. The most relevant questions asked have concerned how an organization can systematically guide technological development. The work of Marquis (1969), and von Hipple (1976), is representative of this area. More recent research in this area is represented by the work of Betz (1988) and the Task Force on the Management of Technology (1987). Another group of researchers have more directly studied the strategy-technology link. They are represented by the work of Friar and Horwitch (1985), Mitchell (1985), Butler (1988), Rosenbloom and Burgelman (1989) and Tornatzky and Fleischer (1990).

The streams of research presented by the evolutionary economists and the strategic management of technology find a common meeting ground in the area of overlap between the three circles. The issues discussed by these groups as they relate to the SET intersection will be the primary area from which this book will draw.

Initially, the technology-environment area of overlap must be examined. The basic approach that is taken by the evolutionary economists, and in particular, how this approach differs from previous work done by neoclassical economists, shall be discussed. It is important to understand these differences, since the evolutionary economists represent a departure from standard economic theory. Following that, our central concern will focus on the work of Richard Nelson and Sidney Winter, particularly as it relates to determining paths of technological change.

The second part of this chapter shall examine the work of those scholars concerned with the strategic management of technology—the area of technology-strategy overlap. Of primary concern in this section will be examining the process by which the resources necessary for technological innovation are acquired and organized. The implications of this for competing in an industry are then discussed.

In the final section of this chapter, the beginnings of a synthesis of these two areas of overlap into the SET area will be reached. Since much work is still being done on these issues and many areas of research are still unexplored, the synthesis arrived at in this book will undoubtedly evolve. What is presented in this book is a useful starting point for further research.

MARKET DYNAMICS AND EVOLUTION

This section examines the thought of scholars concerning the connection between changes in technology and the development of markets—what is called by many the dynamics of Schumpeterian competition. The dynamics of technology development will be looked at first. They will then be related to market development.

Technological Change and Market Change

Schumpeter (1936) was the first to recognize the importance of the connection between the dynamics of the innovation process and the dynamics of markets. While he was the first to tie market dynamics to those of technological change through innovation, and present an alternative to the standard theory of economics, many of his ideas remained dormant for years. This was due partially to the lack of empirical interest in testing his ideas, and to the state of their conceptual development compared to neoclassical economic theory. Then the work of Robert Solow (1957) brought to light a problem in neoclassical theory.

In attempting to explain the growth of the U.S. economy over a period of years through the use of the standard neoclassical inputs of capital and labor, an extremely large residual was found. This residual was labeled technological progress (Solow, 1957). Since that time, economists have been interested in technology and technological change, and, while making passing reference to Schumpeter, have essentially studied change using a static model (Nelson and Winter, 1982, p. 6; Sahal, 1981, p. 77).

More recently, models which specifically take a dynamic view of the technological change process and market development have begun to appear (Nelson and Winter, 1982; Sahal, 1981; Mensch, 1979; Phillips, 1971; Ayers, 1984). Each of these models presents a framework in which the market is driven by technology, as embodied in the processes and products of that market. Firms compete in terms of quality and performance of products rather than simply in terms of price, as in the neoclassical model. The changes in technology, whether driven by demand or supply considerations, present a series of challenges and opportunities to the firms in the market. Firms, through their actions, either overcome or are overwhelmed by the challenges. They are either able to exploit opportunities and survive, or fail to do so and consequently die off.

While they are competing they may enjoy temporary monopoly profits, but these are lost over the long term by the continued change in the technology brought about by research done within the firms or among outside sources. Thus, the time frame for these models is long-term, as opposed to short-term for the neoclassical model. Further, these models recognize that competition can come from anywhere. In a demand elasticity sense, there are no monopolists, since any firm can compete in any industry if it is technologically vigorous enough (Kamien and Schwartz, 1982, pp. 22–24).

It has also been recognized by some researchers that technologically competitive industries may contain the seeds of their eventual downfall and replacement by another industry. This may occur because the technical problems confronted are too great for the current scientific base to support, and progress in some substitutable technology is greater (Sahal, 1979). Or it may be due to the successful erection of economic barriers that cannot be breached (Kamien and Schwartz, 1982). These barriers are the result of previous technological progress (Tilton, 1971). The existence of such barriers can create conditions which lower the incentive to compete technologically for the firms in the industry. The conditions in the U.S. automobile industry prior to the emergence of powerful Japanese and European competitors was such a case.

Beyond this, the effect of the dynamics of both technologies and markets has been related to the broader economic cycles (Mensch, 1979; Klein, 1984). The causes for the undulation of these cycles and the issues of inflation, recession and productivity are viewed differently when technological dynamics come into play. A number of scholars have suggested that technological innovation is the wellspring for overcoming depressions and powering the Kondratief long wave cycle of economic growth (Mensch, 1979). Consequently, the perspective in which the various private sector strategy and public sector policy instruments are viewed changes if the dynamic model of economics is utilized.

Diffusion

One area where major rethinking has occurred is in the conceptualization of the diffusion stage. Often innovation has been thought of as a one-shot perturbation of the market. The innovation would pass through the technology and bring about only a one-time change. Now it is being recognized that an innovation in one technology may stimulate an innovation in another technology against which the first innovation must compete (Sahal, 1979, p. 80). The current debate in the empirical literature as to whether the diffusion process is really sigmoidal is an outgrowth of this recognition.

It has also been recognized that an innovation itself undergoes change and development as it is diffused throughout an industry; it may in fact be reinvented with each use (Rogers, 1983). Because of this change and development in a technology, markets can be described as going through various stages of growth based on the degree of innovation that is occurring in their production technologies (Mueller and Tilton, 1969). The economic conditions resulting from the differences in the degree of innovation that exist at each of the stages create differences in strategic imperatives that firms confront.

Innovation as a Dynamic Process

To what extent is the evolutionary path along which a technology moves knowable? In order to answer this question, the distinction between radical innovation, major innovation, and improvement innovation which we have made in the first chapter is important. As noted, radical innovation results in a discontinuous jump from one type of technology to another while serving the same market need. The invention of the transistor and its triumph over the vacuum tube is an example. A radical innovation results in the birth of an entirely new industry which may or may not replace an already existing industry.

In one respect all innovations can be radical in that they may greatly alter the given technology of some industry. For example, a process change which allows for more flexibility in the styles of automobiles that proceed down an assembly line may be a minor change in terms of the product produced, but will require some major changes in the machinery used to carry out those style changes. Thus, the change for the machine tool industry may be quite radical. Still, in spite of this nested impact of technology change across industries, within an industry changes can be considered as radical, major, and incremental.

The definitions given for the differences between major and incremental innovations range from economic, concerned with changes in quantity and price of a product, to engineering, concerned with pushing back some previous technical limit (Kamien and Schwartz, 1982, p. 38; Sahal, 1979, pp. 57–58). As noted in chapter one, a major change within an industry is one where a product or process is introduced which had not existed previously. Incremental innovations are changes in the process or product which result in improvements of the quality or efficiency of the process or product. Thus, major innovations allow for the development of new products or processes within an established industry, whereas incremental innovations are improvements to those products or processes. Incremental innovations should not be considered unimportant. It is through incremental changes in industrial processes that a product moves through its learning curve.

Technological Trajectories

The evolution of a technology can be understood using the distinctions between major and incremental innovations. The recognition that innovations come in clusters, usually with a major innovation followed by a series of incremental ones, is not new (Kuznets, 1979, p. 449; Mensch, 1979), but the process underpinning this phenomenon is only now being explored. While there is a random component to the innovation process, there do appear to be some clear paths, at least in hindsight.

These paths or trajectories exist along definable technical or economic signposts (Nelson and Winter, 1977, pp. 56–60; Sahal, 1979, pp. 32–36). As an example of the economic signposts, as the technology becomes more mechanized, it also becomes more capitalized. Thus, there are levels of capital expenditure which would be associated with the maturity of the technology. Further, the exploitation of economies of scale would also serve to guide a technology through a defined path of innovation (Nelson and Winter, 1977, pp. 58–60).

Along technical lines, the size of the product, its power consumption, or its capacity to do work are what guide development. To decrease size while maintaining the same ability to do work, for example, confronts the engineer with a whole set of limits that must be met. These economic and technical signposts are best thought of as obstacles to be overcome or opportunities to be achieved. The precise path to overcoming the problem and achieving the solution are not always evident as single best solutions. Multiple solutions, different potential paths, compete in the marketplace for dominance. The existence of multiple paths is what makes it difficult to predict, a priori, which innovation will succeed, even when technical or economic signposts are clearly defined.

In proceeding along these paths, the resources required to bring about the desired goal change as the technology changes. As a consequence, the firm is confronted with a continuously shifting equilibrium. There is no stable, well-defined production function. Consequently, technical change does not allow for the maintenance of economic equilibrium (Nelson and Winter, 1977, pp. 46–49).

This has import for the development of firms and markets. While the theoretical origins for the combination of technical change with market change date back to Schumpeter and, still earlier, Marx, the development of a theory to challenge the current neoclassical theory of economics is only recently underway (Kamien and Schwartz, 1982, pp. 6–18; Nelson and Winter, 1982).

Key Market Dynamics Issues

Technology changes through innovation. Non-drastic innovation occurs along definable paths or trajectories. These trajectories are marked by economic and technical signposts which act as channeling devices for the innovations. Each innovation requires resources in the form of capital and information to be successfully brought to fruition.

The composition of these resources changes as major innovations occur in a technology, because the innovations alter the stock of the technology. This alteration process, as well as the dynamics of the innovation process, is reflected in the market. The ability of an innovation to be diffused throughout a market will bring about a change in the market structure, which in turn sets the stage for the next round of innovations. Thus, the change in markets through technology and the change in technology through innovation come together in the diffusion process. Once again, the standard neoclassical theory of the firm and market is inadequate to handle these issues.

Since innovation changes an existing technology, it is natural to think that evolutionary economists present the best model for studying innovation. Evolutionary economists are concerned with financial resources and recognize the importance of informational resources. Management of the innovation process is carried out through what are called "search routines" that are internal to the firm (Nelson and Winter, 1982).

Strategy, to the evolutionary economist, concerns search routines. The firm either works on the next technological innovation through its own efforts, or acquires it through imitation or other means from its rivals. In the first case, without the diffusion of the original innovation there is no incentive for the innovating firm to continue because it already possesses the most efficient technology and can drive rivals out of business. In the second case, non-innovating firms would have no other firms to imitate, without the diffusion of innovation. Strategic incentives are very low in either of these cases.

Even if a firm decides to innovate, how it acquires the necessary resources to do this is not fully developed by evolutionary economists. Financial resources do not post as difficult a problem as do the informational resources. It has been argued that through successful innovation a firm acquires enough financial resources, or profits, to continue innovating, or it can attract a bank to invest in the firm and share in the rewards (Nelson and Winter, 1982). The acquisition of informational resources is left to the diffusion stage of the innovation and conceptual problems arise with these resources. Consequently, the strategic management of technological innovation is rather simply presented in the evolutionary economic scheme.

STRATEGIC MANAGEMENT OF TECHNOLOGY

The importance of strategically managing the technological innovation process began to be recognized in the late 1970s and early 1980s (Hayes and Abernathy, 1980). Over the intervening years, the field has developed both in terms of its conceptual underpinnings, and in techniques which can be used by management (Task Force on the Management of Technology, 1987).

Of primary strategic importance to the firm is to identify the relevant technological areas that impact upon a product. Products today are usually a system of components that are combined together to meet some consumer need. Each component has a connection with some technological knowledge base. A computer has, at the minimum, a hardware component and a software component. Even something as seemingly simple as steel is made up of a number of technological knowledge bases related to its production. These knowledge bases have been identified together as a strategic technology area (STA) for the firm (Mitchell, 1985).

Each STA is important to the firm in that the firm must maintain some capability to the STA in order to understand its contribution to the firm's products. The firm needs to evaluate the STAs both in terms of their vertical and horizontal impact upon products (Mitchell, 1985). The key point in this discussion is that the vertical perspective focuses on resource acquisition, while the horizontal perspective focuses on the growth opportunity in technology.

Clark (1985) recognized the vertical aspect of an STA from a different perspective. His work concerns design hierarchies and core technologies. This will be discussed in greater detail later. For now, the important concept is that innovation in certain component parts or processes for a product may be the key to fundamentally altering the product. The change may actually occur in some other industry which is supplying the particular component. Hence, technological change in a particular product may span several industries as well as several firms.

Once the firm has chosen which technological areas it considers strategically important, the firm has several strategic dimensions open to it in terms of technological strategy (Friar and Horwitch, 1985). The first is the degree to which it chooses to compete or cooperate within the industry. The second concerns the locus of inventive-innovative effort. A firm can choose to internally develop some new invention or to acquire it externally. Finally, the firm must choose how to structure its innovative efforts. This can be done in large multidivisional firms with centralized research and development laboratories or through the efforts of smaller entrepreneurial units.

This latter dimension of structure has sparked some controversy among two groups of scholars. The first group of scholars, represented by George Gilder, argues that smaller entrepreneurial firms are the best way to structure innovation (Gilder, 1988). The second group of scholars, represented by Charles Ferguson, argues that only large, well-capitalized firms can successfully carry out innovation (Ferguson, 1988).

This is an important issue and will be examined at length in later chapters.

For now, let us only note that the large versus small question is too confining. The other two dimensions, competition and invention, are equally as important, and when combined with the third can result in a rich array of strategic options for managing technological innovation.

The essential strategic question in all these options is: does the firm have enough of the necessary resources to carry out the innovation process? If it does, it can follow one set of strategic options. If it does not, then it must share its resources and must decide on how to do this. From an innovation resource perspective, then, there is a continuum of strategic options. At one extreme is either a large or a small firm which decides to not to cooperate with its rival, and internally develops its inventions. At the other extreme is either a large or small firm which decides to cooperate with its rivals, and lets all or part of its invention be developed externally. The essential question posed by this continuum is: does the firm decide to share its resources? If so, how? The firm must also keep in mind that there are horizontal and vertical directions for this sharing as well.

Strategic Management of Technology—Institutional Consideration

Whenever there is sharing of any item in a market environment, special institutional arrangements must be made. This is especially the case if the sharing of information is involved, because information has characteristics similar to those of public goods. Consumption of a public good by one person does not reduce the level available for others, and no one can be prevented from consuming a public good once it is produced (Samuelson, 1954). National defense is considered the quintessential example of a public good. Information is most strongly affected by the first characteristic, that of nonreduction of supply, and to a lesser extent effected by the second characteristic, nonexclusion.

Recalling our definition from chapter one, technology is the stock of knowledge on how to get something accomplished. As such, it is the embodiment of all previous innovations including the initial innovation which distinguishes the technology under study from all others. Innovation creates a flow of new information about how to use the technology in a more useful way. This information must be assimilated by those using the technology.

This occurs with all levels of innovation, radical, major, and incremental. In incremental innovations it is the learning curve phenomenon. This curve is the result of learning how to use a new technology or innovation more efficiently. In the early portion of the curve, the flow of information is important because the stock of knowledge is low. As the stock of knowledge is increased, the flow of information becomes less crucial to those who have accumulated and assimilated the earlier information flow into their knowledge base.

Consequently, when an innovation is transferred throughout an industry, the demand for the informational component will play an important role, especially in the beginning. Major innovations are the beginning for the learning curve. As such, the information component is doubly important. Not only does a whole new product technology need to be learned, but it must also be pushed down its learning curve to a point where it is competitive with products that meet a similar market need.

The Information Paradox

In order to determine whether to share the innovation or not, the information about the innovation will have to be verified. In attempting to do this, those sharing the innovation will confront what Kenneth Arrow has called the "fundamental paradox" of information. The paradox is that, for the adopter of the innovation, the informational component's value "is not known until he has the information, but then he has in effect acquired it without cost" (Arrow, 1971, p. 152).

This leads us directly into the intellectual property rights issue of the appropriability problem. In capitalist systems the developer of an innovation has a right to returns from that innovation. In order to show that he has truly created an innovation, the developer must show how it works and explain its basic functions to prospective clients. Once he has done that, however, there is little to stop the clients from copying the innovation and refusing to render any royalty to the original developer. The original inventor cannot appropriate all the returns justified by the effort expended. Thus, the fundamental paradox of information and the appropriability problem are linked.

There are other difficulties which the informational component introduces into the innovation process. In the neoclassical theory of economics, economic units are assumed to be omniscient and omnipotent in the processing of information. Simon (1976) and others have shown that this is not so, that economic units, be they individuals, firms, or groups of firms are characterized by bounded rationality. This property, coupled with imperfections in the modes and language of information transfer, results in asymmetries of information between two parties. In other words, it may not always be possible to convey the proper meaning from a source to a receiver because the medium used is inherently imperfect. This assumes, of course, that a true message was intended to be sent in the first place.

Institutional Considerations and Information

These asymmetries can manifest themselves in a variety of behaviors, but in general their effect is the same. They come under the general discussion of "moral hazard" in the economic literature (Kamien and Schwartz, 1982, pp. 25–26). They introduce inefficiencies into the market systems through the misallocation of the risk bearing activity. These inefficiencies manifest themselves within firms (Jensen and Meckling, 1976) and within markets (Coase, 1960; Williamson, 1975).

Of particular interest is the research related to markets, since it has been used to explain the development of firms as production and trading institutions in markets. A market is assumed to be the most efficient type of organization to the neoclassical economist, and therefore the existence of firms must be explained. One explanation, which will be used here is offered by Oliver Williamson. In a market, a person or group of people gain some knowledge about the environment that gives them an advantage over others; asymmetries of information result.

This asymmetry of information results in a state characterized by "information impactedness" (Williamson, 1975). Information impactedness results from the interaction of the uncertainty/complexity of the environment with the opportunism of the parties involved in a transaction set. Each transaction has a cost associated with it, and this cost is a direct function of the degree of information impactedness. Information impactedness in a system tends to push that system to one of small numbers. This lacuna in competition is what Williamson refers to as a prime mover or first mover advantage. If the first person to enter the market can hold a near-monopoly position, then that person will have an advantage in the next round also.

SYNTHESIS OF THE PREVIOUS FRAMEWORKS

In this section the key issues addressed by each of the conceptual frameworks will be integrated into·a more unified approach to the issue of technological innovation. Evolutionary economic concepts, especially those related to technological trajectories, will be adapted to be more amenable to the issues raised by the strategic management theorists. The attendant problems raised by the information component of innovation and the institutional arrangements needed will also be addressed.

Technology and Innovation Trajectories

From the firm's perspective, the strategically most relevant elements of the evolutionary economic arguments is that technological changes occur along paths. These technology paths, or trajectories, can be traced by both economic and engineering singposts (Nelson and Winter, 1977; Sahal, 1981). Specific examples of these signposts will vary from technology to technology. In the following section a definition and generic examples of signposts will be given.

Innovation Signposts

For purposes of this book, a signpost can be defined as the next set of technical or economic challenges that must be overcome for improvement to continue in a given technology. Examples of generic technical signposts include issues of size of a product, weight, power consumption and heat dissipation (Sahal, 1981). The challenge confronting a research engineer may be to reduce the power consumption of a component. Doing so brings about an improvement in a technology. If this improvement can be commercialized in a product, an innovation in that product's technology has occurred.

Examples of generic economic signposts include capitalization and economies of scale in production (Nelson and Winter, 1977). The challenge facing the research engineer may be to substitute capital for labor in the production of a component. Doing so would increase productivity and lower the cost of a component. By incorporating this improvement in a production process, an innovation has occurred.

Nelson and Winter argue that these signposts gives direction to innovative activity. Confronting each subsequent set of challenges in a particular technology gives rise over time to innovation trajectories (Nelson and Winter, 1977). It has further been argued that these trajectories exist within a particular product technology (Nelson and Winter, 1977; Clark, 1985).

Within a given product technology, trajectories are defined as a sequence of designs, each building and improving upon the previous design. The direction of a product technology's trajectory is defined by the technical and economic signposts specifically related to that product technology (Clark, 1985). Hence, specific manifestations of signposts will vary with the product technology under consideration.

Further, some signposts are more important than others. In electric power generation, increased electrical output of a turbine is more important than decreased size or weight. The relative weight given to each signpost may change for either technical or market reasons. For example, fuel economy has increased in importance over horsepower improvement in internal combustion engine technology. The important point for this discussion is that since these signposts exist, the direction and character of innovation can be anticipated and incorporated into a firm's product technology strategy (Tushman and Moore, 1982).

Strategy and the Innovation Envelope

The concept of signposts for innovation trajectories is consistent with the synergistic relationship that has been found to exist between product innovation and process innovation (Abernathy and Utterback, 1982; Abernathy and Wayne, 1974; Betz, 1987). Strategically, as pointed out by

Figure 2.2
Relationship between Product Technology and Subtechnology A

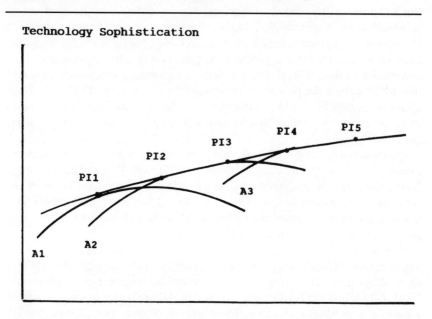

Technology Sophistication

Mitchell (1985) and Friar and Horwitch (1985), it would be more useful to envision the technology trajectory of a given product as embodying a number of crucial subtechnologies needed to produce a given product, each with its own trajectory. These technologies would make up a set of process subtechnologies related to a given product. Each of these subtechnologies exhibits all the properties of technology described in chapter one. What makes them subtechnologies in their relative position in the technology "food chain." These technologies are crucial in supporting the development of a technology associated with a given product. Each of these subtechnologies, then plays a dual role. This duality is as both an end in one technology chain and as a means to some other "end" technology embodied in a given product. The given product's technology trajectory would form the outer curve of an innovation envelope of these crucial process subtechnologies.

A diagrammatic representation of the innovation envelope is presented for a generic product's technology trajectory in Figure 2.2. Improvement in the technical performance is measured along the vertical axis with time along the horizontal axis. Major innovations in the product are indicated by the nodes along its trajectory, which are labelled PI1, PI2, and so forth in the figure.

For ease in presentation only one subtechnology is shown in each figure.

Figure 2.3
Relationship between Product Technology and Subtechnology B

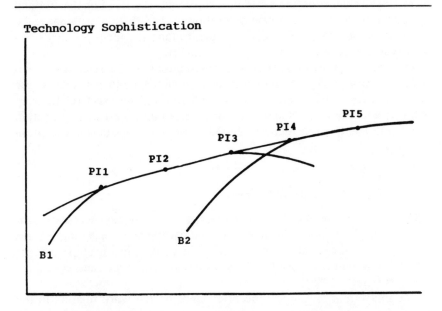

Major improvements in the first process, or subtechnology, is shown in Figure 2.2 by the series of curves labelled "A." Each curve represents a new generation in the equipment needed to produce the given product. The first generation of the subtechnology, curve A1, has technical performance which is adequate for the first generation of the product, PI1. The second generation of the product, PI2, requires technical performance, that is, engineering tolerances, greater than the current subtechnology equipment, A1, is capable of delivering. Hence, for PI2 to occur, improvement in the "A" subtechnology must occur. This improvement is represented by the A2 curve. By our definition of technology as a process and innovation as a probabilistic event, the movement from A1 to A2 represents a recognition that A2 increases the probability of PI2 occurring. It should also be noted that the "A" subtechnology is made up of supporting technologies that must be innovated in order to jump from the A1 curve to the A2 curve. This is also a probabilistic event.

As it is represented in the figure, no new generation of the "A" subtechnology is needed for the PI3 generation of the product to be introduced. For the next two innovations in the product, PI4 and PI5, however, a new generation of the "A" subtechnology is required. This is represented in the figure by the A3 curve.

The relationship between the main product technology and the "B" subtechnology is shown in Figure 2.3. The level of technological change needed in the "B" subtechnology is less than in the case of the "A" subtechnology. Between the PI1 to PI3 product generations, the "B" subtechnology remains on the same trajectory with the B1. For the PI4 and PI5 generations to occur, a new generation of the "B" subtechnology, the B2 must be developed. Hence, movement along the main product's trajectory is less dependent on the "B" technology.

The above figures present two representations of the relationship between a given product technology and two subtechnologies; that is, the innovation for a hypothetical product. Obviously, the exact relationship will vary with the product and subtechnology. Only empirical investigation can determine the exact relationship that exist along a product's innovation envelope.

Interaction of Product and Process

As Clark noted for the development of the V-8 engine, necessary subtechnology development included work in casting and machining (Clark, 1985). Hence, the argument put forth by the innovation envelope concept is consistent with the work by Clark on design hierarchies and core technologies (Clark, 1985).

The innovation envelope concept expands on the work relating to the logic of process and product innovation and the importance of process subtechnologies in propelling movement along a given product technology (Clark, p. 249; 1985). Consequently, the innovation envelope suggests that movement along a given product's technology trajectory, from one product generation to the next, is connected to concurrent movement along technology trajectories of the subtechnologies. In other words, innovation in one product is a probabilistic event dependent upon other probabilistic events, or innovations in subtechnologies.

Institutional Factors

The innovational envelope concept explicitly recognizes the importance of institutional arrangements for the design hierarchies. Since innovation occurs along an envelope of change in subtechnologies, innovation in one industry will often require advanced notice to suppliers of crucial subtechnologies. Consequently, successful commercialization of an improved product design is no longer the solitary act of a single firm, but an interdependent effort between firms at various levels of the technological hierarchy.

The innovation envelope also can highlight the degree of interaction that must occur between firms at the various levels of the technological hierarchy. Certain subtechnologies may become more important than other subtechnologies at different periods of time. As noted in Figure 2.2 and

2.3, changes in the "A" subtechnology occurred more frequently than changes in the "B" subtechnology.

The institutional effect of this technical difference, is that failure of the firms producing the "A" subtechnology to innovate will have a direct, negative impact on the firms producing the main product "P" in introducing the next generation of their product. Consequently, a firm developing a given product technology must identify the crucial subtechnologies needed for each new generation of its product and interact with firms which are developing these subtechnologies. This is particularly necessary when change in those subtechnologies requires large amounts of resources or entails much technical risk which could delay the introduction of the innovation.

LESSONS FROM THEORY

The framework will now be applied to the previous discussions of the innovation and diffusion processes and several research questions will be developed for empirical testing. As noted in the first chapter, the central question posed by the rise of Japanese companies, particularly in high technology industries, calls for a discussion of the interaction between strategy, and its attendant institutional needs as expressed in market structure and technological innovation. Further, what would be the appropriate government policy to facilitate the innovation process.

In order to facilitate the analyses which will be conducted in the following chapters, a shorthand expression will be introduced measuring the movement of a technology along its trajectory. This shorthand expression relates to the sophistication of a technology. A technology will become more sophisticated with each succeeding innovation and this process alters the supply and demand for the financial and informational resources. Technological sophistication is defined as the capacity of a technology to perform a function over the efficiency of performance; it is a measure of effectiveness divided by efficiency. It combines the notions of complexity of a technology with maturation of a technology and, in so doing, it provides a more complete indicator of changes in the technology and need for resources.

The demand for capital is small in the initial period of introduction. With each succeeding innovation, the technology requires higher capital outlays to bring it about; that is, the demand for capital increases. This is a result of the inherent engineering characteristics of technological development. Likewise for the information resource, in the early period of a technology's life cycle, information about an innovation may be scarce, but it is simple to understand with the appropriate background. As the technology becomes more sophisticated the innovation cannot be understood in its entirety, because of the increasing volumes of information necessary to bring about the next generation. A technological imperative is established in the industry. Firms must continue to innovate in order to compete. Hence, the discussion arrives at the first research lesson: as the technology becomes more sophisticated through succeeding innovations, it will require more financial and informational resources.

The degree of sophistication in a technology has an effect on the development of market structure through the need for greater levels of resources. The increasing need for capital resources will favor those firms which can secure a ready supply of financial resources either from internal or external sources. The strategic approach that firms take towards technological innovation will affect the ability to acquire the resources necessary for innovation.

For the information resource, as noted above early in the period of a technology's life cycle, information can be communicated from one person/firm to another person/firm with the appropriate background and the innovation will be understood. As the volume of information increases with each succeeding innovation, it cannot be understood by one individual, and now requires a team. The team is needed to acquire and process the increasing volumes of information necessary to bring about the next generation through innovation. Again, the strategic approach of firms is expected to effect their capability to assemble and maintain such teams.

From the discussion of the strategic management of technology, three areas of firm strategy will be examined. First, there is the strategic competitive approach that a firm takes towards innovation: is it a leader or a follower? Firms which are innovators will have greater access to the resources needed for continued innovation. This may result from a long period of time when the innovating firm has no real competitors, or from being "designed into" their customer's own products. In either case a secure market is available. Second, the horizontal strength of the firm's strategy is exhibited by whether the firm is a broad-based supplier of products or more of a niche supplier. Firms that are broad-based suppliers can take advantage of a "portfolio effect," since the demand for all the products may not follow the same cycle. Finally, we must note the strategic approach that a firm takes towards vertical integration; that is, linkages with suppliers or customers. The ability to coordinate product development cycles will allow for greater access to resources as well as more effective use of the resources available.

As a technology becomes more sophisticated, the size of the firms should increase, which should result in higher levels of market concentration. Further, the increased need for resources should also be reflected in strategies which increase the linkages both horizontally and vertically. Consequently, the movement among these characteristics is towards an oligopolistic market structure containing highly integrated firms. The rapidity with which this movement occurs depends on whether first mover advantages exist with the innovations; that is, whether imitation is successful. These issues are incorporated in the second research lesson. As a technology requires more financial and informational resources through succeeding innovations, the firms which follow a strategic approach that is innovative, broad-based in the supply of products, and vertically integrated will be better able to acquire these resources and continue to innovate.

As the market structure becomes more concentrated, and the firms more interlinked both horizontally and vertically, it should become more difficult for firms not already established in the industry to enter. From this, a third research lesson can be derived. As the market structure becomes more concentrated, the diffusion rate will decline.

As the technology matures, as suggested by the second research lesson, firms will grow in size because it takes more capital to produce the product and the information becomes embodied in a team. Extending the third lesson, oligopolists can generate the necessary funds but they are loath to share information. Thus, an innovation in a mature technology will encounter high information impactedness and thus high transaction costs. As a corollary of the above two research lessons, it is expected that firms which can best capture both the financial and informational resources will prosper and come to dominate the industry.

The public policy implications of this revolve around the role of government in affecting the amount of resources available for innovation. The type of market structure that exists and the resource which is most constrained must be considered. Thus, for a competitive type of market structure, the most important resource, because the firm cannot supply it, is the financial resource.

Any policy which further restricts the amount of capital resources available will tend to lower the number of firms that can compete in the next innovation round. Likewise, in the oligopolistic market structure, the most constrained resource is information. To constrain it further will lower the amount of innovation. Hence, policies must be developed which allow for the increased flow of information about innovation while balancing the appropriability problem. The policy must not swing too far or it will eliminate the incentive to innovate.

With this, a fourth research lesson is open for consideration. A public policy instrument which alters either or both the financial and informational resources will affect innovation.

SUMMARY

In this chapter, the relationship between strategy, technology and the environment has been explored along two selected streams of thought. The work of evolutionary economists such as Nelson and Winter has been chosen because it considers the dynamics of the endogenous relationship between market structure and technological change. The work of strategic management of technology theorists, such as Mitchell, and Friar and Horwitch, has been chosen because it provides insights into how technological innovation can be channeled by firms.

The institutional implications of both the evolutionary economic and strategic management perspectives have also been examined. The work of Williamson is found to be adequate for discussing the informational economics of technology. A combination of the above provides a new approach which centers on the concept of a technology innovation envelope has been derived. From this modified approach, four research lessons have been generated. The first is that the technology becomes more sophisticated through succeeding innovations, it will require more financial and informational resources. From this a second is derived: as a technology requires more financial and informational resources through succeeding innovations, the market structure will become more concentrated and the relationship between firms more integrated. The third states that as the market structure becomes more concentrated, the diffusion rate will decline. Consequently, it is expected that firms which can best capture both the financial and informational resources will prosper and come to dominate the industry. The fourth research lesson is that a public policy instrument which alters either or both the financial and informational resources will affect innovation. These research lessons will guide our analysis in each of the following four chapters.

3

Technological Evolution and Innovation Resources

OVERVIEW

As noted in chapter one, American companies have been challenged by Japanese companies in a number of industries. Also as noted, these industries range from steel and automobiles to finance and electronics. Of particular interest in this book is the rise of Japanese companies in high technology industries. Technology, it will be remembered, is a crucial engine of growth, not only for companies, but for a country's economy as well.

Technology has been defined as a process composed of a stock of tools and a stock of the knowledge to use them. These two stocks provide a company with the capability to compete in a market by producing products that meet the needs of customers. Improvements in technology occur through inventions which yield innovations in products. The discussion in chapter two focused on recent scholarly thinking concerning the effects of technological change, through innovation, on competition in industries. Competition based on innovation in products creates a technological imperative. Firms must continually improve their technological capabilities in order to successfully remain in the industry. This type of competition confronts the firm with a number of strategic decisions to make.

In this chapter, the context of these strategic choices will be discussed. This will be accomplished by examining a high technology industry where U.S. and Japanese firms are locked in intense technological competition. The integrated circuit industry will be the center of this examination.

The first research lesson presented in the previous chapter will be used to guide the analyses of this chapter. This lesson stated that as the technology becomes more sophisticated through succeeding innovations, it will require more financial and informational resources. This research lesson is very closely tied to the evolutionary economic concept of a technology following a definable trajectory along some set of signposts. For the strategic management of that technology, the key issue is what level of resources will be necessary to sustain the company's innovative momentum. Issues of whether the company wishes to lead, stay equal with, or lag the innovative pace will be discussed in later chapters.

The key issues to be explored in this chapter relate to determining the existence of a technology trajectory for the integrated circuit industry. Once this is done, the DRAM segment will be used to visualize the innovation envelope concept described in chapter two. This will form the basis for a discussion of the impact of the innovation envelope on the resources needed for sustained innovation. One assumption is made in this chapter which will differentiate it from those that follow. It is assumed that the Japanese and U.S. firms are confronted with the same innovation envelope. Consequently, the analyses presented in this chapter will not draw distinctions between U.S. and Japanese firms.

CHOICE OF INDUSTRY

Importance of the Integrated Circuit Industry

The electronics industry is currently at about $330 billion in sales. The core of the electronics industry is the integrated circuit industry. The integrated circuit industry is currently at fifty-nine billion in world-wide sales. Projections are that by 1993 the integrated circuit industry will grow by fifty percent to eighty-one billion dollars in sales in a total electronics industry which will be over $740 billion in sales (McClean, 1989). More significant is the fact that the automobile and aerospace industries are, increasingly, end users of integrated circuits.

Let us take the automobile industry as an example. Both product and process innovations in that industry are becoming more dependent on integrated circuits. It is expected, for example, that the electronic content of automobiles will increase from a current figure of $550 per car to $1,100 per car in 1990 and $1,450 per car in 1995 (McClean, 1986). In the area of improvements in process technology, the shift to computer aided design (CAD), and computer aided manufacturing (CAM) could not take place without the integrated circuits in the computers. The current shift to computer integrated manufacturing (CIM) will require even more powerful integrated circuits. Similar trends are occurring in industries ranging from steel to aerospace to pharmaceutical. Consequently, improvements in those industries as well are being tied more closely to improvements in the integrated circuit industry.

U.S. AND JAPANESE TRADE PATTERNS IN INTEGRATED CIRCUITS

Patterns of global market share have been changing in the integrated circuit industry. The dominance of the world market in integrated circuits by U.S. firms has been decreasing. Concurrent with the decline of U.S. firms, Japanese firms have been ascending in market share terms. U.S. firms held 80% of the world market share in semiconductors in 1974, against a 10% share held by the Japanese. Throughout the late 1970s and early 1980s U.S. firms, both merchant integrated circuit producers, such as Motorola and National Semiconductor, and captive integrated circuit producers, such as IBM and DEC, lost market share, but only gradually. The period from 1982 to 1985 was pivotal. Japanese firms gained momentum in the market share race during this period. By 1987 the U.S. share of the world market had declined to 50% while the Japanese had increased to 41%, European companies held 7%, while companies from the rest of the world held 2% (McClean, 1988).

It should be noted that the combined world share held by the Japanese and U.S. firms is about 90% and this has been constant since 1974. What has shifted is the relative market share, with the Japanese gaining and the United States losing over the thirteen year period. The European and other countries are essentially non-players in the global integrated circuit industry of today.

As global competition is increasing in the integrated circuit industry, the dominance of U.S. merchant firms has been decreasing. Japanese firms have been ascending in market share terms. This is particularly true for the merchant integrated circuit producers, like Intel or AMD. It is these merchant integrated circuit producers which will be studied throughout the remainder of this book. In 1982, U.S. merchant firms held 51% of the world market for integrated circuits, Japanese firms held 25% (McClean, 1989). By 1987 the Japanese had surpassed the U.S. merchant firms, with the respective market shares being 36% and 33%. Japanese firms in 1989 held 39%, while U.S. merchant firms held 31%.

This trend is also reflected in the change over of firms which are considered world producers. In the 1970s, Japanese firms such as NEC, Toshiba, and Fujitsu were not considered important integrated circuit firms. Today Japanese firms occupy six out of the top ten spots in overall integrated circuit production. In addition to the growing proportion of Japanese firms, it should also be noted that technological changes have effected the rankings. Many large U.S. companies, such as Clevite, Philco, and Fairchild, that initially entered the semiconductor industry in 1966 were not able to keep abreast of the technological changes and exited the industry, well before the advent of competition from Japan. Throughout this book, the focus will be on how U.S. merchant IC producers have faired. Merchant firms are those firms that were begun as entrepreneurial start-ups and have grown through sales in the open market. These have been the most dynamic firms technologically, and as such their fate is of the utmost importance to all U.S. consumers of integrated circuits. Even captive suppliers of ICs, firms which produce ICs only for internal use such as IBM, have become highly dependent on merchant firms.

Importance of the DRAM in U.S.-Japan Integrated Circuit Competition

It should be noted that the competition from Japan has occurred primarily in the memory segment of the integrated circuit industry, particularly dynamic random access memory, or DRAM. U.S. firms lost dominance, by world market share terms, in this market segment five years before losing their dominant position in the overall integrated circuit world market. The crossover in the DRAM segment between Japanese and U.S. firms occurred in 1982 and the slide down in market share for the United States has continued up through 1989 (Dataquest, 1989).

The trade balance between Japan and the United States in terms of integrated circuits follows a similar pattern. Prior to 1980 the United States enjoyed a surplus with Japan. Between 1980 and 1982 rough trade parity existed. In 1983 the trade balance tipped in favor of Japan. The United States has run a deficit with Japan since then. The deficit narrowed in 1986 by $250 million, but has increased since that time. In 1988, the most recent year for statistics, the deficit increased to $800 million (McClean, 1989).

Most of the deficit is due to the strength of the Japanese firms in the DRAM segment. Choosing 1985 as a representative year, as it marks the midpoint between when the United States began to run significant deficits and the present time, it has been shown that of the one billion worth of integrated circuits imported from Japan in 1985, 65 percent were memory chips. The importance of the memory segment is that it drives the basic fabrication technologies needed in producing other types of integrated circuits, such as microprocessors (McClean, 1986; Gramlich, 1987).

Because the DRAM is one of the most important integrated circuit technologies, by tracing its development this work will:

- explore and evaluate the technical factors most responsible for the development of the DRAM;
- explore and evaluate the strategic factors which most influenced the development of the DRAM;
- examine the interplay of the technological and strategic factors;
- determine the consequences for company strategies and government policies for technology intensive industries and;

• assess the directions of change in current socioeconomic-political arrangements within and between nations.

Focus on Diffusion

The idiosyncratic quality of the innovation process as it is practiced in various industries is well recognized today (Nelson, 1982). What the above discussion should also bring out is that the innovation process possesses internal idiosyncrasies. These idiosyncrasies arise from the stages that innovations progress through. Consequently, while the entire innovation process will be examined, the diffusion stage will provide the primary focus for this book. This will enhance the clarity of our findings.

The diffusion stage is chosen for two reasons. First, it is considered to be the stage which offers the greatest opportunity to examine the external factors effecting the strategic management of technological innovation. Second, it is in the diffusion stage that the fruits of innovation are released to fuel technological growth and economic development (Mansfield, 1971; Rogers, 1983). This stage also sets the economic conditions for further innovation. A firm's ability to gather and maintain necessary resources for its next innovation will be determined in the diffusion stage of the current innovation.

The primary focus of this book will be on the strategic management of technology and the differences in the approaches used by Japanese and U.S. firms to the issues posed by technological competition. These differences will help to explain why the Japanese have come to dominate the DRAM segment of the integrated circuit industry. From this a better understanding of where Japanese companies are going technologically can be derived.

This increased understanding of the innovation process will be accomplished through the collection and analysis of both qualitative and quantitative data. The quantitative data is archival data collected through various published and unpublished sources. These sources included industry trade associations and research from companies which study the industries. The qualitative data consists of interviews with government and industry leaders in the respective countries done through field work in each of the countries. The data on Japan was initially collected during a six month stay from October 1983 until April 1984 and subsequent stays during June to August in 1985 and 1989. The data on the United States has been continuously collected from July 1984 until September 1989.

The DRAM device has also been chosen because of the important role it plays in advancing integrated circuit technology in general (Sanger, 1987). It is considered one of the key products for developing process technologies used in manufacturing other integrated circuit devices. Further, as indicated, this market is an area of intense competition between United States and Japanese firms. As will be shown in later chapters, the Japanese have come to dominate this crucial integrated circuit product technology. The importance of the innovation envelope concept to the strategy of the Japanese in DRAM product technology will then be examined.

SIGNPOSTS AND TRAJECTORIES FOR THE INTEGRATED CIRCUIT INDUSTRY

Economic Signposts and the Integrated Circuit Industry

The discussion presented in chapter two will now be operationalized in the integrated circuit industry. As noted above, it has been suggested that technologies follow along paths or trajectories which can be traced by determining the signposts or "markers" of the technology (Nelson and Winter, 1977). One important set of signposts is economic. While a number of economic signposts for the integrated circuit industry have been examined, one will be used to illustrate some of the characteristics of the trajectory followed by integrated circuit technology (Methé, 1985).

The economic measure chosen is the amount of initial investment needed to enter the integrated circuit industry with a fully functioning manufacturing facility to produce state-of-the-art integrated circuit (IC) devices. This measure was chosen because it summarizes factors seen in two other measures that are sometimes used—R&D expense and capital spending. Each new production facility embodies the R&D and capital spending needed to develop and produce the product.

The investment necessary for the integrated circuit industry over a number of years is shown in Table 3.1. As can be seen in the table, the initial investment needed in the early years, the 1950s, was between $100,000 and $350,000. By 1967, the needed investment had increased to two and one-half million. The ten-year period between the late 1950s and the late 1960s saw the introduction of the integrated circuit as the predominant semiconductor product technology. Prior to the 1960s, discrete semiconductor devices, such as transistors and diodes, were the dominant product technologies.

The period from 1967 to 1987 showed a vast increase in the needed investment for a state-of-the-art integrated circuit facility. Necessary investment increased from two and one-half million to about ten million between 1967 and 1977. This coincided with the movement of integrated circuit technology from small scale integration (SSI) to large scale integration (LSI). This change in technology relates to the number of circuits, or transistors, that can be inscribed on each device and hence to the com-

Table 3.1
Estimated Investment Necessary for Entry into U.S. Integrated Circuit Market

YEAR	INVESTMENT (million dollars in year noted)
1957	$ 0.1-0.35 Million
1967	$ 2.5 Million
1977	$10 Million
1979	$18.5 Million
1980	$19.5 Million
1984	$60 Million
1987	$100 Million
1989	$250 Million
1993	$750 Million*

Sources: Tilton, 1971; Wilson, Ashton and Egan, 1980; Strauss, 1981; Strauss, 1984; McClean, 1988; McClean, 1989; Robertson, 1990.
*Forecast

plexity of the integrated circuit devices produced. While the implication of this technology trend will be discussed in greater detail in the next section, it is important to note that changes in the level of integration mark significant advances in the sophistication of integrated circuit technology.

The next major jump occurred in 1984 with investment increasing from twenty million to sixty million. This marks the movement in integrated circuit technology from large scale integration to very large scale integration (VLSI). These movements in required initial investment have also been found to exist for the R&D and capital spending signposts for the period 1977 to 1987 (Methé, 1985; Ferguson, 1988). In 1989 the cost of establishing a state-of-the-art fabrication facility was estimated to be $250 million, and the projections are that by 1993 it will cost over $750 million (Robertson, 1989). This indicates that the integrated circuit industry is moving into the ultra large scale integration (ULSI) era. If the past is a prologue, the R&D and capital expenditures will have to increase accordingly.

In order to understand these economic signposts more fully, the technical signposts which parallel them must be examined. The importance of the relationship between both sets of signposts will be examined in the next section. The interrelation of the two sets will then be operationalized for a representative integrated circuit product.

Technical Signposts and the Integrated Circuit Industry

When examining a complex, technologically intensive industry such as the integrated circuit industry, determining technological trajectories and signposts may appear difficult. The number and types of products, ranging from dynamic random access memory (DRAM) and read only memory (ROM), to microprocessors (MPU) and programmable logic arrays (PLA) is at first daunting. However, a number of characteristics are common among these products. Further, all of the products share common technological traits in their design and production.

First, products in the integrated circuit industry are broadly classified into two major groups, logic and memory devices (Wilson, Ashton and Egan, 1980). All memory devices, such as DRAMs, store information in the form of bits (zeros or ones) on the device. All logic devices, such as microprocessors, are associated with the processing of these bits of information; that is, manipulating the bits of information according to some set of instructions to perform some task.

While specific products in each group perform specific tasks and has a specific product trajectory, all products share common technological characteristics which allow for comparisons of their trajectories. For example, in the microprocessor trajectory, the engineering signposts are associated with the number of bits of information that can be processed at one time. Hence, the trajectory for the microprocessor (MPU) went from four bits to eight bits to sixteen bits to the current thirty-two bit microprocessor device. This corresponds to the three levels of integration discussed in the previous section. Small scale integration (SSI) would correspond to the four bit MPU, while large scale integration (LSI) would correspond to the eight bit MPU. Very large scale integration (VLSI) corresponds to the sixteen bit and thirty-two bit MPU.

A similar progression is exhibited by memory devices, such as the dynamic random access memory (DRAM) device. The relevant engineering signposts for its technological trajectory are the 1K (K = Kilobit = 1,064 bits), 4K, 16K, 64K, 256K, 1Mb (Mb = Megabit = 1,089,536 bits) devices. Again, SSI would correspond to the 1K, with LSI corresponding to the 4K and 16K devices. VLSI corresponds to the 64K, 256K and 1Mb devices. The introduction of the 4Mb in 1988 marked the beginning of the ULSI era. Each memory and logic device follows a similar path as measured by the number of bits that are either stored or processed by the device.

While other technological signposts exist, the number of bits of information is a highly salient one, since it acts as a demarcation line between product generations. The number of bits of information is also important as a signpost because of the direct relationship it has with another engineering signpost, circuit width. For the integrated circuit firm, circuit width is a key guidepost for the designing and production of IC devices. As the number of bits of information increases, the circuit width must decrease. Consequently, the circuit width and number of bits of information are interchangeable as engineering signposts.

Because circuit width can be substituted for number of bits of information as a signpost, comparisons can be made between devices that perform different tasks, such as microprocessors and DRAMs (McClean, 1986). For ease of presentation, the relationship between the number of bits of information and circuit size is presented for only one integrated circuit device, the DRAM.

SOPHISTICATION

In chapter two, the concept of technological sophistication was defined as the capacity to perform a function divided by the cost to perform the function; that is, an effectiveness measure divided by an efficiency measure. As noted above, a good measure of the degree of effectiveness exhibited in the DRAM technology is the increasing number of memory bits per integrated circuit device.

The number of bits per device is a measure of the increase in capacity of the devices to perform the function of memory storage; it is a purely technical measure. There are other measures of capability, such as access or cycle time, electrical power usage, die size and number of pins on the chip (Hazewindus and Tooker, 1982). These will not be used since they change over the life of the chip, as will be explained below.

The efficiency measure is the cost to the user per bit. The price per bit is a reflection of the cost of the capacity to perform the function. This economic measure must be distinguished from other measures related to cost, such as the price per chip. The price per chip is a reflection of the cost of producing the chip, and the resources needed to fabricate it.

While this is the price that a user must pay to acquire the memory chip, the price per bit is the actual cost of the use of the memory function. It is a measure of efficiency for the user of the integrated circuit, but since price is related to cost it is a measure of efficiency of production, especially at the time of introduction of the integrated circuit.

The price that will be used to compute the price per bit will be the average selling price of each chip at its introduction. This price will be divided by the number of bits contained on the chip to determine the price, or cost to the user, per bit. The comparison will be made between innovations at the time of their introduction.

As the innovation matures and moves down its learning curve, the average selling price drops. Consequently, a DRAM chip that sold for $200 at its initial offering may be selling for as little as ninety-nine cents several years later. Therefore, the initial price is used. Further, during the maturation process, the chip may undergo several quality improvements in cycle time, electrical power usage, and the like (Hazewindus and Tooker, 1982). These are considered minor innovations to the basic technology and are not covered in this study.

FINANCIAL AND INFORMATIONAL RESOURCES

Once it has been established that the sophistication of the DRAM technology is increasing, the level of resources needed to support the increase will be examined. The need for financial resources will be measured by the price per chip at the time of introduction, and the level of investment needed to enter the integrated circuit market.

Archival data on the use of informational resources are not readily available. Therefore, a surrogate measure was devised to indicate the level of resource use with each DRAM device. In the integrated circuit industry it is customary to circulate samples of chips that are new. There exists an interval of time between when the chips are first sampled and when they are available at significant production levels.

This period of time represents the time needed to learn the various new production technologies associated with the new chip. This "sampling time" is a reflection of the level of information resources needed to produce the new DRAM device. While it is not a measure of all the information resources needed since it does not reflect the invention phase for the new device, it does reflect an important portion of the innovation process.

Recalling information from Figure 1.1, sampling time would be the equivalent of the information resources needed to move from design to mass manufacturing. To the firm, merely having a few prototype devices is not as economically important as being able to produce large quantities of the device. As such, the firm will attempt to gain the resources necessary to move from prototype to pilot to mass manufacturing. Once the firm mass-produces the device, it begins to gain a return on its earlier investments.

In summary, major innovations will be used are measured by the introduction of new DRAM devices. Sophistication will be measured by the number of bits per chip, an effectiveness measure, and the cost per bit, an efficiency measure. The indicators used for the financial resources include the price per chip, the entry investment, and the level of capital expenditure and research and development expense. The informational resources are measured by the "sampling time" for each device.

TECHNOLOGICAL SOPHISTICATION AND RESOURCE NEED

In this section, technological sophistication for the DRAM technology is measured and its effects on innovation resources determined. In order to

Table 3.2
Effectiveness and Efficiency of Various DRAM Devices for Year of Introduction

YEAR	DEVICE	EFFECTIVENESS	EFFICIENCY
1974	4K	4096	0.9765
1976	16K	16384	0.3662
1978	64K	65536	0.1376
1980	256K	262144	0.0763
1985	1Mb	1048576	0.0143

Source: Dataquest, 1984; 1989

illustrate the first research lesson, for the DRAM technology, the sophistication of the technology will be determined. Then both the financial and informational resources are measured. In order to be conservative in illustrating the research lesson, both the level of sophistication of the technology and resources needed for innovation are expected to increase.

Technological Sophistication in the DRAM Technology

As noted above, technological sophistication is a combination of effectiveness and efficiency for a technology. These two measures are displayed in Table 3.2.

It is evident from the table that both the effectiveness of the technology and the efficiency of the technology are increasing. With each succeeding generation of DRAM devices, the number of bits, or capacity, of the device has increased and the price per bit has fallen. The fall in the price per bit indicates that a ninety cent drop in the price of storage of one bit of information occurred between the 4K DRAM and the 256K DRAM which currently dominates the DRAM market. The drop occasioned with the introduction of the one megabit DRAM (1Mb DRAM) is even more precipitous, from ninety-seven cents to one cent.

Since the price per bit is the price at the introduction of the device, and this price decreases over the life of the device, the figures presented in the table are conservative. These two trends are combined in Table 3.3 to yield the sophistication measure for the DRAM technology. In this table, both the sophistication measure and a sophistication index are presented.

Computation of the Sophistication Measure and Index

The sophistication measure is computed by dividing the effectiveness of the technology by the efficiency of the technology and taking the log of

50   Technological Competition in Global Industries

Table 3.3
Degree of Sophistication for Innovations in DRAM Technology

YEAR	DEVICE INNOVATION	SOPHISTICATION	SOPHISTICATION INDEX
1974	4K	3.622688	1.000
1976	16K	4.303869	1.188
1978	64K	5.332546	1.472
1980	256K	6.508638	1.797
1985	1Mb	7.865200	2.1711

the result. Because of the technical/engineering aspects of the technology, a curvilinear trend exists in the data which is removed by taking the log. These are the figures that appear in Table 3.3.

The index is computed with the 4K DRAM as the base. From both the sophistication measure and the accompanying index, it is apparent that the sophistication of the technology is increasing. The sophistication index indicates that the 16K DRAM is 18.8 percent more sophisticated, that is, more effective and efficient in carrying out its design function, than is the 4K DRAM. The 256K DRAM is 79.7 percent more sophisticated. The 1Mb DRAM is more than two hundred times as sophisticated. Consequently, as the DRAM has become more sophisticated, the number and variety of applications has increased (Methé, 1990). The importance of this for changes in the market for the DRAM will be discussed in chapter five in this book. It should also be noted that the rate of change of increase in sophistication is also increasing. The difference between the 16K and 64K DRAM devices is 0.284, while the difference between the 64K and 256K DRAM devices is 0.325 and for the 256K and 1Mb it is 0.3741.

Since the technology for the DRAM is the same for the Japanese firms, the results hold for both sets of producers. This is not surprising, since it is expected that the technology will not differ in its general composition from country to country. The relevant question to be discussed is how does this increase in the sophistication impact the resources needed for the innovation process. In order to answer this question, it is necessary to understand that DRAM technology is composed of a number of such technologies. These technologies are closely coupled so that a change in one cannot come about without change in the others.

TECHNOLOGICAL TRAJECTORY IN DRAM DEVICES

The various generations of DRAM devices, the 4K, 16K, 64K, 256K and 1Mb, all perform the same function, that is, to store information. The

Table 3.4
Technological Change Required in Selected DRAM Production Technologies

DRAM DEVICE (DESIGN RULE)	PHOTOLITHOGRAPHIC TECHNOLOGY	ETCHING TECHNOLOGY	CLEAN ROOM TECHNOLOGY
4K	Contact Printer	Wet	Class 10K
(8-6 micron)	$10,000-50,000	$2.45 Million	$4 Million
16K	Proximity Printer	Wet	Class 10K
(6-4 micron)	$125,000	$2.45 Million	$4 Million
64K	Projection Printer	Wet/Dry	Class 1K-10K
(3-2 micron)	$250,000-750,000	$2.45 Million $3.85 Million	$6 Million
256K/1Mb	Stepper	Dry	Class 100-1K
(2-1.5 micron/ 1-0.5 micron)	$500,000-1 Million	$3.85 Million	$10 Million

Sources: Pickar, 1982 p. 58; Eklund and Strauss, 1982, p. 19; Strauss, 1984, pp. 76–83.

trajectory along which this technology has moved is affected by a number of signposts. Since there are more bits per chip, that is, the density of the chip has increased, the cell size, or the area on a chip covered by a transistor, must be smaller. As a result, the circuit geometries connecting these cells must work with more precise design rules.

The design rules for each DRAM device described in this book, and the effect that these design rules have on the technologies needed to produce the device, are presented in Table 3.4. For the 4K, the design rule is that the width of the connecting circuits is between six to eight microns. As the density of each device increases, the design rules demand greater precision. Thus, the design rules of the 16K device are between four and six microns, while the design rules for the 64K device are two to three microns and for the 256K device are between one and one-half to two microns. For the 1Mb, the design rule requires that sub-micron technologies be used. This is also the case with the 4Mb, although it is not shown.

Changes in the design rules will impact the various production technologies differently. These production technologies are considered subtechnologies for the parent DRAM device technology. The movement of the DRAM along its technology trajectory cannot be accomplished without concurrent movement among the subtechnologies. Certain of the subtechnologies become more important than others for making the change from one set of design rules to another. As will be discussed below, identifying these subtechnologies is crucial to the strategic management of the DRAM technology.

OPERATIONALIZATION IN A PRODUCT TECHNOLOGY

DRAM Product Technology's Innovation Envelope

Innovations in the dynamic random access memory (DRAM) segment of the integrated circuit industry are used to illustrate the technology innovation envelope. These were measured by the introduction of new DRAM devices in the United States and Japan between the years 1974 to 1988. These data were collected by the author during field trips in Japan and the United States.

The technical signpost chosen for the DRAM product technology was circuit width. As noted above, circuit width is an important technical signpost (Hazewindus and Tooker, 1982). Again, circuit width determines the capacity of the DRAM device to store data. The trajectory follows the design rule that to increase data storage capacity requires a decrease in circuit width. Therefore, each new device type requires stricter design rules. This is illustrated in Table 3.5.

Three subtechnologies were chosen because of their critical importance in meeting the circuit width rule changes (Strauss, 1984). Photolithographic technology is the means by which the circuit patterns are projected onto the DRAM chip. Etching technology is the means by which the circuits are carved into the DRAM chip, following the pattern laid down during photolithography. Clean room technology is the means by which dust and other contaminants are prevented from destroying a circuit during fabrication.

The stricter design rules for circuit widths affect the three subtechnologies differently, but each must be altered to meet the new requirements. This results in increased cost for the machines needed to produce the new devices. These increases in cost are a proxy measure for the increasing complexity of the equipment subtechnologies and provides an economic signpost. Hence, Table 3.4 illustrates how the DRAM technology creates an innovation envelope which affects the production subtechnologies.

To further illustrate the innovation envelope of the DRAM, each of the subtechnologies shown in the above table are displayed in Figure 3.1. The main product technology trajectory is the DRAM device. Major innovations are indicated as the 4K, 16K, 64K, 256K and 1Mb. Each of the three subtechnologies and their respective relationship with the DRAM technology is also displayed.

As can be seen in Figure 3.1, the photolithographic subtechnology has shown the most change. Each generation of the DRAM product, with the exception of the 1Mb, has required a new type of photolithographic equip-

Figure 3.1
Relationship between DRAM Product Technology and Photolithographic
Subtechnology

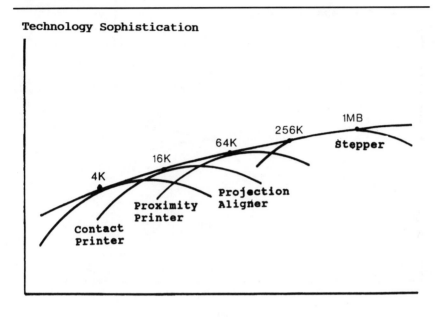

Technology Sophistication

1MB

256K

64K

Stepper

16K

4K

Projection
Aligner

Proximity
Printer

Contact
Printer

Time

ment to produce it. For the LSI DRAMs, the 4K and 16K, the contract printer could be used. The advantage of the proximity printer is that it does not directly touch the integrated circuit device, and consequently there is less chance of contamination with dust particles. This is an important consideration in terms of increasing the yield of the manufacturing process. The issue of yield will be discussed in more detail below.

There was not an overlay between the LSI 16K and the VLSI 64K. In order to produce the 64K, the projection aligner was needed. This is also the case with the 256K. In order to produce this DRAM device, the Stepper must be used. The Stepper has proven remarkably robust, since it is still being used for the 1Mb and the 4Mb. Indication are that for the 16Mb, however, a shift to either X-ray or E-beam lithography will have to be enacted (McClean, 1989).

The etching subtechnology shown in Figure 3.2 has had the least change, with a break occurring at the introduction of the 64K DRAM device. Again, as illustrated with the photolithographic subtechnology, some overlap exists for the use of wet etching could continue through the 64K DRAM device. However, with the advent of the 256K DRAM, dry plasma etching had to

Figure 3.2
Relationship between DRAM Product Technology and Etching Subtechnology

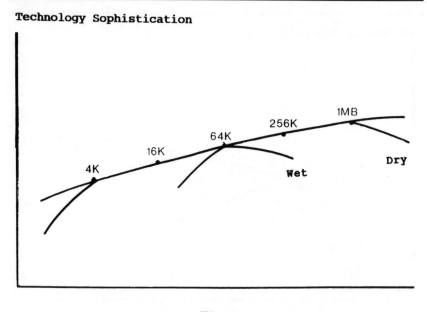

Technology Sophistication

Time

be used. Dry etching allows for more precise cuts to be made in the silicon material used in IC chip. This precision is necessary in order to eliminate one circuit on a chip from touching another, rendering the chip useless. Dry etching is also being used for the 1Mb and the 4Mb. This particular subtechnology has been less constraining to the development of the DRAM devices.

The clean room subtechnology shown in Figure 3.3 is between the other two in the number of changes needed to support advancement along the DRAM's technology trajectory. As noted above, clean room technology is the process by which dust particles and other contaminants are kept out of the production area. The various "classes" shown in the table refer to the number of particles of greater than 0.5 micron in diameter per square foot of air that are tolerated in the production process. In the LSI period, class 10,000 environments were acceptable. For the production of the first VLSI, the 64K, initial production could be at class 10,000, but in order to maintain yield, the production environment had to become a class 1,000. For the 256K and 1Mb devices even more stringent environments are needed. These range between class 100 and class 10. For the 4Mb and other ULSI devices, a class 1 environment will be required.

Figure 3.3
Relationship between DRAM Product Technology and Clean Room Subtechnology

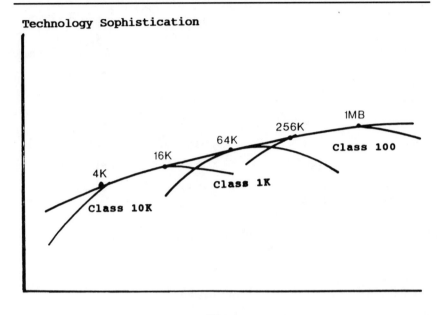

Time

While these figures vary within the production process of each device, they represent the minimum tolerance acceptable during important phases of each device's production. As with the above technologies, clean room technology is very important in increasing the yield of the production process. It is important to note that as the tolerances increase for the clean room, so does the cost. The impact that these design rules have on the three selected technologies of production is to demand greater performance from them and this is achieved only with greater cost.

The interrelationships between the DRAM product technology and the various subtechnologies is important not only in terms of cost and in indicating which subtechnologies are more crucial in effecting improvement in the main product technology, but also because each subtechnology is generally produced by a firm which specializes in only that subtechnology. Hence, the strategic relationships between the firm producing the DRAM and the firms producing each of the three subtechnologies is important for the innovation process.

Differences in these strategic arrangements should affect the innovation process in a given product's technological trajectory. These differences will be examined in later chapters, for now the important issue is how the

Table 3.5
Initial Average Selling Price for Each DRAM Device

YEAR	DRAM DEVICE	TECHNOLOGY	AVERAGE SELLING PRICE (dollars in year introduced)
1974	4K	LSI	$ 40.00
1976	16K	LSI	$ 60.00
1978	64K	VLSI	$200.00
1980	256K	VLSI	$200.00
1985	1Mb	VLSI	$150.00
1988	4Mb	ULSI	$452.00

Source: Dataquest, 1984, 1989.

DRAM's innovation envelope effects the resources needed for continued innovation.

INCREASES IN FINANCIAL RESOURCES

As a result of the layering of technological change for the various production technologies within the technological change of the DRAM device, the capital requirements for producing DRAMs has increased. Recalling Table 3.1, the figures presented clearly show that the capital need is increasing. The cost of establishing an integrated circuit facility is increasing. Capital costs for an integrated circuit facility can be used for building and land as well as equipment. The trend, however, is for equipment to take up a greater portion of these costs. In the mid-1970s equipment made up forty percent of the costs. In the mid-1980s that percentage had increased to fifty-five percent. This percentage is forecast to increase to seventy percent in the mid–1990s (McClean, 1988). While these figures are for integrated circuit facility costs in the U.S. integrated circuit industry, it is estimated that the Japanese industry is facing similar trends.

This is first indicated by the increasing initial average selling price per chip for each of the DRAM devices in Table 3.5. This price is at the time of introduction of the device, before learning curve economies have set in. In this way it is an approximation of the capital expenditures and research and development expenses needed to product the device. The significance here is the difference between the large scale integration (LSI) techniques (4K and 16K devices) and the very large scale integration (VLSI) techniques (64K, 256K and 1Mb devices). The differences within each group are not great and the decline in the 1Mb can be accounted for

Table 3.6
Average Capital Expenditure per Year for Top Five Merchant U.S. Firms and Top Five Japanese Firms (in millions of dollars)

YEAR	UNITED STATES	JAPANESE
1979	619	307
1980	780	478
1981	643	658
1982	587	774
1983	790	1193
1984	1724	2330
1985	1195	2005
1986	760	1150
1987	1055	1405
1988	1465	2160

Sources: United States, annual reports of Texas Instruments, Intel, National Semiconductor, Motorola, and Fairchild; Japan, Denki Kiki Shijo Chosa Kaihen, 1971–1980 and Nihon Kaihatsu Ginko, 1984. McClean, 1985–1989.

by the use of similar production technologies between it and the 256K DRAM. The price of introduction for the 4Mb may mark the beginning of the ULSI era. It is more than double the cost of introduction of the VLSI DRAM devices. The capital expenditures for each device market which underlie the trend in these prices are presented in Table 3.6.

Table 3.6 indicates that the level of capital expenditures has been increasing throughout the time period under study. In the U.S. industry, the increase was steady up until 1981, when a decrease occurred. During that year, the integrated circuit industry was hit by a severe recession. A similar situation occurred in 1984 through 1986. This recession was more severe and lasted longer than the 1981 recession. The severity of this recession is indicated by the slow recovery of capital expenditures.

In the Japanese case, the pattern has been the same except at a higher absolute level. While the Japanese have experienced the same recessionary conditions as the United States, they have been better able to maintain increases in capital expenditures. Possible reasons for this will be explored in the next chapter. The important point for this portion of the analysis is that the increase has occurred.

The increases in capital expenditure are mirrored in the research and development expense trends of each country, presented in Table 3.7. These

Table 3.7
Average Research and Development Expenditure per Year for Top Five Merchant U.S. Firms and Top Five Japanese Firms (in millions of dollars and billions of yen)

YEAR	UNITED STATES	JAPANESE
1980	529	376
1981	620	441
1982	730	527
1983	900	633
1984	1151	748
1985	1283	1142
1986	1353	1222
1987	1516	1160
1988	1746	1451
1989	1926	1656

Sources: United States, annual reports of Texas Instruments, Intel, AMD, Motorola and Analog Devices; Japan, Denki Kiki Shijo Chosa Kaihen, 1971–1980, Yano Keizai Kenkyu Jo, 1984b and Nihon Kaihatsu Ginko, 1984; annual reports Hitachi, Matsushita, Toshiba, NEC, Mitsubishi Electric, Fujitsu.

expenses reflect the effort needed to bring about the next generation of a technology, while the capital expenditures more accurately reflect the effort to produce efficiently the current generation. As such, the research and development expenses are a better indicator of the resources needed in innovation.

In both countries, the research and development expenses have increased consistently, even during periods of recession. From the evicence presented in Tables 3.5 through 3.7, it is evident that the need for financial resources has increased.

THE ECONOMICS OF INTEGRATED CIRCUIT PRODUCTION, YIELD, AND THE LEARNING CURVE

Before proceeding into the analysis of the informational resource needs, it is important to understand the economics of integrated circuit production. By doing so, the coexistence of decreasing price per bit and increasing capital requirements can be explained.

There are three factors which are important. The first is simply that more bits can now be placed on the devices. The increase in the number of bits has been faster than the increase in costs of production. This can compensate for the increase in cost as long as the percent increase in the number of bits is greater than the percent increase in cost.

The second factor of importance is the yield of production. The production process for integrated circuits is made up of a number of steps. Each of these steps is related to a production subtechnology. The relationship between the steps in the production process is multiplicative, so that a small variation in the yield from one step will result in a large variation in the yield for the total process. One of the factors that affects yield is the precision of the machines which is directly affected by the quality of the subtechnologies.

As each production subtechnology is perfected, the quality of capital equipment embodies that improvement. Thus, with the production of each photolithographic system, for example, improvements are made in the machine which increase the yield for DRAM devices.

Improvements in etching, clean room and other subtechnologies will also affect the yield for the DRAM device. Again, the importance of the technological envelope comes in. Movement along the DRAM device technology trajectory can only occur if the subtechnologies also move along their respective trajectories. In other words, innovation in the DRAM device technology is dependent upon innovation in the subtechnologies.

This process is affected not only at the points of major innovation, as with the introduction of a new DRAM device, but also where minor improvements result in increases in yield and continued technical reliability in each device market.

The third factor, which is related to yield, is the learning curve phenomenon. As the workers involved in the manufacture of a particular device become more familiar with the machines used in that device's production process, less mistakes are made and the yield increases. The familiarity with the process occurs through learning, or the acquisition of information. The learning curve followed by most integrated circuit devices is about seventy percent, this is also true for the DRAM device (McClean, 1989). The importance of this fact will be explored below.

INFORMATIONAL RESOURCES

Increases in Informational Resources and the Learning Curve

The need for informational resources will now be discussed. It is difficult to determine the need for informational resources because archival data for this particular type of resource is not available. From the discussion on the learning curve, however, one way to measure the need for such resources is apparent.

Table 3.8
Mean Sampling Time for Informational Resources for the DRAM Market

Estimate of Means

Sampling Time (quarter years)	4K	16K	64K	256K	1Mb
	1.21	1.75	4.17	3.56	4.27

It is argued in this book that as the technology of the DRAM becomes more sophisticated, it should take longer to move down the learning curve from the point of initial introduction of the device to some predetermined point on the curve. Thus, the informational resources needed should be reflected in the time it takes to obtain a given level of production.

Many firms do not begin producing large volumes of chips until the problems of production have been worked out. The producers will, however, send samples of the chips to potential customers. As the producer's knowledge of the production process grows, that is, as the amount of information acquired about the new machines needed to produce the device increases, the number of chips shipped to customers increases.

Initially the demand for the new chips is low, since customers have not yet designed them into their own products. Consequently, in the early stages of production the most important factors are supply factors: factors affected by information acquisition. Eventually the demand for the new chips increases and becomes more important than the supply factors.

DRAM Informational Resource Needs

To be conservative in our analysis, the level of production is chosen to be 50,000 units per quarter. This is a small quantity, and the importance of the demand factor is thus minimized. The difference between the quarter in which initial samples were sent to customers and the quarter when shipment was greater than 50,000 units is then taken; this is called the sampling time.

The average sampling time is determined for each device type by averaging the sampling time across the firms that introduced the device. The difference in these averages are calculated and the results for all the firms in the DRAM market are presented in Table 3.8.

As seen in Table 3.8, the averages increase as the innovations move from the 4K to the 64K devices. The 256K device shows a small drop in the average, but the 1Mb device sees the average in sampling time increase. The 4Mb is not included in this analysis because currently firms are still entering that market. The mean sampling times for the firms that have entered is presented for comparison. As can be seen from the table, the data for the LSI devices, the 4K and 16K, and the VLSI devices, the 64K

Table 3.9
U.S. Firms, Mean Sampling Time for Informational Resources for the DRAM Market

Estimate of Means					
Sampling Time	4K	16K	64K	256K	1Mb
(quarter years)	1.27	2.40	4.44	4.50	5.67

Table 3.10
Japanese Firms, Mean Sampling Time for Informational Resources for the DRAM Market

Estimate of Means					
Sampling Time	4K	16K	64K	256K	1Mb
(quarter years)	1.0	0.67	3.09	2.80	3.75

through 1Mb, shows the same break that was seen with the financial resources.

Differences between the 4K and 16K devices are not large, but the differences between the 4K and 64K and the 16K and 64K are. Furthermore, the mean sampling time for both the 256K and 1Mb DRAM devices follows the same pattern for the earlier devices, both being larger than the 4K and 16K. These findings indicate that the informational resource needs for innovation have increased for the overall DRAM market. To determine the relationship within the two market segments under study, this analysis is done for both the U.S. and Japanese segments of the DRAM industry. The same procedure is followed for the U.S. firms in the market and for the Japanese firms in the market. These results are presented in Tables 3.9 and 3.10.

The results are similar to the findings for the overall DRAM market. One exception is with the Japanese firms in the 16K market. Sampling time decreased from the 4K sampling time. Further, for the Japanese samples there was a drop in the sampling time for the 256K DRAM from the 64K DRAM. This drop did not occur among the U.S. firms. With each innovation, the information needs increased for U.S. firms. Sampling time increased for the 1Mb in the Japanese sample and continued to increase for the U.S. sample.

From this analysis, it is evident that the first research lesson does apply to the DRAM device. The sophistication of the DRAM technology is shown to increase with each new innovation. The DRAM technology follows a trajectory which affects the production technologies. This results in increased cost for the machines needed to produce the new devices.

As a result, capital expenditures increase as do research and development expenses. Each new machine requires learning, and therefore information, before it can be operated properly and produce a yield of sufficient quantity. This is reflected in the increase in sampling time. The impact of these changes in resource needs on the strategic management of technology will be discussed in the next chapter.

As noted earlier in this chapter, the integrated circuit industry is divided into logic as well as memory devices. From a technological perspective, does the innovation envelope concept hold for logic devices as well? This is particularly important for two types of logic devices, microprocessors (MPU) and Application Specific Integrated Circuits (ASIC), since these are the major logic devices in terms of market share. Studies of the increase in density for logic devices indicate that there is a 1.35 times increase per year in density of transistors on a single integrated circuit chip. This compares to the 1.5 times increase per year for the DRAM (McClean, 1989). Consequently, memory devices have tended to lead the logic devices in terms of movement along the innovation envelope, but both have followed the same technological trajectory.

Improvements in microprocessors occur in terms of the amount of information that can be inputed and processed as well as the number of transistors per chip. Hence, microprocessors are referred to by the amount of "bits" of information that can be processed. However, the number of transistors on the chip for a microprocessor indicates the number and complexity of the functions that can be carried out. Consequently, two microprocessor devices may be 16-bit devices, but one may have more transistors per chip and be able to carry out more functions. In terms of a comparison of logic and memory devices, the 1K DRAM is roughly equivalent to the 8-bit microprocessor in terms of the number of transistors per chip or density. The 16K DRAM is equivalent to the 16-bit microprocessor. The 256K DRAM is equivalent to the 32-bit microprocessor. Current generations of 32-bit microprocessors are continuing to improve by adding more transistors per chip. Hence, Intel's latest 32-bit microprocessor, the 80486, is roughly equivalent to the 1Mb DRAM device in terms of density.

Both the logic and memory devices follow the same technological trajectory. Both use the same manufacturing techniques, so the innovation envelope concept is equally applicable to both types of devices. As will be shown in a later chapter, however, the subtechnologies key to each type of device will differ. These differences and the implication of these are important in understanding the competition between companies in the integrated circuit industry. However, the technological similarities that have been discussed above are more important. These indicate that both sets of integrated circuit devices can be described in terms of the innovation envelope concept. The implications of what occurs in the DRAM segment can be applied to the logic device segment.

INFORMATION RESOURCES AND INSTITUTIONAL FACTORS

Before proceeding to the discussion of the next research lesson, the dips in the mean sampling time for the 4K–16K and 64K–256K devices in the Japanese sample and the steady decline in the 64K–256K–1Mb device sample time for the United States need further discussion. Information comes in a variety of forms. As can be gathered from the analysis done above, the forms of the information are not considered crucial to the innovation process. What is considered crucial is the reception point for the information among individuals.

INTERNAL INSTITUTIONAL FACTORS

In a company competing in a technology intensive industry such as the DRAM industry, two segments of the company's employees are vital to the success of using the information resources efficiently. The first set of people are the engineers—both design and process engineers. Both are equally important for the process of major innovation to continue. This is because of the technological envelope discussed above. For a new device to be introduced, not only must design challenges be overcome, but process challenges as well. Consequently, design and process engineers must be given equal support, especially as the technology becomes more sophisticated.

The second set of people are those on the production line. These people play an equally important role as the engineers in the area of increasing the yield. When economists study movements along the learning curve, what they are actually exploring is how people on a production line learn to do their job more efficiently.

Often a single person may play a role. On more than one occasion it was pointed out, during studies of fabrication facilities conducted by the author in both the United States and Japan, that one person had a certain "touch" for a machine. This person could make the machine work at near 100 percent efficiency, while other people could not.

Skills that this person acquired could only be passed on by direct contact with other people; a manual would not suffice. It was also pointed out that the ability of the production staff to work as a team was important, especially with the later DRAM devices. Not only was communication with the production staff important, but communication between the production and engineering staff also became crucial with the more sophisticated technologies.

One explanation for the decline in the sampling time for the Japanese with the 16K DRAM can be attributed to faster learning of a technology not very different from the 4K DRAM. Since the Japanese have less employee turnover, both among engineers and production staff, learning occurs more rapidly.

With the 64K DRAM, technologies were so much more complicated that learning again returned to its expected direction and sampling time increased. The results for the 256K DRAM and 1Mb DRAM markets further support the trend.

The results discussed above point to another consideration that companies must confront in technological competition. The issue is one of follow-through on the major technological innovations. The companies which are able to follow through on their major product introductions by continually improving quality and lowering cost are the companies which survive. The learning curve phenomena discussed above is the conceptual embodiment of this industrial phenomenon.

The pace of movement down the learning curve is facilitated by maximum effort spent in improvement of process technology. These innovations require close communication between the integrated circuit design engineers in the integrated circuit companies and their process engineers and the engineers in the equipment companies. This is especially true as the technology becomes more sophisticated. This communication process is also crucial to the rapid development of succeeding generations of the product, once a technological envelope has formed. The ability to determine the critical subtechnologies and the financial and informational requirements necessary for progression along the correct trajectories will be enhanced by increased communication among the scientists and engineers in these areas. Companies which are better able to organize these resources will have shorter product development cycles.

EXTERNAL INSTITUTIONAL FACTORS

External to the firms are its relationships to its suppliers, customers, competitors and the government. As noted in chapter two, institutional factors are expected to influence the pace and direction of technological innovation. The arrangements of the various players in a market may increase or decrease the flow of the necessary resources, in this case the informational resource. Firms which are able to adopt new types of institutional arrangements will be better able to exploit market and technological opportunities if they exist. The importance of these considerations for firm strategy and market structure will be shown in the analyses presented in forthcoming chapters.

SUMMARY

In this chapter some of the concepts introduced and discussed conceptually in chapters one and two have been operationalized and applied to the integrated circuit industry and the DRAM device segment. The concept of technological trajectory has been introduced as a relevant way of describing the technological development of integrated circuit technology. It has then been applied to the DRAM device technology. This was done by determining the degree of technological sophistication that resulted from each innovation. It was shown that each new introduction of a DRAM device results in an increase in technological sophistication. We expected that the resources needed for continued innovation would also increase. In order to determine if this were so, the innovation envelope for the DRAM had to be determined.

It was evident from our analyses that the changes in the production technologies were layered within the movement along the trajectory of the DRAM device technology. The movement within each of the production technologies that performed the same function but at higher tolerances from one type of machine or process to another formed trajectories for that respective technology. It was shown that there was close coupling of these production subtechnologies with the parent DRAM device technology, which formed an innovation envelope for the subtechnologies.

An innovation envelope was shown to relate changes in one technology to changes in other technologies coupled to it. Each of the subtechnologies formed a dimension along which change occurred. The concepts of an innovation envelope and a technology trajectory are interrelated, although there are differences. A trajectory implies an inexorable movement which abandons the machines of the past. The envelope, however, implies that movement can go forward or backward, depending on the needs of the technology. Thus, even in the production of the 256K device, a class 10K clean room may be used during certain production steps. The use of the stepper photolithographic machine in both the 256K and 1Mb production process is another example. The trajectory concept can be seen as a special case of the envelope concept.

It was further shown that as the DRAM progressed along its innovation envelope, the resources needed to carry out continued improvement in the DRAM device increased. Both the financial and the information resources were shown to increase. Similar findings were true for both the United States and Japan.

4

The Effect of Innovation on Market Structure

OVERVIEW

This chapter will refine the understanding gained in chapter three concerning the technological factors that drive the DRAM device. This concern has focused primarily on innovations in the product technology associated with the DRAM device. As we observed in the previous chapter, the technology trajectory formed by the innovation pattern in the DRAM device interacts with the subtechnologies crucial to the improvement in the parent DRAM technology to form an innovation envelope. Movement along the DRAM technology trajectory can only occur if certain subtechnologies also experience innovations. While these innovations result in more sophisticated machines to produce the DRAM, these machines also tend to be more complicated to operate and the absolute cost increases. Consequently, more of both the information and financial resources are required as the DRAM technology becomes more sophisticated.

A major break is observed between the LSI devices, the 4K and 16K DRAMS, and the VLSI devices, the 64K, 256K and 1Mb DRAMs. Both the 4K and 16K devices are classified as large scale integration (LSI) devices. With the introduction of the 64K device, the DRAM technology moves to a dramatically more complex design, which is called very large scale integration (VLSI).

While at first glance the progression from 16K to 64K may appear no more complicated than the progression from 4K to 16K, because of non-linear changes in the geometries of circuit size, the progression from 16K to 64K is qualitatively different from the progression from 4K to 16K (Hazewindus and Tooker, 1982). As a result, the movement from LSI devices (16K) to VLSI devices (256K), requires major changes in design and production. These changes in design and production result in a dramatic change in the resources required to innovate (Strauss, 1984). The capital investment in plant and equipment increases threefold from the LSI era to the VLSI era (Strauss, 1984). Hence, the demarcation in DRAM technological complexity between LSI and VLSI will be utilized in analyzing the dominance of various strategies and the success of the firms which adopted them.

In order to more fully understand the implications for strategy of these innovations in DRAM product technology, shifts in the process technologies for integrated circuits must also be examined. These shifts in the process technology used for integrated circuits will further refine the innovation envelope of the DRAM device. The combination of these product and process technology changes will set the context for understanding the success and failure of various strategies used by firms in the DRAM segment of the integrated circuit industry. It is the success or failure of the various strategic approaches of firms in the context of the DRAM innovation envelope that results in the types of firm and market structure that exists today.

Before examining the strategies and the results that these have had, the context of technological competition between U.S. and Japanese firms will be discussed. Following this, shifts in the process technology used in manufacturing the DRAM device will be incorporated into the innovation envelope discussion begun in the previous chapter. These two together will set the stage for the discussion of strategy.

In this discussion, the basic strategic approaches to the integrated circuit industries taken by the U.S. and Japanese firms will be compared. This discussion will serve as the foundation for the examination of specific strategic approaches used by firms in the DRAM segment of the integrated circuit industry. These specific strategic approaches were derived from theories related to the strategic management of technology discussed in the second chapter. The implications of the strategic approaches as exhibited in the type of firms playing the strongest role in the DRAM industry will then be discussed.

Innovation Competition in the DRAM Device

As pointed out in chapter three, the DRAM segment of the integrated circuit industry is an area of major competition between the United States and Japan. Japanese firms became dominant as world suppliers of the DRAM device in 1981. The Japanese have become the innovators in this technology, first to introduce each DRAM innovation beginning with the 64K device. Prior to the introduction of that device, American firms had been the first to innovate. It was Intel which developed the first DRAM device, the 1K, in the early 1970s. Throughout the early LSI period, the

Table 4.1
Maximum Market Share in DRAMs by Device for Japanese Companies

Device	Maximum Percent Market Share U. S.	Japan
1K	95	5
4K	83	17
16K	59	41
64K	29	71
256K	8	92
1Mb	4	96
4Mb	2	98

Source: Dataquest, 1989.

4K and 16K, U.S. firms were the innovators. Beginning with the VLSI period, Japanese firms became the innovators. The results of this change in terms of market share held can be seen in Table 4.1. It can be readily observed from this table that the world share of the firms supplying each succeeding DRAM device follows closely which group introduced it first though innovation in the device segment. In the early years of the DRAM industry, the world market share held by Japanese firms was small. The corresponding share held by the U.S. firms was large. But the world market share supplied by Japanese firms has risen steadily throughout the history of the DRAM device.

The maximum world market share held by Japanese firms in each DRAM device has increased from five percent with the 1K DRAM to forty-one percent with the 16K DRAM to seventy-one percent with the 64K DRAM and ninety-six percent with the 1Mb DRAM. Even after several years of competition from American firms, this early dominance in the latter two VLSI DRAM devices still remains. In 1988, Japanese firms held eighty-five percent of the 256K DRAM device segment and eighty-eight percent of the 1Mb DRAM device segment (McClean, 1989). It is projected that with the current level of interest in the DRAM segment by American firms and the entrance into the DRAM segment of other national firms, Japanese firms are still expected to hold eighty percent of the 1Mb DRAM and seventy-eight percent of the 4Mb DRAM world market share in 1991 and 1994, the years of peak demand for each of each respective device (McClean, 1989).

From this it can be seen that the innovative initiative has shifted towards the Japanese. It is obvious that being able to innovate the DRAM device gives an advantage in terms of market share. This advantage has been found to exist for individual companies as well (Davis, 1989). The full importance of this shift will become evident when the changes in process technology that have been occurring in the DRAM device have been examined.

PROCESS TECHNOLOGY IN THE DRAM DEVICE

Process technology in the integrated circuit industry relates to the way the materials, silicon, metals, oxides of metals and nonmetals, are layered on the integrated circuit chip to create the circuit patterns which allow the chip to perform its function. While these will be described in greater detail below, these process technologies can be broadly divided into bipolar and metal oxide semiconductor (MOS). MOS process technology has further evolved into NMOS (negative metal oxide semiconductor) and CMOS (complementary metal oxide semiconductor). What is important is that the type of process of technology chosen gives the DRAM device certain characteristics which make it better suited for different applications, such as use in a VCR or a computer.

The choice of process technology occurs within the innovation envelope of the DRAM product technology. A company can choose to innovate from a 256K to a 1Mb DRAM using bipolar, NMOS or CMOS processing technology. As noted, this choice of processing technology has been related to the application for which the DRAM was to be used. Because of innovations in the CMOS technology, it will be shown that this process technology has come to dominate all others. The strategic implications of this will be discussed initially in this chapter and again in the next. But before doing so, the changes in process technology must be examined.

Shifts in the DRAM Process Technology

There are basically two types of process technologies, bipolar and metal oxide semiconductor (MOS). Bipolar technology was first developed in the 1950s. Metal oxide semiconductor technology emerged in the late 1960s. Thedifference between these two types of technology is the way in which the variousmetals and insulators are layered to make the integrated circuit device. This difference results in transistors that carry electricity in different ways. Bipolar integrated circuit devices carry both positive and negative charges. MOS devices are divided into three types: PMOS for those types that carry positive charges, NMOS for types that carry negative charges, and CMOS for those that carry both positive and negative charges. Each of these processing technologies gave certain characteristics, such as speed, power usage, and heat generation to the integrated circuit devices which first used them.

The advantage that the older bipolar process technology gave to devices was faster speed in carrying out arithmetic functions. This made that process technology particularly appropriate for logic devices. But the disadvantage of bipolar process technology was that devices which employed it used an excessive amount of electrical energy and generated large quantities of heat. The advantage of MOS integrated circuit devices was that they required less electrical power to carry out their functions compared to bipolar devices. But devices made with MOS process technology tended to be slower. Speed in carrying out a function was less of a constraint than information storage capacity for memory devices. With the advent of the DRAM device in the early 1970s, MOS process technology began replacing the older bipolar process technology.

Among the three MOS process technologies, NMOS was faster than either PMOS or CMOS. CMOS used less power and generated less heat than either NMOS and PMOS. PMOS consumed as much power as NMOS and generated as much heat, but was slower. CMOS was also slower but generated much less heat and used much less power than NMOS or PMOS. Since many of the applications, such as large and medium sized computers, that required memory integrated circuits were less constraining in terms of power and heat, but more stringent in terms of speed, NMOS became the processing technology of choice. As a result, NMOS process technology became predominant in the 1970s in memory device production.

Because of recent developments in CMOS technology, the speed differential between CMOS and NMOS and bipolar is now declining, though the power use advantage remains with the CMOS integrated circuits. While both bipolar and CMOS carry both positive and negative charges, CMOS chips have the P and N transistors connected in such a way that they use less power than the bipolar device. Hence, the relative advantage of bipolar process technology for logic production is rapidly decreasing. This is also the case for NMOS memory devices. The speed of chips that use CMOS devices has increased relative to that of chips that use NMOS, while keeping the power use and heat generation advantage. As a result, CMOS process technology is fast becoming the dominant process technology for all segments of the integrated circuit industry and should remain so well into the next century (Barney, 1987). These trends in process technology can be clearly seen in Table 4.2.

Bipolar held the majority share of all integrated circuits until 1978. Between 1978 and 1984, MOS process technology became the dominant choice of integrated circuit producers. The year 1978 was crucial because it marked the advent of the VLSI era. It was during the period 1978 to 1984 that the 64K and 256K devices were introduced. The increasing density required the shift to a processing technology that required less power and generated less heat, which, as noted is a major advantage of MOS over bipolar. With the introduction of the 1Mb and the 4Mb, this trend towards

Table 4.2
Shift in Integrated Circuit Process Technology

		Year		
Process technology	1978	1984	1987	1992
Bipolar	60%	43%	36%	31%
MOS	40%	57%	63%	67%
PMOS	15%	1%	0%	0%
NMOS	20%	40%	25%	10%
CMOS	5%	16%	38%	57%

Source: ICE, 1978, 1984, 1987.

a processing technology that required less power and generated less heat continued. The rapid increase in the CMOS process technology is the result.

CMOS process technology is more complicated than either NMOS and bipolar. It requires more steps in the manufacturing process for each of the integrated circuits. As such, in shifting from bipolar to NMOS to CMOS, firms must first learn how to use each process technology. They must also invest more in a comparable CMOS facility than either a bipolar or NMOS production facility. Consequently, the latter portion of the VLSI period is somewhat different from the earlier portion.

In the earlier portion of the VLSI period, the 64K and 256K DRAM device, NMOS process technology dominated. It was with the 1Mb DRAM device that CMOS gained the dominant position. This is also true for the 4Mb DRAM device. Both the 1Mb and 4Mb DRAM devices were innovated using the CMOS process technology. As a result, for purposes of examining firm strategies, the VLSI period will be divided into two sub-periods. The first will be the 64K and 256K devices, where NMOS process technology is dominant. The second will be the 1Mb device where CMOS process technology is dominant. Although the 4Mb device is still in its introductory stage, the firms producing the 4Mb DRAM device will also be analyzed.

As noted in chapter one, the link between product and process innovation is a recognized phenomenon. The portrayal of that connection as product innovation preceding process innovation may be generally correct, but as the above section on the DRAM has shown, the connection may be more subtle and complex. While it is recognized that the DRAM product, because it is sold in large volume, helps to drive manufacturing efficiency, the contribution of process innovation has been less widely noted. Without improvements in process technology as occurred with the movements from bipolar to NMOS and later with NMOS to CMOS, the DRAM may not have enjoyed as wide a variety of applications. Rather than product innovation giving way to process innovation, the two appear to be mutually reinforcing in fostering technology change. Instead of what is often shown as product innovation dominating in the early years of a technology's life cycle, and process innovation dominating in the latter years, the reciprocal and complimentary relationship between product and process innovation has existed over the life cycle of the DRAM technology. Since the DRAM technology is about twenty years old, the strategic implications have had ample time to manifest themselves. Firms which were sensitive to the interactions of product and process innovation as described above and adopted strategies to reflect the continuous innovation in the DRAM and this innovations impact on subtechnologies throughout the innovation envelope of the DRAM would be better able to survive.

FIRM STRATEGIES

The firm strategies to be examined were discussed in chapter two and include the firm's innovation strategy and horizontal and vertical integration strategies.

These strategic variables are expected to affect the firm's survival chances. As discussed in the second chapter, an essential element of strategy for a firm when it is operating in an environment characterized by innovation is to establish strategic technological areas (STA). As noted, these have both a horizontal and vertical component.

The horizontal strategy for the integrated circuit industry relates to the breadth of market participation. It has been shown that some integrated circuit firms produce a wide variety of integrated circuits, while others are more specialized (Wilson, Ashton and Egan, 1980). Thus, for the integrated circuit market, firms are divided into two groups: those that are specialized integrated circuit producers and those that produce a wide variety of integrated circuits.

Previous studies have shown that the innovation strategy may be important to firm survival (Spital, 1983; Flaherty, 1983). It has been suggested that innovation strategies can be divided into two types, innovative and imitative (Wilson, Ashton and Egan, 1980; Nelson and Winter, 1982).

The innovative firm follows a strategy of producing major innovations and of being a primary source for a device, while the imitative firm follows a strategy of incremental change and of being a secondary source for a device. This study will divide the firms in the DRAM market into the two categories of innovative and imitative to determine if these strategies have any effect on the survival of the firms.

Also, the degree to which an integrated circuit firm is vertically integrated is an important strategic variable. This is the second component of defining a firm's strategic technological area. The degree of integration with downstream firms that use integrated circuit, or with upstream firms that produce the equipment that makes the circuits, will provide our basis for examination. The degree of integration for firms will be measured by the existence of equity involvement of upstream and downstream firms with the integrated circuit firm.

In summary, then, the firm characteristics will be measured in the following manner. The horizontal strategy will group the firms into two categories depending upon whether the firm specializes in one type of integrated circuit device or produces many types of integrated circuit devices. The innovation strategy variable will group the firms by whether they are innovators or imitators. The integration structure will be determined by the degree of equity integration between the upstream and downstream firms with the integrated circuit firms in the DRAM market.

Research Lesson: Strategy and the Need for Resources

The relationship between the increased need for resources, as described in chapter three, and the role of strategy in managing technological innovation will now be examined. This is done by assessing the changes in firm strategies described above as the DRAM progresses through its five innovations—16K, 64K, 256K, 1Mb, and 4Mb. These have been divided into four periods of technological competition in the DRAM segment, LSI, early VLSI, late VLSI and ULSI.

Previous research has indicated that firms which are vertically integrated, that is, have more deeply defined their STA, should be more have greater longevity. In order to obtain a more complete picture of this, both forward and backward integration must be assessed. It is also expected that firms which define their horizontal STA more broadly should have greater longevity. Hence, it is expected that the horizontal strategy should move from the specialized niche production of integrated circuits to production of a broader, full line of integrated circuits. It is also expected, from the previous research that firms which follow an innovative strategy rather than an imitative one will be able to continue to meet the technological imperative that exists in the DRAM industry.

APPROACHES TO THE STRATEGIC MANAGEMENT OF TECHNOLOGY

It is important before examining the various strategies to make some brief comments on the differences in approach to strategy between Japanese and American firms. It should be noted that for both U.S. and Japanese firms, the resultant strategies are as much emergent as they are intended. Often decisions were made which over the course of time opened up or closed off opportunities. This is particularly true with decisions to adopt one type of process technology or DRAM design.

In 1974, it was not possible to forecast that in ten years, integrated circuit devices made with CMOS would be as fast as integrated circuits made with NMOS or even bipolar processes. Nor was it obvious that a more simplified design approach to the 64K device would work as opposed a radically new approach. These decisions were often originally made to meet a more immediate need, that only over time developed far-reaching implications. The Japanese choose correctly in both cases, but it cannot simply be said that they were more prescient than the Americans. As will be seen below, environmental conditions helped to share those decisions.

This is not to say that real differences do not exist between the Japanese and American approach. A number of researchers, both Japanese and American, have commented on these differences (Abegglen and Stalk, 1985; Kagono, et al., 1985). Of the many issues explored by these researchers, three are of particular salience for the discussion of the strategic management of technology. These three issues correspond strongly with observations drawn from my own interviews of Japanese and American integrated circuit executives.

First, the Japanese integrated circuit firms are interested in technological self-sufficiency. The executives of these firms wish to control each of the crucial subtechnologies that make up the DRAM innovation envelope. This is needed because the DRAM is an important subtechnology in other electronic products which have higher value added, such as computers and VCRs. This kind of approach is only now beginning to emerge in the strategic thinking of U.S. firms. Generally, U.S. integrated circuit firms have taken a much narrower approach to defining the technology and have left to the specialization of supplier industries the issues of subtechnology supply.

Second, the Japanese tend to look at an emerging technological or market area from the perspective of vulnerability rather than risk. They key difference is in the question of how vulnerable is the firm if it does not enter a new technology rather than what are the risks of entering. American strategic decisionmakers tend to be very strong in conducting risk analysis. Consequently, the predisposition among American managers in established firms is to take a conservative "wait and see" approach to new technologies. It is not that the Japanese managers are less conservative or less risk averse, but that the system of decision making imposes a predisposition to enter a new technology to keep up with or gain an advantage on competitors. Entry may often be incremental and cautious, blending as much of the known "old technology" with the unexplored "new technology." But entry is made and often before markets are established.

Third, when the Japanese approach a research project, its from the point of view of multiple applications. Often a risky research project will be

Table 4.3
Strategic Approaches for All Firms in the DRAM Industry for All Innovation Periods

Strategic Approach

Innovation Approach		Horizontal STA	
Innoative	19	Broad Based	17
Imitative	3	Specialized	5

Forward STA Integration		Backward STA Integration	
Forward Integrated	18	Backward Integrated	12
Not Forward Integrated	4	Not Backward Integrated	10

undertaken not because it will solve one particular problem, but because it may contribute to solving a number of seemingly unrelated problems. American companies tend to be more narrowly focused in their research. American integrated circuit firms are not involved in research pertaining to superconductive materials, let alone biotechnology, but Japanese integrated circuit firms are conducting such research.

Strategic Elements: Vertical, Innovation and Horizontal Strategies

In Table 4.3, all the American and Japanese firms which have produced DRAMs from 1974 through 1988 are categorized. Twenty-two firms in all have participated in the DRAM industry. Ten Japanese and twelve American firms have produced DRAM devices. The majority of these firms have followed an innovative strategy, as well as being broad-based suppliers of integrated circuit devices. The participating firms have also been vertically integrated, although more have been forward-integrated than backward-integrated. From this table it can readily be seen that the strategic approaches of firms that engaged in the DRAM industry generally followed the pattern suggested by the research lesson. In order to examine the strategic effect of innovation in the DRAM on these firms, the strategic categories are displayed for each of the innovation periods described above.

In Table 4.4, the LSI, early VLSI, late VLSI and ULSI periods and the strategic approaches of all U.S. and Japanese firms are displayed. As can be seen, the movement of the strategic approaches is in the direction

Table 4.4
Strategic Approaches for All Firms in the DRAM Industry by Each
Innovation Period

	(A) Innovation Approach		(B) Horizontal STA	
	Innovative	Imitative	Specialized	Broad Based
LSI	14	1	1	14
VLSI	15	2	3	14
VLSI	13	2	2	13
ULSI	7	0	0	7

	(C) Forward STA Integration		(D) Backward STA Integration	
	IC Only	Forward Product	Not Integrated	Integrated
LSI	13	11	6	8
VLSI	3	14	6	11
VLSI	0	15	3	12
ULSI	0	7	0	7

expected from the research lesson. What this table represents is the strategies of firms which have survived the changes in the DRAM technology described in chapter three. These firms have been able to acquire the resources necessary to carry out the continual innovation needed to compete in the DRAM industry. this is particularly true of the ULSI period, which is in its early introductory phase. This indicates that these strategic approaches may be even more important in determining whether the firms are able to acquire the resources needed to be successful in producing the next innovation faster than the competing firms and thereby assuring a position of market dominance from which to launch the next innovation effort.

As can be observed from the table, firms which have followed a strategic approach to innovation of developing their own technology and being first to market, dominate throughout each of the periods. It is important to recognize what innovation in DRAM technology means. Recalling from chapter one, the innovation process is made up of steps which move an invention into commercial production. These steps are divided into design and various phases of production. While designing more and more sophisticated versions of the DRAM is not an easy task, the more crucial element of the innovation is translating that design into a working prototype and then into a mass-manufactured device. This is because DRAMs—unlike logic devices where there may exist many different ways to design circuits to carry out the various arithmetic and control functions—have only one function, the storage of information. Further, the different designs available for logic devices may have wide ranges in performance, whereas the different designs in the DRAM have a narrower range. Hence, innovation in the DRAM means bringing the device as quickly as possible from the design to the production stage. The emphasis is placed on innovation in the crucial production subtechnologies. Because of this, the DRAM device is seen by integrated circuit firms as a process technology driver.

From the table it can also be observed that firms which define their STA very broadly are also dominant throughout each of the periods. Since the other technology areas are defined as other integrated circuit devices, there are obvious synergies with the DRAM device. Resources used to innovate in the DRAM can be used to innovate in other integrated circuit devices. This is particularly true in the production subtechnology areas that can be used in producing different kinds of integrated circuit devices. This can also work in the other direction as well, but because of the large volume of DRAMs produced, even when compared to other memory devices, the flow of information tends to be much weaker. From interviews conducted by the author, this was the opinion of both American and Japanese engineers. However, because of the intense price competition that occurs in the DRAM industry, being able to sell other devices that are less price-sensitive may help in acquiring the financial resources needed for continued innovation.

Firms which defined their STA deeply are also dominant throughout each of the periods. This is true of firms which connect forward into industries that use integrated circuits as well as those which connect backward. As seen in the table, the movement for firms connecting backward into the suppliers of the subtechnologies is much more pronounced than the movement towards forward connection. There are two reasons for this difference. First, the number of firms that are forward-integrated in the LSI period is initially quite strong. In each of the succeeding periods, there is only marginal room for expansion. In the case of firms backward-integrated, while more are backward-connected than not in the LSI period, the numbers are more even. In each succeeding period, the number of backward-connected firms increases, and the number not backward-integrated decreases. Second, and more importantly, forward integration allows the integrated circuit firm to be directly involved in a $490 billion market in electronic systems, in 1988 sales (McClean, 1989). Because of the higher value added in electronic systems, firms which are forward-connected are able to draw upon the financial resources of both the integrated circuit industry, valued at $57 billion in 1988 sales, and the electronic systems market. Backward connection into the semiconductor equipment industry, with sales of $8.6 billion in 1988, and/or into the semiconductor materials industry, with 1988 sales of $7.6 billion, are less likely to yield financial resources (McClean, 1989). However, this type of connection will yield informational resources needed to move along the DRAM innovation envelope. Again, because the DRAM is a memory device, it is less likely that information from DRAM users is as crucial as it would be for a multi-function logic device. Further, as noted in the above discussion of the innovation strategy, the DRAM device is a driver of process technologies. Consequently, the ability to link with the suppliers of key subtechnologies and to share information has become more important as the DRAM has become more sophisticated.

As discussed in an earlier section of this chapter, Japanese firms have come to dominate in the DRAM industry, especially after the initiative of the VLSI period. Their ability to compete technologically has increased steadily. In order to gain some insight into this situation, the strategic approaches of the United States and Japanese are examined in turn.

U.S. Firms

The results for the U.S. firms are presented in Table 4.5. Again, the basic pattern that has been observed above is repeated. As would be expected, firms which follow an innovative approach, are broad suppliers of integrated circuits, and are both forward- and backward-integrated dominate throughout each period. Firms following these types of strategies dominate across the periods as well.

Several distinct issues exist. It is obvious from the table that the number of U.S. firms has decreased with each period. It is too soon to tell with the ULSI 4Mb DRAM device, since it is early in its introductory stage. Several other U.S. firms have indicated that they would enter this device category. Some of these firms will be entering under license from Japanese firms, a complete role reversal from the LSI period. Firms which independently develop new products in other integrated circuit areas would still be classified as innovative. The one current U.S. firm in the ULSI segment developed its own proprietary DRAM technology. Most of the firms that have entered are broad-based suppliers of integrated circuits. This U.S. strength in other integrated circuit devices, especially logic devices, will be an important element for further examination.

It is also important to recognize the type of forward integration that exists among the U.S. firms. The pattern of integration closely follows the type of customers, who buy from U.S. firms. This pattern is displayed in Table 4.6. As can be seen in this table, the dominant customers for U.S. integrated circuit firms are the industrial and computer users. This pattern has remained roughly the same throughout the period and is expected to continue to be so. The U.S. firms have either bought into or have been

Table 4.5
Strategic Approaches for U.S. Firms in the DRAM Industry by Each Innovation Period

	(A) Innovation Approach		(B) Horizontal STA	
	Innovative	Imitative	Specialized	Broad Based
LSI	8	1	2	7
VLSI	6	1	1	6
VLSI	4	0	0	4
ULSI	1	0	0	1

	(C) Forward STA Integration		(D) Backward STA Integration	
	IC Only	Forward Product	Not Integrated	Integrated
LSI	2	7	6	3
VLSI	2	5	4	3
VLSI	0	4	1	3
ULSI	0	1	0	1

Table 4.6
Percent of Value of Integrated Circuit Consumption by End User Segment for U.S.

	Year	
End User	1979	1987
Consumer	22%	15%
Computer/Industrial	53%	53%
Telecommunications	10%	18%
Military	10%	14%

Source: Wilson, Ashton, Eagan, 1980; McClean, 1988.

bought by these types of firms. The fact that computer and industrial users are the most important is significant for another reason. As noted above, these type of users would require integrated circuit devices that have high speed in performing their functions. Up until quite recently, this meant producing bipolar and NMOS-type devices, rather than the CMOS-type

Table 4.7
Strategic Approaches for Japanese Firms in the DRAM Industry by Each Innovation Period

	(A) Innovation Approach		(B) Horizontal STA	
	Innovative	Imitative	Specialized	Broad Based
LSI	3	0	0	3
VLSI	7	0	0	7
VLSI	8	2	1	9
ULSI	6	0	0	6

	(C) Forward STA Integration		(D) Backward STA Integration	
	IC Only	Forward Product	Not Integrated	Integrated
LSI	0	3	0	3
VLSI	0	7	0	7
VLSI	0	10	1	9
ULSI	0	6	0	6

device. Hence, American firms have produced most of their integrated circuit using the bipolar and NMOS process technologies.

The number of U.S. firms that are backward-integrated into the semiconductor equipment and materials technologies is quite few. For the U.S. firms, this backward connection is predominantly in integrated circuit firms which also produce and sell some type of semiconductor production equipment, usually integrated circuit testers. This lack of strong backward connection with suppliers of crucial subtechnologies is one factor that has contributed to the decline in the number of U.S. firms in the DRAM device segment.

Japanese Firms

The analysis for the Japanese firms participating in the DRAM market is arrayed in Table 4.7. In a mirror image of the U.S. situation, the number of firms has increased steadily across each innovation period. Again, as expected from the research lesson derived in chapter two, the firms which have followed an innovative, broad-based approach and are vertically connected dominate. The strength of this is quite evident from the table. Only in the late VLSI period is there any variation among the strategic approach

Table 4.8
Percent of Value of Integrated Circuit Consumption by End User Segment for Japan

	Year	
End User	1979	1987
Consumer	55%	39%
Computer/Industrial	19%	46%
Telecommunications	26%	15%

Source: BA Asia, Ltd, 1982, McClean, 1988.

categories. During this period a couple of Japanese firms have entered under license to other Japanese firms. These two firms are fast making progress to become proprietary developers of their own DRAM technology.

The vast majority of the firms take an innovative approach to technology. While these firms produced earlier LSI versions of integrated circuits under license, usually from the United States, each set itself on a path towards self-sufficient proprietary development of technology. In terms of the DRAM, this effort has come to fruition. As noted, some U.S. firms are considering entering the 4Mb DRAM device segment using licensed Japanese DRAM technology. It should also be noted that Japanese firms were important in innovating in CMOS process technology (Bylinsky, 1983). Each of the Japanese integrated circuit firms also produces a broad array of devices. Some of these are produced under licenses from the United States, while some are not. Again, the movement is to become proprietary developers in each of these areas.

In examining the vertical integration strategic approach, Japanese firms are strongly connected both forward and backward. In examining the forward integration aspect, it is useful to determine which type of company buys from the Japanese integrated circuit products. This information is presented in Table 4.8. It is clear that in the LSI and early VLSI periods that the majority of sales from Japanese integrated circuit was to producers of consumer electronics. These type of electronic producers would require devices which have low power needs and low heat output. As noted above, CMOS process technology is ideally suited for these types of applications. In the later VLSI and ULSI periods, the Japanese have begun to shift their sale to computer manufacturers. Because of the improvements brought about in CMOS, the Japanese integrated circuit firms are having an easy transition. It should also be noted that many of the integrated circuit devices produced by Japanese firms are used in-house, both within the firm and

Table 4.9
Percentage of Domestically Supplied Production Equipment for Selected Machines for Japanese Integrated Circuit Market

EQUIPMENT	1977	1979	1981	1983	1989
Surface Grinder	20	40	80	85	100
Edge Processor	30	70	100	100	100
Electron Beams	20	40	40	55	88
Coater/Developer	15	40	50	59	na
Alignment	10	30	40	50	61
Plasma Etcher	40	50	70	71	96
Wet Chemicals	90	100	100	100	100
Stepper	0	30	40	50	94
Ion Implant	0	10	40	50	79
Diffusion	100	100	100	100	100
C V D	60	60	80	80	91
Metal Deposition	70	60	50	50	na

Sources: Nihon Kaihatsu Ginko, 1984; BA Asia Consulting Group, 1982; Strauss, 1983.

to firms affiliated with the integrated circuit firm through its keiretsu group. The range of in-house use for divisions within the integrated circuit firms is from twelve percent to fifty-five percent, and sales within the keiretsu group of up five percent to sixty-three percent (Borrus, 1988).

The Japanese integrated circuit producers are also strongly connected backward. All the firms that have participated in the DRAM segment except one is connected with suppliers of subtechnologies crucial to the design and production of DRAM devices. Many of these firms are affiliated with the integrated circuit firms through the keiretsu groups. The strength of these suppliers has grown over time. This trend is shown in Table 4.9. From the table it can be seen that in each subtechnology area, Japanese supplier firms have grown stronger in their ability to meet domestic demand. This strength has spilled over into the world market as well. Japanese semiconductor equipment and materials firms dominate in such areas as photolithography, testers, silicon production, ceramic chip carriers, and photomasks. This is reflected in Table 4.10 which shows the market share for the top two companies in several key subtechnologies in 1989. As can be seen, Japanese firms hold the top two positions in four out of the fourteen subtechnologies. They hold the top spot in eight of the fourteen

Table 4.10
Top Two Companies in 1989 Worldwide Market Share in Selected IC
Subtechnologies

Subtechnology	Top Companies	Market Share
Deposition	Applied Materials	15%
	Varian	10%
Resist Processing	TEL*	25%
	Dainippon Screen*	20%
Steppers	Nikon*	45%
	Canon*	20%
Dry Etch	Applied Materials	30%
	TEL*	10%
Ion Implant	Varian	30%
	Eaton	20%
Diffusion Furnaces	TEL*	40%
	Kokusai	15%
Process Diagnostics	KLA	20%
	Hitachi*	5%
Wafer Cleaning	Dainippon Screen*	25%
	FSI	20%
Dicing Saws	Disco Abrasive	60%
	Kulicke & Soffa	10%
Die Bonders	Shinkawa*	25%
	ESEC SA	20%
Wire Bonders	Shinkawa*	30%
	Kulicke & Soffa	20%
Packaging	Yamada*	15%
	Towa Electric*	15%
Automatic Test	Advantest*	20%
	Teradyne	10%
CIM Software	Consilium	20%
	Advantest*	20%

Source: Electronic Business, May 14, 1990.

*Japanese semiconductor equipment company

and at least the number two spot in seven of the fourteen. Each of these firms is connected to one of the major IC producing firms in Japan through the keiretsu groups. The importance of these connections for innovating in the DRAM technology and the differences between the U.S. case and Japan will be explored in greater detail in the next section. This strength in supplying the key subtechnologies is one of the key elements in contributing to the rise of Japanese integrated circuit firms in the DRAM device segment. These developments and the differences between the U.S. case and the Japanese case will be explored in greater detail in the next section.

For this portion of the analysis, it is important to note that each of the strategic approaches is in the expected category. It is also interesting to note that, as expected, the dominance of these strategic approaches grows as the DRAM technology becomes more sophisticated. Each of these strategic approaches allows for the acquisition of the resources needed to continue innovation in the DRAM technology. By being innovative, firms are better able to gain market share and with it the revenue needed to continue to innovate. It also allows for learning to occur which increases the information resource available for continual innovation. Being a broad-based supplier of integrated circuit devices allows learning to occur across difference devices. Further, financial resources can be drawn from a larger pool. The vertical integration strategy is playing a critical role. Both forward and backward integration allows for the flow of information and financial resources. Because the DRAM is more of a process technology driver, rather than a design technology driver, the information component is stronger with backward integration. Forward integration links integrated circuit firms in with firms producing higher value-added products, opening up a larger pool of financial resources. There is also found to be a differential between U.S. and Japanese firms in terms of vertical integration. For the U.S. firms it is forward integration into the downstream users of integrated circuit, and for the Japanese it is backward integration into the upstream producers of integrated circuit equipment and materials. It is this stronger backward connection that is one of the most important reasons for the rise of Japanese firms.

SYSTEMIC AND BEHAVIORAL ILLUSTRATION

The interaction of the strategic approaches and technological factors and a further elaboration of the results presented above is in order. The backward integration of the Japanese firms has been identified as an important difference between the LSI and VLSI time periods in acquiring the information resource. The forward integration of the U.S. and Japanese firms likewise differed between the LSI and VLSI periods and was seen as an important factor in acquiring financial resources. The details of these relationships will be examined. The information that appears below was generated from a series of interviews with executives and engineers of integrated circuit firms, and equipment supplier firms in both the United States and Japan, as well as industry experts in market research and consulting firms.

BACKWARD LINKING IN THE JAPANESE MARKET

In the early 1970s, the Japanese did not domestically produce much of the integrated circuit machinery, or the other materials that make up the important subtechnologies that go into the production of integrated circuits, according to a senior executive vice president of a large Japanese integrated circuit firm. This executive went on to explain that it was recognized that in order to obtain a competitive position in the world market, the materials and equipment industry would have to be developed to the point that it could also compete in the world market. This same observation was also made by a director of the international division of a large independent materials supplier.

He explained that in the early 1970s most, if not all, of integrated circuit equipment and materials were imported through trading companies representing the U.S. manufacturers. Recalling Table 4.9, even in 1979, much of the sophisticated subtechnology equipment was still being imported. He went on to state that because of the "no maintenance" policy of Japanese firms, the U.S. equipment manufacturers were obliged to explain how their equipment worked so that the Japanese integrated circuit makers could provide their own maintenance. This the U.S. companies willingly did in order to sell in the Japanese market and because of the complexity of providing maintenance in the foreign setting. In the period of the early- to mid-1970s, the decision made sense to many American equipment supplier firms.

Information Resources and Backward Integration

What emerged was an informal flow of information which the Japanese were able to use to help develop their own equipment industry. The Japanese integrated circuit makers also began to concentrate their own resources in the potential equipment firms. Several researchers who have studied the Japanese economy noted that the productive sector was made up of industrial groups or keiretsu; firms in various product markets related to each other through various financial and economic means (Allen, 1981; Clark, 1979; Kagono, et al., 1985).

Within these groups were a large number of firms in the industrial segment, some growing and some declining. Some of those industrial segment companies that were either flat in terms of sales growth or in declining segments were selected by the major integrated circuit firms in the keiretsu to redirect into the semiconductor equipment industry. One example is Kaijo Denki, which belongs to the NEC group. Its primary product area in the late 1960s and early 1970s was in manufacture and sale of fish detection sonar. This company is now producing bonding equipment for the integrated circuit industry.

Also, each industrial group had several equipment firms attached to it which were usually already established firms selling related products such as lenses, industrial chemicals and gases. However, the equipment firms were not wholly owned subsidiaries of the integrated circuit firms, even if there was shared equity. As an example, in the Mitsubishi group, Nippon Kogaku (Nikon) was a primary producer of photographic equipment and is now a primary producer of photolithographic equipment. Another example is Ando Denki, a producer of testing equipment, which is associated with the NEC group, within the larger Sumitomo group.

Some started out as independent companies and fell on hard times, but were then brought into a keiretsu group and turned around. One example is Takeda Riken, which produced testing equipment. When it ran into financial difficulties Fujitsu, Ltd. bought into it and rehabilitated it. It is now the world leader in integrated circuit testers, under the name of Advantest. Some of the companies began as joint ventures between Japanese and U.S. companies and were later bought out by the Japanese partner. One example is Anelva, a producer of dry etching and sputtering equipment (Dodwell Marketing Consultants, 1982, 1984, 1986).

In the area of materials suppliers, one executive of a materials company explained that Osaka Titanium was associated with NEC; Komatsu, of the Mitsui group, was associated with Toshiba of the same Mitsui group; and Nippon Silicon was associated with the Mitsubishi group. These associations were confirmed in a Japanese trade journal (Denki Kiki Shijo Chosa Kaihen, 1980). These companies, along with Shin Etsu Handotai, an independent Japanese silicon supplier, and one American and one European company, supplied 90 percent of the silicon wafer market in 1988 (McClean, 1989).

In essence, the Japanese have developed "industrial teams" which confront movement along the DRAM's innovation envelope. Each of the firms in the team becomes an expert in one or several important integrated circuit subtechnologies. Each develops the innovations in its subtechnology, which can be used in helping the integrated circuit firm innovate in the DRAM. In this way the product development cycle for DRAMs and other integrated circuit devices is shortened for the Japanese firms. The relationship between the integrated circuit firm and the supplier firms is particularly helpful in shortening the portion of the product development cycle that starts with design and progresses to pilot production.

One recent example of this was seen in the co-development of an electron cyclotron resonance (ECR) plasma etch process by Anelva Corporation and NEC. Anelva and NEC, as noted before, belong to the same Keiretsu. The ECR plasma etcher will be crucial for producing the 64Mb DRAM. NEC has already installed this equipment in its production facilities and plans to begin using it for the 16Mb DRAM (Electronic News June 11, 1990). This illustrates two important aspects of the Keiretsu relationship in fostering innovation in the DRAM. First, the cooperative effort of both Anelva and NEC have resulted in the development of this crucial sub-technology earlier than in the U.S. using a more market based relationship between IC firm and equipment supplier firm. Second, the early development and use of the equipment allows for learning in advance of when that equipment will be needed. The ECR plasma etcher is not critical for the 16Mb DRAM, but will be used to provide learning so that when it is critical, with the 64Mb DRAM, most of the defects will be eliminated. Eliminating defects allows for increasing the yield and therefore the profitability for these devices. This benefits NEC. Anelva is benefitted by having the best equipment to sell in its respective market.

While there is certainly coordination among the team members so as to match the variety required by the technology with the appropriate member of the industrial team, this coordination is not so rigid and fixed that member's products cannot be substituted by higher quality ones found outside the team. Hence, the members of the team are able to draw on the informational and financial resources of other team members but are not isolated from technological or market pressures as a captive supplier would be.

In addition, these industrial teams each have their own history, and from that, their own dynamic for approaching the integrated circuit industry. In some cases, as with Fujitsu, the integrated circuit department became independent of the computer department, as explained by the director of a marketing research firm. This may explain why Fujitsu still has a high rate of in-house integrated circuit sales, as reported by Borrus (1988). In other cases, closer ties were forged with a downstream user such as a computer manufacturer, as was the case with Hitachi (Nomura Sogo Ken Kyu Jo, 1984). Some companies, such as NEC, which perceived themselves strong technically, but weak from a marketing standpoint, set up special integrated circuit marketing sections directly connected to the production departments (Denki Kiki Shijo Chosa Kaihen, 1978).

Innovation Resources and Forward Integration

Another advantage provided by the close connections between integrated circuit producer and user is the in-house development of integrated circuits. One senior executive of a large integrated circuit firm indicated that they had developed a 64K DRAM in 1975, but only used it in-house initially in order to work the bugs out of it. The 64K DRAM was then introduced for sale in the open market in 1978. This pattern of development has been repeated for the 256K, 1Mb and 4Mb devices. Once enough production experience is gained through in-house use, so as to be quite far down on the learning curve, the integrated circuit is then offered for external or merchant sale. This helps to shorten the portion of the product development cycle that proceeds from pilot production to mass production.

Not only are gains in information available, but gains in financial resources as well. In chapter three, the expenditure for capital equipment and research and development funds for the Japanese manufacturers has been displayed. In the Japanese case, the trend moves constantly upward. This is because, as explained by a senior executive of a large Japanese integrated circuit firm, the various integrated circuit producers are connected to computer, communication, and commercial users of integrated circuits, so that when one market is down another market is up. In financial theory, this is called the portfolio effect. In practical terms, the Japanese have less variance in their income streams and, therefore, less variance in their capital investment in integrated circuits.

The picture that emerges is one of a close confederation of firms that are connected to one another yet stand alone. While they can derive technical and financial support from other group members, they must compete on their own merits and are not restricted to selling to or buying from other group's members. This creates a dynamic tension both within the firms and the industrial teams which disciplines the firms for the rigorous environment established by the innovation imperative of the DRAMs innovation envelope.

Influence Patterns Between Firms

The firms that have the most influence within these industrial teams are the integrated circuit manufacturers. This is especially true in the relation between equipment maker and integrated circuit producers. As explained by the director of the international division of a large independent material supplier, the integrated circuit producers are the buyers and the equipment producers are the sellers. In any Japanese market relationship, the buyer is in a stronger position relative to the seller. In Japan the buyer has the right to ask a great many things of the seller.

As an example, a buyer of silicon ingots can demand from a supplier a high grade of silicon at below market price. The "carrot" offered to the supplier is a long-term relationship. The buyer, with high grade silicon, can produce a higher quality integrated circuit, raising the market share of the integrated circuit manufacturer. This in turn increases his demand for the silicon supplier's material. The "stick" is that the material supplier is often dependent on the integrated circuit producer for technical information or financial aid.

Even if the Japanese material supplier is totally independent of the integrated circuit producers, he must sell in a setting where six or seven firms control seventy percent of the total integrated circuit market. One executive explained that even the independent firms have difficulty resisting such pressure. The relationship is not "arm's length," he said, so often the material and equipment firms forgo a normal short-run return on their sales.

The Japanese market, then, can be characterized as one that does not allow for the "game theoretic cooperation" of its participants. Taking the perspective of the two-person prisoner's dilemma game, the Japanese market is set up in a way whereby one of the players [the IC makers] can alter the payoff table to their liking. The participants are not independent from oneanother and of equal power. This is particularly true of any type of vertical relationship, such as buyer and seller.

Another way that integrated circuit manufacturers maintain influence in the equipment market was explained by the director of sales for a large U.S. equipment manufacturer in Japan. The Japanese integrated circuit producers have emphasized process technology in the training of their engineers. Thus, the engineers from the integrated circuit producers know as much or more about the process and the equipment needed as do the engineers of the equipment firms. Since the integrated circuit producers are the buyers, they often send their engineers to the plants of equipment makers to inspect the equipment as it is being assembled.

Because of their training, the integrated circuit product engineers often know as much or more about the equipment as the equipment engineers. Their evaluations of the equipment assembling process can influence, for well or ill, the equipment firm's relationship with its main integrated circuit firm. This attention to process engineering shows up in the types of papers presented at technical conventions. The papers on process development are often Japanese (Nishimura, 1983, pp. 87–91).

Is life for the Japanese equipment supplier operating within these groups all that bad? As noted above the "carrot" held out is that if the integrated circuit producer is doing well the equipment producer will also do well. As seen in Table 4.11, the ranking according to worldwide sales for 1988 and 1989 for equipment suppliers has three of the top spots going to Japanese equipment suppliers. Both TEL, Advantest and Canon moved up over in ranking from 1987 to 1988 (Electronic News, April 24, 1989). What is even more remarkable is that in 1979, none of these firms were in the top ten rankings. Life for Japanese equipment suppliers does not appear to be that bad, at least in terms of sales.

One other point often brought up by the people interviewed was that the Japanese market was characterized by intense rivalry, among not only the integrated circuit producers but also among the equipment and material suppliers. Each firm was out to be number one in its field, and the firms competed head to head in all segments of the markets. Of the top five integrated circuit firms, all except one produce MOS, bipolar and hybrid ICs. Each firm jealously guards its secrets, both technical and marketing, and attempts to outdo the others. Each firm aids in guarding its secrets

Table 4.11
Top Ten Semiconductor Equipment Firms in Worldwide Sales (1979 and 1989)

1979	1989	1988
Fairchild	Tokyo Electron Ltd (TEL)*	2
Perkin-Elmer	Nikon*	1
Applied Materials	Applied Materials	4
GCA	Advantest*	3
Teradyne	Canon*	6
Varian	General Signal	5
Tektronix	Varian	7
Eaton	Hitachi*	11
Kulicke & Soffa	Teradyne	9
Balzers AG	ASM International	13

Source: Microelectronic News July 12, 1980; Electronic News May 21, 1990.

*Japanese semiconductor equipment firm

and outdoing the others by having supplier firms which are top in their industries. As members of the same industrial teams, information is quick to pass among team members and slow to leak outside the team. A Japanese integrated circuit firm with links to supplier companies within its own team need not show its proprietary designs to other supplier firms. In essence then, the Japanese firms follow strategies which may be suboptimal to members of the group in the short run, but optimize the group's performance in the long run. All the members of the group share in this, but some more than others.

LINKAGES IN THE U.S. INTEGRATED CIRCUIT INDUSTRY

Within the U.S. integrated circuit industry, the predominant trend in recent years has been the acquisition of device firms by either "high technology" conglomerates, such as United Technology's acquisition of Mostek, or General Electric's acquisition of Intersil; or by integrated circuit user firms, such as the IBM partial equity buy-in of Intel. None of this activity has been between IC firms and equipment producers. In discussions with officials of industry trade associations, the primary reasons cited for these acquisitions have been the need for capital by the device firms coupled with the general attractiveness of investing in "high technology."

Need for Financial Resources and Vertical Integration

Integrated circuit executives often point to the high volatility of orders and, therefore, the sensitivity of cash flows to the state of the economy as a major reason for the shortage of capital investment. User firms will place double or sometimes triple orders when times are good. With the onset of a recession, the inventory of user firms is so high, because of the double ordering, that the integrated circuit firms are placed under tremendous cash flow strain.

The severity of the 1984–1986 recession is attributed to this double- and triple-ordering process. Computer manufacturers overestimated their need for integrated circuits. When the demand for computers did not materialize, inventories were overstocked and slow to drain. This ordering phenomenon acts to create a high elasticity for the integrated circuit producers so that small changes in user markets translate into large swings in the integrated circuit market. This is particularly true for memory devices like the DRAM and less so for logic devices like the microprocessor or the new market for application specific integrated circuits (ASIC). This is because most electronic devices will need only a few logic devices, but many memory devices to operate properly. It is not uncommon to have as many as ten memory devices for each logic device that is a piece of electronic equipment. During years where there is strong demand for computers, consumer electronics and other type of electronic equipment, memory producers cannot keep up with demand. During the slow years, memory producers suffer. This is reflected in the capital expenditure for U.S. firms presented in chapter three. It also helps explain why so many American firms have exited the DRAM industry. Because of the feast or famine cycle that exists in the DRAM market, not enough market-generated financial resources are available for U.S. firms to meet the increasing needs created by the innovation envelope.

It is generally acknowledged that many of the mergers and acquisitions have opened up an adequate source of capital for improvements. However, it is noted by some industry observers that many of the device firms that have been so acquired have not fared well in adjusting to changes in the market. The poor performance has occurred in spite of the fact that the acquiring firm is either in the electronics industry or in some other closely related high technology industry.

Unintended Consequences of Mergers

Several engineers and marketing people in device firms have pointed out that the technical characteristics of an integrated circuit device are still of prime importance in selling in the market. Within the MOS process technology alone, during the past five to ten years, numerous process technologies (e.g., PMOS, NMOS, CMOS, HCMOS, BiCMOS) have been developed by various firms. Each of these process technologies has advantages and disadvantages associated with it. Further, the success of these various technologies depends upon several integrated circuit user firms finding them superior enough to their competitors that they will buy and use the devices made with them.

Often device firms that have been acquired are committed to a particular technology by their new parent firm before that technology has become an industry standard. If the technology fails to become an industry standard, the parent firm is reluctant to pull away from the technology it has chosen, and continues to support it with money and manpower. The independent firms, because they have less financial resources and because their upper management has to justify their decisions only to themselves, will pull out of a dead end technology much more rapidly than their acquired brethren.

Also, when a vigorous company is acquired, many of its best engineers and managers leave, either to other yet-unacquired companies, or to start their own company. The result of this exit is that the necessary critical mass of engineering and managerial talent needed to use and interpret the informational resources is not available. The acquired company suffers a loss in the continuity of its engineering staff, even if it can replace the personnel who leave. This loss in continuity among key personnel causes disruptions in the company's production and innovation process. Consequently, the gain in the financial resources cannot compensate for the loss in the ability to use the informational resources.

The key to success, as has been pointed out by several officials of industry trade and research associations, is the degree of control exerted by the acquiring firm over the integrated circuit device firm. If the acquiring firm does not attempt to substitute its own management structure, systems or personnel for that of the integrated circuit device firm, then the device firm still has the expertise in place to contend with the changing integrated circuit market and can remain flexible with respect to technology.

Information Resources and Asymmetries of Knowledge

Connections between integrated circuit device manufacturers and equipment and materials suppliers are not as strong as the connections between integrated circuit users and integrated circuit device manufacturers. It is an arms-length relationship that exists between equipment firms and integrated circuit firms. This relationship has developed over the long history of the two industries.

In the early days of the semiconductor industry, the late 1950s and the 1960s, much of the equipment was designed by the device firms. The equipment was then either built by the device firms or given to start-up firms from the machine tool industry. Consequently, the equipment industry of today is an outgrowth of the integrated circuit industry and the machine tool industry. According to a vice president of a market research firm which studies the equipment industry, during the early to mid-1970s, the device manufacturers still maintained the crucial knowledge for equipment design. In the latter part of the 1970s and early 1980s, the asymmetry in knowledge began to swing in favor of the equipment firms.

Movement along the technological envelope pushed for greater complexity of the machines needed to produce the tolerances required by the new devices. From an institutional perspective, the device makers, because they designed the new generations of devices, were slow to recognize this shift in knowledge and attendant need for increased information flow about the equipment needed for the new devices. As a result, friction developed between device firms which supplied the specifications for the machines and the equipment firms which had the knowledge of what was feasible.

According to the same industry official, the device firms would request new machines based on specifications they had developed. Some equipment firms would turn the request down because of their inability to build such equipment. Other equipment firms would be contacted by the device firms and would build the machine. When the machine was delivered, it would not perform up to specifications and the device firm would either spend six months debugging the machine or would sue the equipment firm for breach of contract. In either case an unsatisfactory situation for both firms resulted because time and resources had to be expended to correct a problem which should not have occurred in the first place. This slowed the progress along the DRAM technology envelope.

In order to prevent this situation from occurring, Applied Materials, Inc., and other firms initiated what it termed the "entire solution"—a system perspective approach begun in 1982. Instead of building one machine for a device firm based on the "specs" supplied, the entire process would be specified and then all the machines necessary would be built. This has required some cooperation between IC firms and equipment firms and coordination among equipment firms. In this way, the integrated circuit could be specified from beginning to end.

There are problems with this type of institutional arrangement which come to fore during the diffusion of a major DRAM innovation. These will be considered in detail in the next chapter. What is crucial to note is that the relationship between the integrated circuit producers and integrated circuit equipment manufacturers cannot be classified as an "industrial team" in the U.S. case. It resembles more a collection of all-star players who are choosing up sides for a sandlot game. Each time the game is played, the members of each side may change. Consequently, there is little continuity at the macro-firm level. In essence, American firms attempt to be optimal in the short run and ignore the long term synergies between firms which come from the innovation envelope.

This has led to a drastic decline in the competitive ability of the equipment and material supplier firms in the United States. This is illustrated for one crucial subtechnology area, photolithography. Late in 1989, one of America's biggest suppliers of photolithographic equipment, Perkin-Elmer, indicated that it would sell off its semiconductor equipment division. The only buyer that Perkin-Elmer claimed they could find was Nikon. Nikon, you will recall from Table 4.10, was the largest equipment supplier in 1988. It was only when this was made public and there were implied threats of U.S. government intervention, that Nikon withdrew its interest. This situation is not unique to the photolithographic subtechnology. It exists in silicon ingot supply, ceramic casing supply and could occur in the photomask subtechnology. If U.S. semiconductor equipment manufacturers continue to exit their respective industries, this will leave U.S. integrated circuit manufacturers about in the same position as U.S. computer manufacturers are in with respect to DRAMs.

Because so few manufacturers of DRAMs are American firms, U.S. computer manufacturers must buy their DRAMs from the Japanese. These same Japanese firms are also competing against the American computer firms. The Japanese integrated circuit firms win either way they sell in terms of market share. The revenues and information acquired by selling to American computer firms can then be used to improve the designs of Japanese computers. This will ultimately give the Japanese computer manufacturers an edge over their American counterparts. If the equipment industry goes this same route, the entire electronic "food chain" will belong to Japanese firms.

SUMMARY OF THE FINDINGS

In this chapter, the strategic approaches of firms that operate in the DRAM industry were examined. It was expected that these firms would be innovative, broad-based suppliers of integrated circuits with some degree of forward and backward integration. This expectation received support. The firms entering first in the more sophisticated VLSI and ULSI DRAM technologies were the larger firms. The firms were also more equity-integrated in the sophisticated technology. The U.S. firms tended to become integrated with downstream, integrated circuit user firms, while the tendency for the Japanese firms was to develop ties with upstream firms which made the equipment for producing integrated circuits as well as with downstream firms.

In the U.S. case the primary motivation for this movement was described as financial. The need for more capital resources created the opportunity for mergers. The need for more information played a secondary role in the mergers, but was shown to have strong organizational consequences. The failure to maintain continuity among the engineering and managerial staff after the takeover weakened the ability of the acquired firm to obtain and process the informational resources.

In the Japanese case, both the financial and informational resources played a role. The need for informational resources played the more important role. Another crucial aspect of the relationship between the Japanese firms involving vertical integration was revealed in the same section. The firms were not wholly owned subsidiaries, as is likely to be the case in the U.S. industry, but had to compete as independent firms within their respective industries.

Consequently, the links between the firms in Japan were not as strong, when looking at equity considerations alone, as they were in the U.S. industry. Broad-based definition of a firm's STA was also seen as more important as the technology became more sophisticated. Further, the number of firms that followed an imitative strategy rather than an innovative strategy did not fare as well as the technology increased in sophistication; the trend favored the innovation strategy.

The relative youth of the integrated circuit industry plays a role in determining what is the primer mover in the evolution of the industry. Since the industry is still young, it is still affected by more changes in technology, even though market effects are evident.

5

Industrial Dynamics and the Diffusion Process

OVERVIEW

This chapter will extend the findings presented in the previous chapters. As will be recalled, firms competing in the DRAM industry are confronted with increased information and financial resource needs. These increased resource needs are generated by the innovation envelope created by the innovation imperative of the DRAM technology. Firms which have followed certain strategic approaches have been better able to acquire the needed resources. Firms which have been innovative, rather than imitative, have focused their research efforts and the resources necessary to support those efforts toward entering the market with proprietary DRAM devices. By entering before other firms, innovative firms can command higher returns for their innovation. These returns form the resource base for the next innovation attempt.

Firms which define their STAs broadly are able to use the knowledge gained from innovation in the DRAM with other integrated circuit devices. They are also able to spread the risk of market influence, such as downturns in demand, and are better able to insure a constant flow of the financial resource. This strategic approach will be examined more fully in this chapter. It was also seen that firms which defined their STAs deeply were also better able to acquire the needed resources.

Those firms which were backward connected were able to acquire the necessary information resources to stimulate the innovation in the crucial subtechnologies needed for each generation of DRAM device. Information could flow freely between the firms that produced DRAMs and those that produced semiconductor equipment without fear of loss of proprietary product knowledge. This was observed as a pivotal reason for Japanese firms gaining the innovation initiative in DRAMs.

Those firms which were forward-connected were able to gain information about the market and the products that the DRAM devices would be used in. These firms were also able to gain more financial resources, first, by being able to spread the risk from demand downturns in integrated circuits, and second, by connecting into markets that use DRAMs and thus into higher value-added products. The impact of these strategic approaches will now be examined. The focus of this chapter will be on how the changes in the DRAM technology and industry have been experienced by the firms in the integrated circuit industry. This will be done by focusing on the process of diffusion of innovations in the DRAM.

Initially the characteristics of diffusion in the DRAM will be examined. The pacing of the innovations, the introduction to peak sales and the life cycle of the DRAM device will be examined. Other factors such as the learning curve for each DRAM device and the shift in process technology will be examined. Following that discussion, the impact of these and the various strategic approaches will be examined.

This will be done by examining the types of firms that have survived the DRAM industry. Also the types of firms that have entered and exited the industry will be examined. In examining the existing firms, it will be necessary to examine where exiting firms left to and why other firms entered the new industry. From this a fuller picture of the integrated circuit industry will emerge. Finally, the emergence of international strategic alliances will be discussed in light of the trends examined in this chapter.

DYNAMICS OF THE DIFFUSION PROCESS AND THE S-SHAPED DIFFUSION CURVE

Before summarizing the results of the analyses done on the third proposition, the implications of these results for the shape of the diffusion curve and the dynamics of the diffusion stage is the focus of the investigation. Hence, it will be useful to examine the current research on that stage a little more closely.

Diffusion Literature Findings

The initial point of investigation is the pattern of diffusion. Mansfield (1961) was the first to determine that the S-shaped curve was appropriate for diffusion of innovations in the industrial setting. The sigmoid curve has been used in other social sciences for some time and was used to study the spread of infectious disease for many years (Rogers, 1983). Since its use by Mansfield, economists have regularly adopted this logistic epidemic curve as the best for studying diffusion patterns.

However, the sigmoid curve has recently been called into question by a number of researchers (Gold, Rosegger and Boylan, 1980; Nabseth and Ray, 1974; Davies, 1979). In their study of diffusion, Nabseth and Ray (1974, p. 16) questioned the use of the sigmoid curve because of the inability to determine empirically the appropriate population of adopters. Gold, Rosegger and Boylan (1980, p. 13) summarized several earlier studies, including the one conducted by Nabseth and Ray. They questioned the use of the sigmoid curve as a predictor of the patterns of diffusion and suggested that the population of potential adopters must be adjusted for changes in the innovation and in the needs and resources of potential users.

While both of these studies criticized the use of the sigmoid curve, they did not suggest and test any alternatives. This was done by Davies (1979) in his study of the diffusion of process innovations in the United Kingdom. Davies criticized, not so much the use of the sigmoid curve, but the parameters that underlay it. His criticism was of two parts. The first was that the sigmoid curve used in economics assumes a constant rate of diffusion over time and that each individual firm has an equally likely chance of adopting the innovation. Davies tested his criticism and found that the diffusion pattern, while still a sigmoid curve, varied in its relation to the type of innovation under study. Hence, he divided his innovations into two groups, one made up of minor innovations, the second of important innovations. He postulated that differences in the learning curves for each innovation would affect their diffusion patterns. For the minor type he felt a cumulative lognormal time path would result and for the major type of innovation a cumulative normal time path would result. His empirical findings support his ideas. Second, he tested to see if economic cycles would affect the curves and did not find any strong effect, but did suggest that further testing was necessary.

The change in the shape of the sigmoid diffusion curve was affected by the learning curve associated with the new technology. The impact of the learning curve on innovation in general and diffusion in particular has been recognized by many researchers (Mansfield, 1971, p. 83; Spence, 1981). As noted in chapter one, the learning curve for a technology reflects the process of debugging that occurs when it is being implemented. In their study of the development of a high technology industry, Mueller and Tilton (1969) suggested that it goes through four phases: innovation, imitation, technological competition and standardization.

This same scheme could be applied to the diffusion of a technology within an industry. First, the innovation is introduced by one firm in an industry. Then it is imitated by other firms. In order to gain an advantage over the original firm, the imitating firms will begin to "re-invent" on the original innovation. Finally, the innovation becomes standardized, or "beat'n down" as engineers say (Rogers, 1983, p. 16). Thus, the diffusion stage is a dynamic one that is driven by the learning curve. With the process of reinvention or improving on the original innovation, a series of minor improvements occur and are diffused out into the industry much like the ripples from a stone thrown into a pond diffuse out over the water, first in a major wave, then followed by several minor ones. Eventually the technology becomes the standard, the waves are dampened down, and the new technology becomes the starting point for the next innovation.

In summing up the literature on the diffusion process, several findings can be noted. First, while the standard logistic sigmoid curve may not be always appropriate, some types of sigmoid curve is reflective of the diffusion pattern. This curve, in turn, is affected by and affects the learning curve of the new technology. Thus, the diffusion process is a dynamic one that reflects the changes of the innovation as it is implemented as well as the changes in the potential adopting population.

DIFFUSION IN THE DRAM TECHNOLOGY

In this section the examination of changes in the DRAM product and process technologies begun in the last chapter will be examined in greater detail. Initially certain characteristics of the DRAM product technology will be examined. These include the interval between introduction of the various DRAM innovations, the interval between time of introduction and peak sale in each DRAM device segment, and the learning curve for each DRAM device. Following this the changes in integrated circuit process technology, especially the change form NMOS to CMOS will be examined.

Diffusion in the DRAM Product Technology

As seen in chapter three, innovation in the DRAM product technology has followed a pattern of fourfold increases in circuit density; beginning with the 1K, then the 4K, 16K, 64K, 256K, 1Mb, and now the 4Mb device. Currently, American and Japanese companies are working on prototypes for the 16Mb, and some Japanese companies are engaged in design work for the 64Mb device. While the increase in density has been a straightforward quadrupling, the timing of introduction has varied.

The date of introduction, interval between introduction, and the device type are displayed in Table 5.1. The first DRAM device, the 1K, was introduced in 1971. The 4K was introduced two years later in 1973. It took three years before the 16K device was introduced in 1976. The 64K device was introduced two years later in 1978. The 256K device came four years later in 1982. The 1Mb followed on that by three years in 1985. Finally, in 1988, the 4Mb arrived three years after the introduction of the 1Mb. The pattern of introduction has been fairly consistent over the life cycle of the DRAM product technology.

The average time for introduction has increased slightly over the three

Table 5.1
Year of Introduction of Each DRAM Device Type

Device	Year
1K	1971
4K	1973
16K	1976
64K	1978
256K	1982
1Mb	1985
4Mb	1988

innovation periods. For the LSI period, the average, including the 1K to 4K interval, is 2.3 years between new product introductions. For the early VLSI period, the 64K and 256K, the average span of time between new product introductions is 3 years. For the last VLSI period, the 1Mb, it is also 3 years. The interval between the late VLSI and the beginning of the ULSI period, with the 4Mb, is also 3 years. It is too early to determine, but it is expected that the next ULSI DRAM device, the 16Mb, will be introduced in 1991. It appears from the above that the pace of innovation has slowed somewhat. This is not surprising, given the increased need for resources that have been described in chapter three. This indicates that strong innovative and technological competition exists across the DRAM device segments. However, the interval from new product introduction to new product introduction is only part of the story. Several other measures of diffusion should be examined.

Another way of looking at diffusion is to determine how fast the industry went from introduction to ramping up for volume production. Estimates of volume production may vary. A measure was chosen which was the interval from when one-half of all the firms that would introduce the device had begun producing above 10,000 units per year. In examining each of the DRAM device segments, the pattern was the same for both measures, except that the absolute number of years for the interval changed. These are displayed in Table 5.2.

It took one year for the 1K to reach volume production, two years for the 4K, one year for the 16K and two years for the 64K device. For the 256K and 1Mb devices it took one year each. If the second set of numbers in the table are used, it can be seen that about one-half of all the firms that were going to enter a device category had done so by the second year of the 1K, the second of the 4K, the second of the 16K, the third for the

Table 5.2
Ramp Up Interval between Introduction and Volume Production for Each Device Type

Device	Ramp Up Interval
1K	1 year
4K	2 years
16K	1 year
64K	2 years
256K	1 year
1Mb	1 year

64K, the second for the 256K, and by the second year for the 1Mb. Entry occurred rapidly in each of these device segments. Further, volume production occurred rapidly after entry. This indicates strong innovative and technological competition within each DRAM device segment. It should also be noted that within two years from the beginning of the second measure of volume production, all the firms that were going to enter each of the device segments had entered. This second wave of firms coming into each segment had to compete with the firms that already had two years of production experience and were thus able to set standards for the product. As such, these firms were more at the mercy of market as opposed to technological competition; that is, returns for these firms were more sensitive to demand conditions.

Another measure of diffusion is to look at the time interval between year introduced and year of peak production. When this is compared to the total life cycle of each DRAM device, some measure of the shape of the diffusion curve can be derived. Again, it is expected that some form of S-shaped curve will result. These two measures are seen in Table 5.3.

All the firms had entered before the peak year of production. In the case of the 1K, the peak year came three years after introduction. In the case of the 4K, 16K, and 64K DRAM devices, the peak year came seven years after introduction. The projected peak for both the 256K and 1Mb devices is six years after their introduction. This shows that firms are not only competing within each device segment, but must also compete across device segments. It is difficult to determine when a product goes out of production. Market research firms stop tracking a device after a certain level has been reached in their declines. Hence, the dates offered as termination dates and the life cycle durations are the most accurate estimates available. With the exception of the 1K, all the other DRAM devices peak

Table 5.3
Year Introduced to Peak Production Interval and Total Life Cycle by Device Type

Device	Intro to Peak Interval	Life Cycle
1K	3 years	10 years
4K	7 years	12 years
16K	7 years	12 years
64K	7 years	14 years
256K	6 years	14 years
1Mb	6 years	14 years

Table 5.4
Learning Curve for DRAM Device Type

Device	Learning Curve
16K	77%
64K	77%
256K	76%
1Mb	83%

Source: Dataquest, 1988.

about midway through their product life cycle. These are a little over the midway point for the 4K and 16K, at the midway point for the 64K, and a little under the midway point for the 256K and 1Mb devices. This would seem to indicate that a classic S-curve is being followed from the point of view of demand for a product. There is about a five-year period from introduction to maturity, one to two years at maturity, and about a five-year period from maturity to decline. However, given the rapid rate of entry of the firms within each DRAM device segment, it appears that diffusion from the point of view of firm entry, or supply of the product, does not follow a classic S-shape.

One last look at diffusion of the product occurs with the learning curve. Since it is difficult to calculate the learning cost curve, because of the proprietary nature of cost data, price data is substituted instead. As can be seen in Table 5.4, the learning curve is fairly constant throughout the 16K to 256K DRAM device introductions. It is also evident that these are not far off from the classic learning curve for integrated circuit devices in general, which is 70 percent. With the 1Mb device introduction, however,

Table 5.5
Dollar Value in Millions and Units of Millions of DRAMs Produced in NMOS and CMOS for World Market (1986 through 1990)

	Year				
	1986	1987	1988	1989	1990
CMOS					
Units	4.6	45.8	192.6	466.6	761.0
Dollar Value	50.6	520.6	3043.6	5340.0	5170.0
NMOS					
Units	844.7	803.6	983.7	825.5	505.0
Dollar Value	1478.7	1838.6	3346.2	2682.8	1060.0

Source: Electronic News, December 11, 1989.

there is a significant decline in the learning curve. As will be seen below, this has to do primarily with the rapid introduction and use of CMOS process technology in preference to the previously used NMOS process technology.

Diffusion of Process Technology in the DRAM Industry

Throughout most of the history of the DRAM, NMOS was the dominant process technology. From the 4K DRAM through the 64K DRAM device, NMOS offered better characteristics than either bipolar or CMOS. While there were bipolar DRAMs produced, by 1985 the percentage of DRAMs bipolar was less than one (McClean, 1985). Recalling from the previous chapter, innovations had begun to occur in the CMOS process technology in the early 1980s. By 1983, it had become apparent to industry experts that CMOS was going to be superior to NMOS. Even with this knowledge, the majority of 256K DRAM device introductions were made using the NMOS process technology.

It was with the introduction of the 1Mb DRAM device that CMOS became the dominant process technology. All the new 1Mb device introductions were in CMOS. Even with this, and the introduction of some 256K DRAMs using CMOS, only three percent in dollar value terms of all DRAMs produced in 1985 were using CMOS (McClean, 1986). From that point on, however, the rise in the use of CMOS in the DRAM industry has been rapid, both in terms of units produced and in dollar value. As can be seen in Table 5.5, in terms of dollar value CMOS held fifty percent of the market in 1988. It can also be seen in the table that the number of DRAM produced using the CMOS process technology will be greater than the number of NMOS DRAMs in 1990.

From this is easy to understand the decline in the learning curve for the 1Mb device. Not only is more sophisticated DRAM device being produced, from a product technology point of view, it is also using a different process technology. As the firms use this process technology, the learning should return to its previous level of about seventy-seven percent. If it does not, then some other factor, related to the product technology side, will most likely be the cause.

Having examined the diffusion of the DRAM device from both the product technology and process technology sides, it is appropriate to examine the effects that these had on the firms in the industry. Several measures will be used to determine effects. The number of firms entering and existing the DRAM industry will be determined, as well as the staying power of the firms. The level of return for the firms in general will also be shown.

DIFFUSION AND FIRMS IN THE DRAM INDUSTRY

It was shown in the analyses presented in chapter four that the firm strategic approaches did react in accord with the research framework described in chapter two. In the following section, the impact of the strategic approaches and the diffusion forces described above will be discussed. In doing so, the type of firms that entered in each DRAM device segment will be assessed. Also the number and type of firm which has existed and from which DRAM device segment will be determined. From this the level of continuity across device segments will be assessed. This will help to show if learning is occurring across the DRAM segments. Following this the impact of the strategic approaches and the diffusion forces on the return earned by firms will be examined. This will be done for the firms in general.

Firm Entry into DRAM Device Segments

As was seen in chapter four, twenty-two firms have participated in the DRAM industry. Not all these firms participated at the same time or in the same DRAM device segments. Some firms participated in some of the DRAM device segments and not in others. Some have been able to participate over all the device segments. By examining the firms that entered and participated in the various device segments, a clearer view of the firms and the diffusion process can be gained.

In each of the innovation periods, LSI, and early and late VLSI firms have entered. Using the 4K DRAM as a starting point, eleven firms have entered the merchant end of the DRAM IC industry. Four firms entered

Table 5.6
Demand for DRAM in Millions of Dollars and Percent Change from Previous Year

	Year										
	1978	1979	1980	1981	1982	1983	1984	1985	1986	1987	1988
Dollars	350	650	1000	600	900	1500	3550	1550	1650	2550	5900
% Change	+40	+63	+54	−40	+50	+88	+137	−67	+7	+55	+131

Source: McClean, 1989.

in the 16K, two in the 64K, three in the 256K and two in the 1Mb device market. Of the four that entered with the 16K, one was American and three were Japanese. The one American firm, Zilog also exited soon after entering. Of the two that entered with the 64K one was Japanese and one was American. Of the three that entered with the 256K, two were American and one was Japanese. Both of the firms that entered with the 1Mb were Japanese firms. It should be noted that in the 64K, 256K and 1Mb devices one of the entering firms, has been an entrepreneurial start-up firm. Micron, in the 64K, Vitelic in the 256K and a venture start-up, albeit a well financed venture firm from Japan, NMB, in the 1Mb device have each innovated these VLSI devices. As of the first quarter of 1990, no new entrants have emerged in the 4Mb device market. One question that may be asked, is why a firm would wish to enter this industry, if the technological and market competition is as intense as described above and in the preceding chapters.

One reason is that the DRAM is a process technology driver, and as such allows for a firm to become knowledgeable in process technology which would be useful for integrated circuit device segments other than the DRAM. Second, while the DRAM is a complicated device to manufacture, it is relatively easy to design. A firm wishing to enter and become a broad-based supplier of integrated circuits may choose the DRAM as a way to learn about other aspects of integrated circuit technology. Third, as can be seen from Table 5.6, the DRAM segment of the integrated circuit industry has time intervals of tremendous growth in demand. Recalling from chapter three, the sophistication of the DRAM device was shown to be increasing with each innovation. One of the results of this increased sophistication was the increasing variety of applications for which the DRAM could be used. DRAM devices are found in most electronic equipment, from compact disc players to computers. The demand growth was 131 percent in 1988 for the entire DRAM market, but the CMOS portion of that market grew even faster at 387 percent (McClean, 1989). Consequently, there is a fair financial return to be made by firms that take the appropriate strategic approaches to acquire the resources necessary for continued innovation.

What type of firms were those that entered? With the Japanese firms, all but one were large, broad-based suppliers which were both forward- and backward-connected. These are Matsushita, Mitsubishi Electric, Oki Electric, Sanyo, and Sharp. The one atypical firm NMB that entered could be classified as a venture start-up firm, but in a different sense than American start-ups. It has received the backing, both financially and in terms of access to distribution channels, from one of Japan's large firms, Minebea. In the case of the American firms, of the four firms that have entered, three Zilog, Micron and Vitelic were classic entrepreneurial start-ups and one was a large fully-integrated manufacturer of electronic equipment, AT&T. Consequently, seven out of the eleven firms that entered were large firms which defined their STAs both broadly and deeply. Of the seven firms that entered, six were following innovative strategic approach, and one an imitative strategic approach. The other four firms were smaller entrepreneurial start-ups. Two of the four followed innovative approaches and two followed imitative approaches. Two were forward connected and two were not. None of the four entrepreneurial firms were backward connected.

In order to obtain a more complete picture of the diffusion of firms in the DRAM industry, the degree of continuity and exist must be assessed. Continuity for the firms in the DRAM industry depends on where one begins to measure. For our purposes, the beginning point for measuring continuity will be the LSI period. In this period, however, four firms entered with the 16K device. Hence, both the 4K and 16K will serve as jump-off points. Another measurement issue that must be addressed is the ending point. For the strongest statement, the most recent device should be used. The most recent device is the 4Mb device, however, this device is still in its introduction phase. As a result, firms are still likely to enter. In order to strengthen the analysis, both the 1Mb and 4Mb device segments will be used as ending points for continuity.

In examining the 4K to 1Mb interval, six of the fourteen firms that are producing the 1Mb began by producing the 4K DRAM device. Furthermore, all six of the firms had produced the intermediate DRAM devices. Hence, a little under half of the firms in the DRAM industry had sustained the innovative effort necessary to keep up with the technological competition required by the innovation envelope. In examining the firms that had continued to produce throughout the 4K to 4Mb device interval, similar results were found. Four out of the seven firms had innovated and produced all the preceding devices down to the 4K DRAM device. In this case the percentage is a little over one half.

If the 16K DRAM device is taken as the starting point, the case for continuity becomes even stronger. Of the fourteen firms producing the 1Mb device, nine had innovated and produced DRAM devices beginning with the 16K DRAM device. This is well over half the firms. The number of firms that are innovating and producing the 4Mb DRAM device that had begun with the 16K device is six out of seven: almost the entire segment. This clearly indicates that learning is going on across the DRAM device categories. It also indicates that this learning may be helpful in being early into a new product segment. The methods of this learning and some of the implications of these will be discussed in another section of this chapter. Before leaving this portion of the analysis, however, the issue of exiting firms needs to be addressed.

Not all firms were able to sustain themselves throughout the 4K to 4Mb time period. Three had exited at the end of the LSI period, six during the VLSI period, two at the 64K level, and four at the 256K level. One of those firms later reentered into the 1Mb DRAM device segment. All the firms which exited were American firms. Of these nine firms, five are still independent firms that produce in other integrated circuit device segments. Of the other four, three have been absorbed into other firms as integrated circuit producing divisions. The remaining firm has been taken over by another firm, but is treated as a subsidiary and retains its own name.

During this period, the firms which adopted the strategic approaches that were suggested in chapter two were able to survive the rigors of the DRAM innovation envelope. As noted in chapter four, the degree and type of forward and backward integration exhibited by U.S. and Japanese firms differed. U.S. firms tended to concentrate on financial objects and securing financial resources but also the information resources necessary for new product development. These firms were also able to grow more rapidly and indications are that the returns for these firms were also greater. Japanese firms were able to grow at about 29 percent between 1975 and 1980 while U.S. firms grew about 23 percent if they were independent and 17 percent if they were forward-integrated (McClean, 1987). In the period 1980 to 1985 the Japanese firms were able to grow at a 22 percent rate per annum, while U.S. firms grew at 12 percent and 8 percent per annum (McClean, 1987). While U.S. firms with greater independence grew more rapidly than did firms with some forward connection, the return on equity for the latter is greater than for the former. Comparisons between Intel and Motorola, as representing each of these groups, indicates that during the VLSI era, Motorola has been able to maintain a higher and more stable return on equity than has Intel (McClean, 1987). This is because of the broader and deeper definition of STAs by Motorola.

One of the issues which will be examined later in this chapter is what other integrated circuit segments these United States firms retreated to. This is an important issue, because it will help to set the stage for understanding where the next competitive challenge will come from. For now,

Table 5.7
Top Ten Producers of IC by Process Technology (in 1988)

	Process Technology		
	Bipolar	MOS	CMOS
Rank	Company	Company	Company
1	TI	NEC	NEC
2	National	Toshiba	Toshiba
3	Philips	Hitachi	Hitachi
4	Motorola	Intel	Motorola
5	Hitachi	Fujitsu	Intel
6	AMD/MMI	Motorola	National
7	NEC	TI	Fujitsu
8	Toshiba	Sharp	Sharp
9	Fujitsu	Mitsubishi	Oki
10	Matsushita	National	Matsushita

Source: McClean, 1988.

the most recent technological competition in DRAM innovation belongs to the large, broad-based, and deep STA firms that follow an innovative approach to both the product and process. For the most part these firms are Japanese. This can be seen for process technology in Table 5.7. In this table the leading firms in the various processing technologies discussed above are displayed. In the older bipolar process technology, U.S. firms tend to dominate. There is, however, a strong showing from Japanese firms. These firms make up five of the top ten slots. The dominance grows with the move into MOS process technology. In the NMOS segment, the Japanese occupy six of the top ten slots, and clearly dominate the top positions. This dominance is even more clear in the CMOS process technology segment. Japanese firms occupy seven out of the top ten slots. Again, as with the NMOS segment, the Japanese hold the top three slots of the CMOS process technology segment.

The clear dominance of Japanese firms is also shown in the product technology area. Table 5.8 shows the ranking of firms for 1988 in the 1Mb DRAM segments. Of the eleven firms listed, nine were Japanese and three were American. In terms of the ranking, the Japanese held the top five spots. Only one American firm, TI entered into the top ten. The next American firms were ranked twelfth and fourteenth. As with pro-

Table 5.8
Top Japanese and American Producers of 1Mb DRAM Devices and Respective Rank (in 1988)

Company	Rank
Toshiba	1
NEC	2
Mitsubishi	3
Hitachi	4
Fujitsu	5
TI	6
Oki	7
Matsushita	10
NMB	11
Micron	12
Motorola	14

Source: McClean, 1989.

cess technology, Japanese firms dominate in the DRAM product technology.

In the next section, some of the mechanisms by which diffusion took place will be examined. In this section the process by which learning occurred will also be explored. The implications of these various methods will also be discussed, especially as these relate to issues of information sharing and protection of proprietary knowledge. This protection of proprietary knowledge is known as intellectual property rights, and will be discussed in greater detail in the next chapter.

SYSTEMIC AND BEHAVIORAL ISSUES

Shape of the DRAM Diffusion Curve

As was noted above the shape of the diffusion curve was not found to be sigmoidal for entry into the DRAM segment. The number of firms adopting the various DRAM innovations was far short of the total number of firms in the integrated circuit market. The rate of adoption did not follow the standard sigmoidal pattern of increasing up to the fifty percent point and then decreasing, when measured against time.

At least in terms of the firms producing the DRAM innovations, the results favor the interpretation that the diffusion curve is not S-shaped. The results for the diffusion of the DRAM product and process technologies appear to follow the S-shaped curve more closely. These and the results on entry, exit, and continuity agree with the studies that indicate the diffusion process is a dynamic process.

Changes that have occurred also raise questions for such managerial and economic concepts as the product life cycle and industrial shakeouts. As is indicated by the framework developed in chapter two, larger, more vertically-integrated firms survive longer. During the diffusion process the overall tendency in the DRAM industry is toward large integrated firms. It is important to note that the one U.S. merchant firm to continue throughout the DRAM industry is TI, and it is integrated both forward and backward. This is also the only merchant firm which has entered the 4Mb DRAM market.

INDUSTRIAL TEAMS AND DIFFUSION

The firms which are now dominating the DRAM industry are members of "industrial teams," that is, they either have in-house capability in subtechnologies for the DRAM or have close connection to firms which do. As the DRAM technology progresses along the technological envelope, the industrial team is better able to utilize the informational resources needed for further innovation. As noted, a shakeout has occurred in the U.S. segment of the 256K DRAM industry. While on the surface it appears to be a traditional shakeout caused by a drop in demand, it is not. Demand for the DRAM, as shown in this chapter, goes through cycles of boom and bust, but the trend is increasing with each new product.

In order to ride that increase in demand, however, a firm must continue to innovate. As shown in chapter three, as the technology becomes more sophisticated, larger quantities of innovation resources are necessary. The shakeout which occurred in the U.S. segment, and which failed to occur in the Japanese segment, is as much as technological shakeout as a demand shakeout.

Firms which were not able to keep up technologically with other firms, and were confronted with the decreased revenue which follows the drop in demand, had to exit. The implication of industrial teams for financing and gathering information innovations is important. Since most U.S. firms are equity market financed, while Japanese firms have relied more on debt based financing (Zysman, 1983), the ability to generate capital resources for innovation differs. It has recently been noted that because of the success that Japanese firms have had, their ability to generate financial resources internally has increased (Abegglen and Stalk, 1985). What has not been emphasized as strongly is the difference in using informational resources which is also necessary to match the variety of changes in subtechnologies as the DRAM parent technology moves along its technological envelope.

The ability to track development along the various subtechnologies' trajectories plays a crucial role in which companies are first to the market. This becomes even more important as the technology becomes more sophisticated, as the introduction of the next generation DRAM, the 4Mb, illustrates. Toshiba and five other Japanese firms (NEC, Hitachi, Fujitsu, Mitsubishi Electric, Oki Electric) and two other firms (TI and the European firm Seimens) are readying development. All of these firms are large integrated firms which can generate a team approach to the innovations in technology. There is a major difference in how the team is generated in the U.S. and how it is generated in Japan. These differences will now be explored.

INFORMATION FLOWS AND EXCLUSIVITY IN JAPAN

As explained in the previous chapter, the Japanese have the equivalent of industrial teams which match in variety the complexity of the technology. Within these teams, the information resource is exchanged among members. As was seen, the relationship between the various material, equipment, and integrated circuit firms differs according to which group the company is in. While there are many firms in the materials and equipment industry which are independent of the main integrated circuit makers, the existence of them within group firms provides leverage for the integrated circuit makers. This is because these firms within group firms provide an accessible pool of knowledge on the state-of-the-art in equipment and materials. As explained by an executive vice president of research for a large integrated circuit manufacturer in Japan, these equipment firms will also receive valuable information on the designs for the next generation of integrated circuit devices which they can use to develop the best processing equipment.

The close link between upstream and downstream operations was confirmed by a general manager for marketing of another large integrated circuit producer. Links are established with the end user of integrated circuit devices in order to design the best chip to fit the required product. A market analyst for a large securities research institute explained that attempts were made to standardize the use of the integrated circuits as much as possible; that is, to use the same integrated circuit devices in large mainframe computers, minicomputers, personal computers and consumer electronics. In this manner, the learning curve for a given integrated circuit device could be exploited to its maximum.

As was noted in the previous chapter, the links of backward connection between integrated circuit producers and equipment producers are not unbreakable. For the integrated circuit makers and users, the links are not so solid that one cannot break them and go outside the group. Several of the executives from Japanese firms mentioned, independently of one another, that buying from rival firms did occur. This holds for both downstream and upstream relationships. A downstream VCR maker from one group would buy the integrated circuit devices of a rival if they were of better quality or if a particular integrated circuit was in short supply or not produced by an in-group firm. This is because, it was explained, while each firm is a member of the group, it must survive as a stand-alone venture. For the upstream relationship, one executive explained that buying the best equipment was most important in providing the highest yield, even if it meant buying from a rival integrated circuit firm's within-group equipment maker. Buying from rival integrated circuit firms' equipment makers was indicated to be a major form of diffusion in the Japanese industry.

CHANGES IN THE DIFFUSION PROCESS IN THE U.S. INTEGRATED CIRCUIT INDUSTRY

This section examines the changes that have occurred within the integrated circuit industry. Special attention is devoted to the movement from methods common when integrated circuit technology was new to what methods are now used. The diffusion of technology has changed more in quantitative aspects than in qualitative aspects over the decade of the 1970s and into the 1980s. In discussions with industry people on how information is diffused, references to the "Wagon Wheel Method" still come up, but more formalized procedures are beginning to predominate. The Wagon Wheel was a restaurant/bar near Fairchild Semiconductor where engineers from many semiconductor firms would gather at the end of the day and converse.

While such establishments still abound in the silicon valley area, and may yet play a role in launching new companies or technologies, the processes of second-sourcing, patent trading and other types of formal licensing agreements are playing a more important role.

Recent issues of trade journals devote entire sections to the second-sourcing and technology licensing that is currently occurring in the integrated circuit industry (McClean, 1985). While these activities have always existed, this increased awareness indicates the growing importance of these methods. The increasing technological complexity of integrated circuit innovations, and the diversity of sources from which it can spring, has lead many firms to seek out licensing arrangements in a very loose-fitting industrial team approach. This has occurred between U.S. and Japanese firms as well. These are often referred to as "strategic alliances." The importance of these alliances will be discussed later in this chapter.

Also still important is the constant hopping of engineers from one company to another. It is this diffusion phenomenon that the Japanese were trying to recreate in the VLSI Project. This project will be examined in greater detail in the next chapter. For this discussion, it is important to note that the positive aspects of this phenomenon are recognized by industry executives. Recognized also is the disadvantage of having an unstable portion of your work force, especially when the more sophisticated technologies require a longer gestation period.

It is also not uncommon for lawsuits to arise out of engineers leaving one company for another. This is especially true when the engineer leaves to start up a new company. While few of these suits are successful in stopping a new company, they do delay the effective entrance of the company by tying resources up in litigation battles (Hoefler, 1974, 1975; McClean, 1988, 1989).

In spite of the threat of litigation, the entry of new firms is enjoying a renaissance, not only in the silicon valley but in other parts of the United States. Oregon, Arizona, Texas, and New York are but a few of the states which have experienced an increase in integrated circuit activity. The technological opportunities that are available to new firms is evidenced by the rise in the application specific integrated circuit (ASIC) device. The importance of this device will be examined below. For now, it is important to note that as a method of technology diffusion, the entry of new firms still plays a role. It provides competition for existing firms and thus a motivating force for existing firms to innovate.

Entering firms can also be a source for existing firms of information on new technologies. The process by which this occurs is through the use of "silicon foundries." New companies may not have production facilities such as a wafer fabrication site in place. These are known as "fabless start-ups." These firms often have an understanding of a new product or process technology that other firms do not possess. Fabless start-ups have the information resources necessary, but not the financial resources as manifested in production facilities. They will often make an agreement with an already established firm to use their facility.

This facility then becomes a foundry for the new firm. Since the established firm does not understand the new technology, it learns from the start-up through the production of the new device. The established firm receives information on a new design or process technology that the entering firm has expertise in and the established firm does not. In this way an exchange of financial for information resources results. Both firms appear to benefit from this exchange. The entering firms can come on-line and begin selling product much more rapidly and at a lower initial investment than would otherwise be the case. The established firms are able to learn new technologies which will lead them into growth markets.

INFORMATION RESOURCES AND THE INFORMATION PARADOX

The major difficulty with the approach described above is that the device firms feel that they will loose proprietary information on their devices by giving the equipment firms the information needed to develop the entire process. There is much resistance on the part of the device firms to this approach even though it is recognized as a more effective approach. Further, the device firms do not want to help in financing the development of new equipment. Consequently, the equipment firms must bear the entire financial risk of new equipment development.

In addition, when specs to a process are supplied, the device firm usually wants the equipment firm to wait six months to a year before selling the new equipment on the open market. If the equipment firm should accept this condition, it places the equipment firm in a double-bind of not receiving adequate financial support and not being able to generate it through sales. Many officials of equipment industry trade and research firms feel that in some areas of equipment technology, the United States is one to two years behind the Japanese.

As a result, equipment firms have recently started hiring process engineers out of the device firms. In this way, the equipment firms are acquiring the information they need to produce the equipment needed in the new processes. The arm's length relationship is still governed by market forces. Therefore, the potential to develop game theoretic cooperation does exist. At the present time, the level of this cooperation is low, but the need for it has been recognized. What remains is for both parties to work out the form and extent of the cooperation. There appears to be the development of groupings between integrated circuit users, such a the recently formed research cooperative Sematech and the failed attempt to form a consortium of companies to produce DRAMs called U.S. Memories, Inc. Extension into the equipment industry by the integrated circuit manufacturers has been slower. It was only after much effort that a single American company was found to buy the photolithographic division of Perkin-Elmer.

As noted from the discussion, the methods of diffusion in the U.S. segment of the integrated circuit industry has changed. As the various integrated technologies have become more sophisticated, firms that have remained in segments that have intense technological competition, such as DRAMs, have sought out other firms to create makeshift industrial teams. Other firms have retreated into integrated circuit device segments that are not yet under the same intense competitive pressure. These device areas are associated with logic integrated circuits and include microprocessors (MPUs), microcontrollers (MCUs) and ASIC devices.

The major stream still influencing the U.S. segment of the integrated circuit industry, however, is the lure of creating a successful firm and the financial rewards that come with it. This has retarded the process by which industrial teams can come about. Not only is it difficult for U.S. firms to maintain the critical mass of engineering and production staff, the internal team, but these firms also cannot or will not link up with upstream and downstream firms to form the external industrial team needed for further innovation.

MOVEMENT TO LOGIC DEVICES

As was noted in chapter three there are two distinct classes of products in the integrated circuit industry. The first class of products is associated with the storage of information; these are called "memory devices." The second class of products is associated with the processing of information; these are called "logic devices." Because of the market demand forces that exist in the integrated circuit industry, these two classes of products have become associated with either design technologies or process technologies (Wilson, Ashton, Egan, 1980).

Logic devices, while produced by the same process technologies as memory devices, are generally not produced in the same large quantities. Logic devices also tend to have longer product life cycles than do memory devices. Logic devices, moreover, require considerably more effort to design than do memory devices. Hence, logic devices are used to pioneer new design technologies. This is particularly true of the computer-aided design systems that are now being used and of the software used to drive these systems. the same design techniques may then be used for memory devices.

Before discussing design technology, it is important to examine some of the economic reasons that firms have entered into the logic segment of the integrated circuit industry. As was seen in the preceding chapters, the memory segments of the integrated circuit industry, especially the DRAM device segment, have come under intense technological competition. This competition has resulted from the inherent technological imperative that exists in the innovative envelope of the DRAM and the emergence of a class of companies which can marshal the resources necessary to drive that envelope forward at an unrelenting pace.

Within the logic segment of the integrated circuit industry, the kind of technological competition that exists in the memory segment has yet to materialize. This is not to say that technological competition does not exist in the logic segment. Competition is quite fierce, but because logic devices can be tailored to meet specific customer needs more closely, these devices do not suffer the kind of market competition that occurs with memory devices. Memory devices, as noted before, are like commodity products, and one company's memory device is easily substitutable with another company's memory device. One company's logic device is not as easily substitutable for another company's logic device. This is clearly the case for the application specific integrated circuits, such as programmable logic devices (PLD), electronically programmable logic device (EPLD), gate arrays, standard cells, and full custom devices. Each of these devices can be tailored to the specification of a customer. Even in the standard logic device category, however, substitutability of one company's MPU or MCU for another company's is difficult.

This can be illustrated in examining the relationship between Intel and IBM, and Motorola and Apple Computer. Both Intel and Motorola make standard logic devices, such as MPUs. For the past ten years, IBM has used Intel's MPUs in their computers. A similar situation exists between Motorola and Apple Computer. Motorola has been designing its newest 32-bit microprocessors so as to fit more into the "graphics mode" of operating that exists with Apple's personal computers. Intel's new 32-bit microprocessors are designed to suit IBMs personal computer's "number crunching" mode of operating. One result is that it would be difficult for IBM to switch to Motorola's MPU for its current generation of personal computers. The same is true for Apple switching to Intel's MPU for its current generation of Macintosh.

The switch could be accomplished for the next generation of personal computers, but requires much lead-time coordination between the companies. The architecture of the computer and the microprocessor would have to be coordinated. This ability to coordinate requires that both firms have had a long relationship, that would allow for the flow of proprietary information between the two companies. As was seen in chapter four, the forward connection of American integrated circuit firms and the early dominance of computer and industrial applications have allowed for such ties to develop. These ties are less visible than those between Japanese companies, but it has not stopped IBM from investing in companies like Intel.

Another consequence of this is that companies that produce and sell logic devices tend to have less direct competition. As was seen before, the classic learning curve for integrated circuit devices is about seventy percent. For Intel's thirty-two-bit MPU, the price learning curve is ninety-four percent (McClean, 1989). While this could reflect a more difficult manufacturing situation, the study indicated that lack of direct competition was the reason (McClean, 1989). Consequently, if the true cost learning curve is close to seventy percent, the return to Intel for the thirty-two-bit MPU is quite large.

An important development that will effect the near monopoly situation of the MPU market is the emergence of a new approach to designing microprocessors. Up until the mid-1980s, all microprocessors were designed using a method called Complex Instruction Set Computing (CISC). In 1986, Reduce Instruction Set Computing (RISC) was introduced. The advantage that RISC-based microprocessors have over CISC-based micro-processors is that the former are faster in carrying out a series of logic functions. Consequently, in applications were speed in processing infor-mation is crucial, such as the engineering workstation market, RISC-based MPUs are being substituted for CISC-based MPUs and are gaining market share. Another important factor in this innovation was that the firms which have played the central role in commercializing the RISC approach have been entrepreneurial start ups like Sun Microsystems and Mips Computer Systems. Since most of the MPUs designed and produced by Intel and Motorola are CISC-based, it is likely that by the mid-1990s the duopoly position of these two firms will be over. The importance of this development for the U.S. competitive position with Japan will be discussed after ex-amining strategic alliance activity in the IC industry.

One other point needs to be mentioned. Logic devices and MPU, whether RISC- or CISC-based, tend to have longer effective product life cycles. While the life cycle of a logic device, like an MPU, may be twelve to fifteen years, quite similar to DRAMs, the effective life cycle is longer. The effective life cycle is the period from introduction to peak demand for the product. Because there are fewer product introductions among the logic devices, the effective life cycle is longer. Instead of the one to two years that were seen for the DRAM it may be double or triple that, depending on the particular device. This gives firms that are in these mar-kets a longer time to recoup their investment in the development of the new product.

These logic devices tend to be higher value-added devices. As such, and because of the economic characteristics mentioned above, firms that par-ticipate in these markets tend to have larger and more stable returns. However, because of the greater difficulty in designing these devices, and the connections to downstream users, barriers to entry do exist.

Design Technology

An important consideration in product design is the end user of the device. The major end uses for logic integrated circuits are computers, telecom-munications, industrial and military applications (Gramlich, 1987). As a result, integrated circuit firms that produce logic devices must concentrate on meeting the needs of these end users. In addition to speed in performing functions, the complexity of functions, that is, the number and type of actions a logic device can perform, is crucial in these applications. These functions range from simple addition to complicated multi-step programs.

Changes in design technology play an important part in developing logic device applications. In the early 1970s design technology was carried out by engineers at a drafting table. Today's logic devices require a design

Table 5.9
U.S. Imports from Japan by Device Type and Process Technology, 1985

	Process Technology	
Device Type	MOS	Bipolar
Memory	60%	5%
Logic MPU	9%	0%
Other Logic	16%	10%
Total (% of U.S. imports)	85%	15%

Source: McClean, 1986, p. 11.

technology that uses sophisticated equipment, such as computer aided design machines, and especially the software that runs these machines.

In computer, telecommunications, industrial and military applications, logic devices are more important than memory devices. These devices control the systems, such as robot or missile guidance, that use them. Designing logic devices to execute more functions is more difficult than designing memory devices which perform only one function. Hence, in order to maintain a competitive advantage in logic integrated circuits, firms must be stronger in the design aspects of integrated circuit products (Gramlich, 1987).

COMPLEMENTARY TECHNOLOGY PATTERNS AMONG U.S. AND JAPANESE FIRMS

Process Technology

Table 5.9 indicates that of the one billion dollars worth of integrated circuits imported from Japan in 1985, sixty-five percent were memory chips. As noted above, the importance of the memory segment is that it drives the basic process technologies needed in producing other types of integrated circuits, such as microprocessors (McClean, 1986; Gramlich, 1987). It has also been shown that the Japanese advantage in market share is even greater in the most important memory device segment, the dynamic random access memory (DRAM). The Japanese hold from eighty percent to ninety percent of the world market in DRAMs (Dataquest, 1984; McClean, 1988).

Of equal significance is that eighty-five percent of the integrated circuit devices imported into the U.S. were of the metal oxide semiconductor (MOS) variety. also as shown above, Japanese firms occupy dominant positions in both the NMOS and CMOS processing technologies. Conse-

Table 5.10
Top Three Companies in Selected Leading Edge Products

Product	
1Mb DRAM	32 bit MPU
Toshiba	Motorola
Hitachi	Intel
NEC	National

Source: McClean, 1988.

quently, the Japanese have a clear advantage in the most important MOS integrated circuit process technologies. In short, Japanese companies dominate the memory market and, because of this, have the greatest experience in utilizing the MOS process technology (Gramlich, 1987).

Design Technology

From Table 5.9, the percentage of Japanese imports that are logic devices is about thirty-five percent. The most important category of logic devices for design purposes, the microprocessing unit (MPU) makes up only nine percent of the Japanese imports, with none of these being in the leading thirty-two bit MPU category. As noted above, the major end uses for integrated circuits in the United States are computers, telecommunications, industrial, and military (Gramlich, 1987). U.S. integrated circuit firms have concentrated on meeting the needs of these end-user applications.

As can be seen in Table 5.10, the three leading thirty-two bit MPU supplier firms are American. What is equally as important is the fact that market share held between these three firms is about ninety-one percent for the thirty-two bit MPU (McClean, 1989). While Japanese firms are making gains in some areas of the logic market, these are usually in devices that are older and are of a less sophisticated design technology. In the most sophisticated MPU, MCU, and ASIC device areas, U.S. companies dominate, much as Japanese companies do in DRAM devices.

Since U.S. companies have generally maintained a competitive advantage in logic, such as microprocessor (MPU) integrated circuits, these firms tended to be stronger in the design aspects of integrated circuit products (Gramlich, 1987). In the early 1970s, bipolar process technology was predominantly used by U.S. integrated circuit firms producing logic devices (Strauss, 1983).

As discussed before, because of their speed in processing information, logic integrated circuits have utilized the bipolar technology, but MOS technology has now become comparable in speed in many applications.

As a result, U.S. firms are attempting to switch to MOS technology. Of twenty-eight fabrication facilities which began production in the United States between 1983 and 1984, twenty-five were MOS-based (McClean, 1985). In 1985, the trend continued with fifteen out of eighteen new wafer fabrication facilities starting up in the United States utilizing the MOS technology (McClean, 1986). This trend continues into 1988 with nine out of eleven new wafer fabrication facilities being MOS-based (McClean, 1989). It should also be noted that of these new start-ups, from the period 1983 to 1988, thirty out of fifty-six were producing logic-type integrated circuit devices, primarily ASIC devices (McClean, 1989).

The stage has been set for understanding a growing phenomenon in the worldwide integrated circuit industry. As noted, the Japanese have gained dominance in CMOS memory production and the United States has gained dominance in logic device design. Because of the higher value-added in logic, most of the start-ups in the 1983 to 1988 period have been in this area, especially ASIC devices. The Japanese have also taken an interest in ASIC and RISC MPU's (Sunohara, June 2, 1990). Because U.S. firms are relatively weak in CMOS process technology, a situation of technological complementarity exists. This has lead to a growing number of strategic alliances between U.S. and Japanese firms.

STRATEGIC ALLIANCES IN THE INTEGRATED CIRCUIT INDUSTRY

In order to understand this phenomenon, a general definition of strategic alliances will be given. This definition will then be applied to the integrated circuit industry. These alliances will be examined by various device categories and type of firm. The implications of these alliance patterns will then be discerned.

Strategic Alliances

Strategic alliances are links between two or more companies for the purpose of sharing technological knowledge in crucial product areas. Hence, these alliances are, ex ante, considered long-term agreements between two companies to share technical information which the companies deem important to the goods they produce or the markets they serve. These alliances imply a contract between equals and the sharing of complementary knowledge.

There are many types of alliance mechanisms. They can occur as cross-licensing agreements; as the sharing or cross-training of personnel; or as joint ventures. These activities have been engaged in for some time between companies in the United States and companies in other countries. What sets current strategic alliance activity apart from previous activity is its strategic intent.

Conceptually, the strategic intent of current alliances is a long-term sharing of information and capital, between partner companies which are roughly equivalent in complementary technologies. The key complementary relationships that may occur are between product design technologies and process technologies (Abernathy and Utterback, 1982). A strategic alliance partnership should enhance the research capabilities and future product development and manufacturing capacity of each company engaging in the alliance (Friedman, Berg, Duncan, 1979).

Three Types of Strategic Alliance

Three types of strategic alliances based on complementary technology emerge from Abernathy and Utterback's distinction between product design and process technology, that was discussed in chapter one. The first type of complementary technology-based alliance arises from the sharing or trading of design technology in one product for design technology-based alliance rises out of trading process technology for process technology, and the third type arises when trading design technology for process technology. Although other types of alliances are possible, these are not based on a strict technology-for-technology trade. Possible examples include a money- or equity-for-technology trade or marketing service-for-technology trade.

In design technology-for-design technology alliances, one company will trade design information on its product for similar information on a product design by its partner. An example of this is the alliance between Apple Computer and Digital Equipment. This alliance links Apple's design strength in personal computers with Digital's strength in minicomputers (Schlender, 1988).

In an alliance based on process technology-for-process technology, one firm will trade information on how a class of products are made for similar information on a different set of production techniques. An example is the strategic alliance between General Electric and PPG in the composite material industry. GE, with processing knowledge in resins technology and PPG with processing knowledge in glass fiber technology, formed a joint venture called Azdel to produce a product which utilizes both resins and glass fiber technologies (De Young, 1987).

In a design technology for process technology-based alliance, one company will trade design knowledge for information on a set of production techniques. This type of alliance may be based on some set of current products and processes, such as the VLSI Technology-Hitachi alliance. VLSI Technology is trading design technology for Hitachi's process technology in integrated circuits (Henkel, 1988). It might also be based on future products and processes as often occurs in the biotechnology industry.

As noted above, alliances can occur when only one party contributes technology. The other party might contribute marketing skills or equity

Table 5.11
Number of Japanese Strategic Alliances Formed World Wide in IC Industry

Year	Number of Alliances
1980	3
1981	6
1982	10
1983	14
1984	30
1985	54
1986	76
1987	83
1988	37
1989	80*

Source: Dataquest, 1989.

*Estimate

funding. In this study, all of the alliances that were formed in the integrated circuit industry during the period under examination were found to be complementary technology-based strategic alliances of the types described above.

Since this section examined strategic alliances which are based on complementary technologies, the dominant design and process technologies of the integrated circuit industry have been examined. This has helped to determine the types of complementary technologies which exist in the industry. Following that was an analysis of world market share by country in the integrated circuit industry. This helped to determine the relative strengths of various countrys' companies in these technologies. It will be argued that the number of each type of strategic alliance formed in the integrated circuit industry will be heavily affected by each country's relative technological strengths.

Strategic Alliance Activity in the World-Wide IC Industry

The number of alliances formed by Japanese firms is given in Table 5.11. The period 1980 to 1988 represents the period for which accurate and detailed data was available. The number of alliances shown in the table only refers to integrated circuit firms. Most striking is the rapid increase in the number of alliances formed after 1982. This corresponds to the year

Table 5.12
Strategic Alliance Activity by Japanese Companies by Country and Device Type (in 1985)

Device Type	Country		
	United States	South Korea	Europe
Memory	10	0	4
Logic	19	0	2
Other	9	1	3
Total	38	1	9

Source: Tatsuno, 1986; McClean, 1986.

when the trade balance in integrated circuits became a deficit for the United States (McClean, 1986). Hence, the increase in the number of strategic alliances coincides with the emergence of Japanese firms as major players in the world integrated circuit industry. The data in this table includes alliances formed with European and South Korean companies. It must now be determined which countries engaged in the majority of strategic alliance activity.

To do this, the years 1985 and 1986 were chosen because these were the latest years for which detailed and accurate data was available. Table 5.12 indicates the number of alliances formed by Japanese companies with various companies from other countries. The number of alliances between U.S. and Japanese firms is 38. The number for Japanese and European firms is 9. Finally, the number of alliances between Japanese and South Korean firms is only one. As expected, alliance activity is more vigorous among the countries which dominate the world integrated circuit market; that is, the United States and Japan.

Strategic Alliance Patterns in Integrated Circuits

Because of the Japanese competitive advantage in MOS production technology, many U.S. firms are seeking aid in the switch over to MOS technology by forming strategic alliances with Japanese companies. Further, because of the higher profit margins derived from producing and selling logic devices, the Japanese have now started to concentrate on producing logic devices. Consequently, Japanese firms are in need of design technology.

As noted in the previous section, there were 38 alliances between U.S. and Japanese companies in 1985 and 1986. Table 5.13 and Table 5.14 break down these strategic alliances for each type of device. Utilizing the three

Table 5.13

U.S.–Japanese Alliance Activity by Type of Alliance and Device Type (in 1985)

Type of Alliance		Device Type			
U. S. for Japanese	Memory	Logic	Other	I	Total
				I	
				I	
Design for Design	0	4	2	I	6
				I	
Process for Process	3	0	0	I	3
				I	
Design for Process	7	12	5	I	24
				I	
Process for Design	0	3	2	I	5
				I	
				I	
				I	
				I	`
				I	
Total	10	19	9	I	38

Source: Tatsuno, 1986; McClean, 1986.

alliance strategies discussed above, and based on the trading patterns observed above, it is expected that the design-for-process alliances should be the most numerous. In Table 5.13, the type of alliance is stated as "U.S. for Japanese." Hence, in the design-for-design row, the technologies traded are U.S. design for Japanese design. The first two types of alliances are symmetrical; that is, U.S. design for Japanese design is the same as Japanese design for U.S. design. The third type of alliance, design-for-process, is asymmetrical. Thus, the fourth category of alliance, Japanese design for U.S. process, results from the asymmetrical nature of the design for process type of alliance.

It is evident from this table that the "Logic Device" area is of particular interest to Japanese companies. Japanese companies formed nineteen linkages with U.S. companies in this area. Alliances in logic devices are often keyed to the development, production and marketing of future logic devices. Of the nineteen alliances formed in the logic device area between U.S. and Japanese companies in 1985, twelve of these alliances follow the design-for-process pattern. Essentially the trade in these alliances is Japanese process technology for U.S. design technology. Of the remaining seven alliances, four are design-for-design based technology trades. Of the four design-for-design based alliances, two are for joint development of future logic devices and two are alliances for devices currently being sold. The remaining three are technology trades for existing logic designs in which the U.S. company is acting as a second source for a Japanese logic device. Similar results for 1986 can be seen in Table 5.14. Sixteen of the alliances were of this design-for-process variety.

Alliances in the "Memory Device" area follow more closely the process technology for design technology pattern described above. Of the ten alliances in this area, seven are trading MOS technology for U.S. designs. The other three alliances are process technology-for-process technology based alliances in 1985. Six of the alliances were of this type in 1986.

For the "Other Device" category, five of the nine alliances follow the U.S. design technology for Japanese process technology pattern in 1985. Two are design-for-design technology alliances. The last two are alliances based on a trade of Japanese design technology for use of U.S. production facilities. In 1986, six of the alliances were of the design for process variety.

Consequently, in the 38 alliances in 1985, among semiconductor makers, 24 or 63 percent follow the Japanese process technology for U.S. design technology pattern. The implication of this pattern will be more fully explored in the next section. At this juncture, it is important to note that this alliance pattern follows the comparative advantage of the two countries' companies in the integrated circuit industry. In 1986, twenty-eight of forty-seven or fifty-nine percent follow this pattern.

An interesting facet of these alliances is that many of the U.S. companies involved are primarily small entrepreneurial start-up companies whose designs are on the cutting edge of integrated circuit technology. In this study, a start-up company was determined to be one that had been in business for five or less years. For the companies engaged in alliances in 1985 and 1986, any one founded in 1980 or later would qualify as a start-up.

As noted in Table 5.15, six of the ten alliances in the memory device category in 1985 were between established Japanese companies and smaller U.S. start-ups. Seven of the nineteen alliances in the logic device category were between established Japanese companies and U.S. start-ups. In the other devices category, three of the nine alliances were between established Japanese companies and U.S. start-ups.

In Table 5.16, the pattern followed is similar. In the memory device category, of the seven alliances begun in 1986, four were between American start up firms and established Japanese firms. In the logic device category the number is eleven out of twenty-four. The number in the other device category was three out of sixteen.

Sixteen of the thirty-eight strategic alliances formed in 1985, or forty-two percent, were between U.S. start-ups and established Japanese companies. Although not shown in the table, it should also be noted that fourteen of these sixteen alliances were of U.S. design for Japanese process technology. The other two were of Japanese design for U.S. process technology. None occurred in the other types of alliances. Hence, sixteen of the twenty-four design-for-process type of alliance or, sixty-six percent, were between established Japanese companies and U.S. start-ups.

In 1986, eighteen of the forty-seven alliances were between large Japanese companies and small American start-ups. This is roughly thirty-eight

Table 5.14
U.S.–Japanese Alliance Activity by Type of Alliance and Device Type (in 1986)

Type of Alliance	Device Type			Total
U. S. for Japanese	Memory	Logic	Other	
Design for Design	1	5	8	14
Process for Process	0	2	2	4
Design for Process	6	16	6	28
Process for Design	0	1	0	1
Total	7	24	16	47

Source: Tatsuno, 1987; McClean, 1987.

percent. Of the twenty-eight design for process technology type alliances that occurred in 1986, sixty-four percent or eighteen out of twenty-eight occurred between American start-ups and established Japanese firms. While detailed data was not available for conducting analysis the 1987–1989 period, preliminary data indicates that patterns similar to that found for 1985 and 1986 exist (Dataquest, 1989). Of particular interest were the alliances formed by Sun Microsystems and Fujitsu and Mips with NEC. Both Sun and Mips are the current leaders in RISC-based MPU technology. Further, Motorola and Toshiba have signed an alliance which trades Toshiba DRAM technology for Motorola MPU technology and Hitachi and TI have signed an alliance to jointly develop the 16Mb DRAM. The implications of these findings are discussed below. The implications of these findings are discussed below.

As noted in chapter four, Japanese firms are strategically guided by a desire to be self-sufficient in the vital areas of technology. Given the growing importance of the logic segment, in particular ASICs and MPUs, it is of little wonder that Japanese firms would wish to gain knowledge of design technology. Recalling from earlier in this chapter, entrepreneurial start-up firms in the U.S. often are fabless. These firms need productive capacity. The exchange of design for production capability seems to be a natural one, and would be provided that the U.S. firms developed production capability at the same rate that Japanese firms developed design capability. In discussion with executives in the U.S. it was indicated that this does not appear to be the case. From Table 5.17, Japanese firms have already established a strong position in the ASIC market. While it is true that U.S.

Table 5.15
Design for Process-Based Strategic Alliance by Firm Size and Device Type, 1985

		Device Type		
Alliance Pattern	Memory	Logic	Other	Total
Total Alliances	10	19	9	38
Established Japanese with U.S. Start-up	6	7	3	16

Source: Tatsuno, 1986: McClean, 1985, 1986.

firms lead in the more sophisticated end of that market, the PLDs, and Japanese at the less sophisticated end, gate arrays, it is precisely with U.S. PLD firms that Japanese firms are forming alliances. The potential exists for Japanese firms to dominate the ASIC market as was done in DRAMs.

This would leave only the MPU technology as a stronghold for American firms. The Japanese have been attempting to break into this marker for some time. Through licensing and second-source agreements, Japanese firms have been able to make a respectable showing in the older four bit, eight bit and sixteen bit MPU. Two major signals of the Japanese desire to be self-sufficient in this technology was seen in the mid-1980s. The first was NEC's development and production of its V series MPU. Development work began in 1982 when Yoichi Yano of NEC was asked to develop a thirty-two bit microprocessor based on proprietary NEC technology. The result of his efforts and those of more than 250 other NEC researchers was the V60 which debuted in February 1986 (Kagawa, November 18, 1989). While Intel soon sued for patent infringement, NEC was upheld. The second was the consortium of Fujitsu, Mitsubishi Electric, Hitachi, and Oki Electric which worked on the TRON (real-time operating system nucleus) based MPU. Neither the V series MPU nor the TRON-based MPU have gained much acceptance in the market. Consequently, the Japanese firms are keenly aware of the opportunity presented by the growth of RISC-based MPUs (Sunohara, June 2, 1990). A window of opportunity has opened up for them through strategic alliances with firms producing RISC MPUs and the relative weakness of Intel and Motorola in this technology. As with the ASIC technology, Japanese firms now have the potential to dominate MPUs as they did in DRAMs.

Summary of Findings on Strategic Alliances

From the analyses above it has been shown that the dominant players in the global integrated circuit industry are companies from the United States and Japan. Further, the Japanese companies have been gaining strength,

Table 5.16
Design for Process-Based Strategic Alliance by Firm Size and Device Type, 1986

| | Device Type | | | |
Alliance Pattern	Memory	Logic	Other	Total
Total Alliances	7	24	16	47
Established Japanese with U.S. Start-up	4	11	3	18

Source: Tatsuno, 1986: McClean, 1987, 1987.

Table 5.17
Top Ten Companies Producing ASIC Devices (in 1989)

Company	Rank
Fujitsu	1
NEC	2
LSI Logic	3
Toshiba	4
AT&T	5
AMD	6
TI	7
Oki Electric	8
National	9
Hitachi	10

Source: Electronic News, July 2, 1990.

in terms of world market share. From the U.S.-Japan trade data it was shown that technologically, the Japanese companies are strongest in the process technologies of integrated circuits, while U.S. companies maintain a stronghold in design technologies.

Strategic alliance patterns mirror these market share patterns. Most of the strategic alliances formed in 1985 and 1986 were between U.S. and Japanese companies. Further, most of the strategic alliances were based on trading U.S. design technology for Japanese process technology. In addition, it was found that many of the U.S. firms engaging in this type of strategic alliance were small entrepreneurial start-ups.

For firms on both sides of the Pacific, technological innovation in integrated circuits is becoming increasingly more complex and costly (Methé,

1985; 1986). Design technology and process technology are still driven by the logic device and memory device segments, respectively. Firms must combine these two complementary technologies in order to compete successfully in a global market. Since Japanese firms have developed an advantage in process technology such as MOS technology, and U.S. firms have similar advantages in design technology, exchanges would appear to be in order. These exchanges were found to exist.

SUMMARY

To summarize, diffusion in the DRAM segment was seen to be a dynamic situation with both the product and process technologies changing rapidly. While the diffusion of the products followed an S-shaped curve, diffusion among firms adopting the DRAM technology did not. Firms had to adjust to change in both product and process technologies in order to survive. Shifts in the distribution of the firms were occurring between the Japanese and U.S. markets, however. The Japanese were adding firms to their market, while in the U.S. market firms were both entering and exiting. This was evident in the discussion of continuity for each market segment.

This had further implications in that the firms which survived in the later, more sophisticated technologies were members of the industrial teams. These firms had the upstream and downstream connection to be able to track the variety of changes occurring along the technological envelope of the DRAM technology. This also allowed for more careful attention to be paid to the follow-through process on an innovation.

For each Japanese IC firm, there was in-group expertise, which could be tapped whenever it was deemed necessary. The firms responsible for equipment technology had to compete on the open market, however. This forced them to maintain innovativeness in their own technologies, a phenomenon which is less likely to occur in a tightly held vertical integration relationship. The IC firm benefits from the loose relationship, since it has first access to the improved equipment technology. This assists it in moving down the learning curve and exploiting its commercial advantage through follow-through.

Consequently, the Japanese showed continuity among their firms, but weak barriers to entry since new firms entered for the 16K, 64K, 256K and 1Mb device markets. This indicated that diffusion was occurring across market boundaries with each innovation, up to the 1Mb device. In the United States, firms showed continuity and the weak barriers exit. As in the Japanese case, some American firms entered. But because of difficulty in acquiring the necessary informational and financial resources, American firms exited into the more stable market for logic devices. This was also seen to be the area of greatest new firm start-ups throughout the VLSI and into the ULSI periods.

This has resulted in a state of technological complementarity in the integrated circuit industry. Japanese firms dominate in memory products and CMOS process technology. American firms dominate in logic, especially MPU and ASIC devices and design technology. Since the logic device segments have not suffered the technological competition that exists in the DRAM area, Japanese firms have shown an interest in entering this device area. Because of their strength in CMOS process technology, Japanese firms have been trading that knowledge for design technology, especially in the ASIC device area. U.S. firms have been gaining access to CMOS process technology in return.

6

Government Intervention and Innovation

OVERVIEW

This chapter shifts the focus away from the strategies of firms in the integrated circuit industry and examines the effect of government intervention on innovation in the integrated circuit industry. In the previous chapters, the driving force behind competition in the integrated circuit industry was seen to be technological innovation. This innovation was seen to take place in both the product and process technologies related to various integrated circuit devices. The innovation was also seen to take place over a number of interrelated technologies in such a way that change in one technology often required change in others. Changes in a product technology, such as the DRAM, were seen as forming an innovation envelope for the other technologies.

While the primary focus on for the product technology was the DRAM, other integrated circuit devices, such as logic devices, were also seen to exhibit the same technological characteristics. Differences between logic and memory devices existed, but these were seen as differences in degree. Differences were found in the market relationship that exists between logic users and memory users which allows for a greater return for established producers of logic devices. This may make the logic segment of the integrated circuit industry appear as a safe haven for American firms, but the same technological competition that exists in memories is moving into logic devices.

From the strategic management of technology perspective, the important consideration has been the acquisition of the informational and financial resources necessary for continued innovation. Those firms which were able to acquire enough of both resources were able to continue to innovate.

The ability to lead in innovation also helped to set the stage for the acquisition of the resources necessary for continued innovation, although it did not guarantee the top spot in terms of market share from one generation to the next.

In terms of government policy, the critical focus should be on the resources necessary for innovation. By making certain that an adequate amount of both the informational and financial resources are available and that firms have easy access to these resources, innovation can continue. Policies which enhance the amount or access to resources should aid in increasing innovation. Policies which restrict the resources should inhibit firms from innovating.

Several of these policies will be examined in this chapter, both for the United States and Japan. Policy instruments available to governments will be described in general. This description will include the impact that each of these policy instruments should have on technological innovation. Following this will be a discussion of the general approach of the Japanese and U.S. governments to the question of technological innovation. Next will follow a discussion of the approach that both countries' governments took towards the integrated circuit industry. Then one specific policy instrument will be examine for each of the countries.

SUMMARY OF LITERATURE ON GOVERNMENTAL INTERVENTION AND INNOVATION

For this study, the governmental instruments will be categorized by their intended and actual effect on the resources of innovation, both financial and informational. All governmental instruments have actual effects on the innovation process, but not all instruments were intended by their enabling legislation to affect the process.

Some instruments, such as patents, direct research, and development funding, are designed to impact the innovation process by directly altering the amount of financial and informational resources available for innovation. Others, such as antitrust legislation or regulations on the environment, are designed for other purposes but have unintended consequences for the innovation process, affecting the supply and demand for resources. Still others affect the general health of the economy through control of inflation or unemployment, or affect the general health of the society through funding for education and the like. The health of these more general systems has an effect on the health of the innovation process by affecting the amount of resources available to the whole society (Gerstenfeld and Brainard, 1979; Nelson, 1982; Gold, Rosegger and Boylan, 1980; Schnee, 1982).

Again, the government effect has been found to exist in all the stages of the innovation process, from invention through commercialization and diffusion (Tilton, 1971; Nelson, 1982). Very little empirical work has been done in the area of governmental policy impacts on the innovation process. Most of the early studies were done by economists proceeding with the neoclassical theory that perfectly competitive markets would optimally allocate resources, and any deviation from this would decrease the optimal allocation of resources from a societal perspective (Noll, et al., 1975, p. 2). Later case studies were less influenced by the prevailing economic theory. In these later studies, there was an explicit recognition that policy effects vary depending upon the industry under study.

The literature on the effects of U.S. government policy is summarized in Table 6.1. The innovation stage is arrayed along the top and the various policies with their intended and actual effects are arrayed along the side.

Patents

The original intent of patent policy was, and still is, to provide to the original innovator the full returns from the innovation. Patents are intended to affect the informational resources through the establishment of a legal monopoly for a set number of years; seventeen in the United States. This legal monopoly provides a demand pull incentive in the research and development and commercialization stages of innovation. In this way patents are also intended to affect the financial resources available for innovation. Consequently, the problem of appropriability, or intellectual property rights, that is associated with the informational component of innovation is ameliorated.

The actual effects are less clear. There is very little empirical work exploring the causal connection between patents and increased innovative output. In general, the effectiveness of patents varies widely with the industry involved. In the electronic, integrated circuit, aircraft, and automobile industries, there is little influence exerted by the patent system since the patentable innovation is quickly made obsolete. in the pharmaceutical, agricultural, and chemical industries, the role of patents has a stronger influence on the innovation process (Grabowski and Vernon, 1982 p. 241; Evenson, 1982, p. 252; U.S. Senate Committee on the Judiciary, 1983). Further, the influence of patents has been tempered by the influence of other governmental policies, particularly regulation, which will be discussed in a later section.

The research work that has been done on the stages of the innovation process shows that the impact in the earlier, research and development stages of the process, ranges from neutral, having no effect, to helpful, having the intended effect (Kitti and Trozzo, 1976, p. 195). The incentive to innovate is increased through the increase in return granted by the patent monopoly. The empirical work done on the commercialization stage also shows similar results.

The work done on the diffusion stage, however, indicates that patents slow the diffusion process and thus have a harmful effect (Kitti and Trozzo, 1976, p. 195). The patent monopoly can effectively limit the entry of new firms into the market opened up by the innovation. The difference in the price between patented pharmaceutical and generic brands that appear once the patent term has ended is one indication of this slowing effect (U.S. Senate Commission on the Judiciary, 1983). Thus, a trade-off is imposed by the patent system between the increased incentive to innovate and the monopoly price paid by consumers for the patented innovation.

These conclusions regarding the earlier stages should be viewed with caution because while patents provide a monopoly, the details of the innovation must be made public. The publication of the innovation opens up the possibility of infringing on another patent. This may provide a disincentive to patent (Little, 1973, p. 39), derived from the uncertainty involved in a patent infringement case (Kitti and Trozzo, 1976, p. 214; Nelson, 1982). But with the institution of a special patent court of appeals, the number of innovations that fail because of patent infringement is reduced. The perceived impact of this may be enough to dampen some innovative effort (Myers and Sweezy, 1978, p. 42).

Government Funding of R&D

Direct government funding of research and development must be examined in two parts. The first is the funding component designed to affect financial resources. The intent of direct government funding of research and development, whether it is done in a government laboratory of under contract by a nongovernmental organization, is to increase the knowledge base in certain scientific areas and to facilitate the spread of that knowledge. The funding aspect of government research has no intended effects on the commercialization or diffusion stages.

The second component of the government funding of research and development is the ownership of the results. The ownership of the rights is intended to increase the diffusion in two ways. Government research and development funds are intended to directly affect the amount and distribution of financial resources available, and thus create a supply push for innovation. The ownership portion is directly intended to make the information available to as wide an audience as possible.

The best sources of knowledge on the actual effects of governmental funding are case studies. For the most part, these studies show that governmental funding is directed at the basic and applied stages of the research process, leaving the commercialization of inventions to the private sector. Substantial governmental funding in developmental research is provided, but this is primarily for the military.

At least for the agricultural and pharmaceutical industries, the actual effect of government funding has been helpful. This is also true to a lesser extent for the aircraft and semiconductor industries (Mowery and Rosenberg, 1982; Levin, 1982), where the importance of government funding was shown to decrease as the industries became more commercially oriented. Government funding was not successful in the automobile industry (White, 1982). There has been on work on the direct impact of government funding on the commercialization and diffusion stages, although by supporting research in firms some indirect stimulation may occur.

Again, certain caveats must be introduced. The validity of government funding of research has never been called into question. What has sparked controversy is the issue of who acquires the rights to the work done by government funding. Up until 1980, the government had a policy of non-exclusive licensing of all findings derived from government-sponsored research. The effect of this was to deter many companies from joining in such research (Nelson, 1982). Since 1980, this policy has been relaxed, first allowing small business and universities exclusive rights, and later, larger firms.

Patents and government funding of R&D are designed to directly affect innovation. The next set of policies that will be examined were not intended to affect innovation, but were often found to do so. The lack of direct intent does not pose any difficulty in understanding the impact of these policies on innovation. It should be noted that these policies were often guided by general principles derived from neoclassical economic theory. To the extent that these principles have fallen into disrepute, shifts have occurred in the use of these policies.

Antitrust

Antitrust policy was designed to maintain competition and therefore efficiency. Efficiency was judged as the effect on price, or the allocational efficiency, of the factors of production. As such, there were on formal procedures related to the innovation process (Kitti and Trozzo, 1976). Antitrust policy does have an effect on innovation, however. It has a direct effect on industry concentration and firm size and in this way affects the supply of resources needed for innovation. Often antitrust policy has been seen as helping innovation where it has not been enforced, for instance with the research cooperative in the glass industry (Kitti and Trozzo, 1976). Studies of these impacts have lead to passage of the National Research Cooperative Act of 1984 which exempts research cooperatives from certain antitrust provisions (U.S. House of Representatives Committee on Science and Technology, 1983). The effect of this act will be discussed later in this chapter.

Procurement Policy

Only case studies done by Nelson and others give any indication that procurement may have an effect on the innovation process (Nelson, 1982; Phillips, 1971; Schnee, 1982). While not designed to have any impact on innovation, procurement policy, especially military procurement policy, was seen as having a strong impact on technologies in their early stages of development. Procurement policies may also have an effect on the diffusion of innovations. In the early years of the aircraft, semiconductor, and integrated circuit industries, military procurement was a major source of revenue for firms (Schnee, 1982; Katz and Phillips, 1982; Tilton, 1971).

While the procurement of large quantities of an innovation may provide the experience needed to commercialize a product, the commercial product is generally not the same as the one produced for the military. Thus, the impact on commercialization is rated as neutral. The diffusion stage can also be affected by procurement policy. In the semiconductor industry the military required an alternative source for an innovated product. This spread the innovation among a larger group of firms than would have been the case without the policy (Wilson, Ashton, and Egan, 1980).

Regulatory Policy

Although regulatory policy also is not designed to affect the innovation process, in order to carry out the mandated regulations, innovations must often occur. Table 6.1 indicates no intended effects because such innovation is not market driven but societally driven. The existence of automobile safety or pollution regulations have stimulated innovations. The value of such innovations is beyond the scope of this book, but their source is relevant. It should also be noted that studies have shown that regulations can inhibit innovations as well (Nelson, 1982; Gerstenfeld and Brainard, 1979).

Hence, the actual effect of regulations on the various stages of the innovation process and the resources needed in each stage depends upon the industry and the other government policies involved. In the pharmaceutical industry, FDA regulations are often criticized as diminishing the actual life of a patented drug. This may decrease the incentive to innovate. In other circumstances, regulations may create a new market for firms to enter, as in the growth of pollution control equipment.

Tax Policies

The final area to be examined is tax policy. The tax system in general is not designed to affect the innovation process, although it can do so through tax credits (Musgrave and Musgrave, 1976). The tax system is designed

Table 6.1
Effects of Government Policy on the Innovation Process

GOVERNMENT POLICY	INNOVATION PROCESS STAGE		
	Research and Development	Commercialization	Diffusion
Patent:			
Intent	Direct effect on informational resources through increased appropriability.	Direct effect on informational resources through increased appropriability.	None.
Actual	Industry dependent, demand pull effect.	Industry dependent, demand pull effect.	Enforcement difficult.
R&D Funds:			
Intent	Direct effect on financial and information resources.	None.	Increase information resources.
Actual	Industry dependent, supply push weakened by nonexclusive licensing.	None.	Industry dependent, no effect.
Antitrust:			
Intent	No original intent.		
Actual	Industry dependent, increases information resource.	No effect found.	Industry dependent, increases information resource.
Procurement:			
Intent	Policy specific, no original intent.		
Actual	Demand pull increases financial resources.	None.	Supply push increases information resources.

Table 6.1, continued

```
Regulation:

Intent     Policy specific,
           no original
           intent.

Actual     Industry          Industry dependent,     Industry
           dependent,        demand pull effect.     dependent,
           demand pull                               demand pull
           effect.                                   effect.

Tax:

Intent     Policy specific,
           no original
           intent

Actual     Industry          Industry dependent,     Industry
           dependent,        supply push effect      dependent
           supply push       on financial            supply
           effect on         resources.              push effect
           financial                                 on financial
           resources.                                resources.
```

the affect the economy at a macroeconomic level. As a result its effects will differ by industry. Consequently, before considering the tax policy, one must consider the industry. Although all the policies discussed thus far differ in effect by industry, this is particularly true for taxes. This is because the tax policy effects firms in a continuous manner through its accounting of costs and revenues.

Even with a tax which is designed specifically to affect innovation, such as an R&D tax credit, the results are not often straightforward. Many times firms will account for expenses in the R&D area that really do not represent true research expenses. In order to take advantage of the tax credit (Kamien and Schwartz, 1982). In such cases it is impossible to determine what percentage of the increase in R&D expenses was real and what was not.

Policy Interactions

Before concluding this discussion, it should be pointed out that several of the case studies noted interactions between the various policies. Some of these interactions have been mentioned, such as the effect of FDA regulations on patent effectiveness. These interactions vary across industry and stage of innovation. Consequently, it is extremely difficult to draw any strong generalizations on how one particular policy will affect innovation in a particular industry. This sends a strong signal to the policymaker, however, in that the needs of a particular industry must be well understood before a policy is applied, if any negative and unintended results are to be avoided.

Government policy is recognized to have an effect on the innovation process by altering the supply and demand for the financial and informational resources needed in innovation. The actual effect is often different from the intended effect, depending on the stage of the innovation process and the industry under study. Further, government policies which were never intended to have effects on the innovation process are seen often to have them.

Again, these effects can be helpful, neutral, or harmful to the innovation process depending upon the stage of the process and the industry under study. As a result, it is very difficult to determine in advance the effect of a particular policy on the entire innovation process in the entire economy. Irrespective of this difficulty, national, governments do attempt to influence the development of their economies by taking distinctive approaches to the issue of technological innovation (Mowery and Rosenberg, 1989). These approaches have both planned and spontaneous elements to them and it is often difficult to determine in retrospect, which were really at work. The results of the policy approaches, whether planned or not, are less difficult to discern. From these results it is possible to trace the general approach taken by a nation towards the issue of technological innovation.

GENERAL APPROACHES TO INNOVATION OF THE UNITED STATES AND JAPAN

In this section, the approaches taken by Japan and the United States toward innovation in their respective economies will be examined. The thrust of this examination will be to set the broad background against which the current and future settings for policy can be determined. In order to facilitate this discussion, a framework will be provided. Following this, the Japanese and U.S. approaches will be examined.

Recalling from chapter one, innovation can be divided into improvements in products and improvements in processes. Further, research can be divided into basic, applied, and developmental types. From the discussion of the previous chapters, we recall that in order to carry out research in either product or process, the proper amount and mix of financial and informational resources must be acquired. There is one other element that has also been discussed for the firm, that is, strategy. The particular direction that a firm takes in marshalling its innovative resources and the problems that it attempts to solve in the research process are guided by the strategic approach taken by the firm.

The variables in the innovation equation are not that much more complicated at the national level. National governments can fund either developmental, applied, or basic research. This can be carried out in government laboratories, university, or other higher education laboratories, or in company laboratories. Researchers can be trained as scientists or engineers, which will often but not always determine whether they will work on developmental, applied, or basic research projects. These projects can be aimed at developing new products or processes. The final variable for the national-level approach to innovation is the vision which is set forth, and the strategy which is used to accomplish this vision.

Both the United States and Japan must work with the same variables. The manner in which each variable is used and combined with the others reflects the environment that national policymakers believe their nation is confronting. In Figure 6.1, the approach that Japan has followed is displayed over time. The U.S. approach is displayed in Figure 6.2. What is presented in each of these figures is a view of the effect of various governmental and quasi-governmental policies. This analysis does not suggest that there were plans that were completely consciously thought out and then carried out through the various policy instruments described earlier. What is reviewed in this analysis is what has been successful or has been glaringly absent, and as such, has left its mark.

In the case of Japan, the primary vision has been the civilian application of technology. From the end of the Second World War until the present, a primary focus of this use of technology has been in improving the methods of production. Process innovation was particularly dominant between 1945 and the early 1970s. Japan's phenomenal success in terms of double-digit growth rates in GNP during this period is related to the large investment in capital and human resources.

While both product and process technology was acquired from abroad during this period, the emphasis was on rebuilding the industrial infrastructure of Japan and educating the training engineers to absorb the incoming information. The acquisition of basic oxygen furnace (BOF) technology is perhaps most symbolic of this early postwar period. The role that the government played in the acquisition, commercialization and diffusion of this steel processing technology has been chronicled elsewhere (Lynn, 1982). The crucial point is that the government played an important role in this and the acquisition of other manufacturing technologies.

Companies were encouraged by the government to place emphasis on finding ways to more rapidly absorb and add to the imported technological knowledge so as to improve efficiency and product quality. It was during this period that the kanban and "just in time" systems were initiated at Toyota (Abegglen and Stalk, 1985). It was also during this time that quality control circles were first initiated and the Demming Prize was begun. This is not to say that the government, in the form of the Ministry of International Trade and Industry (MITI), was always correct, as in the case of their reluctance to grant Sony permission to acquire a license for transistor technology from AT&T. However, MITI did play an important role in the

Figure 6.1
Japan's Strategic Approach to Industry

```
Production-----------------------------------------------------------
(quality/efficiency)



                    Product--------------------------------
                    (features/knowledge utilization)




                                    Technology------------
                                    (Knowledge creation)

```

```
 1945                        1965              1980
```

early postwar period and for the most part, the push to improve production efficiency and product quality was successful (Johnson, 1982).

The base from which this push sprung was created by a high savings rate and high level of education. The high savings rate created a large pool of capital which could be turned into financial resources for innovation. The high education level created a work force and engineers who could not only absorb technological knowledge from abroad but could also substantially add to it. By the early to mid-1970s the Japanese were to shift the emphasis to new product development.

The VCR is perhaps the best symbol of the transition that occurred in the early to mid-1970s from production to product innovation. The VCR was originally developed in the United States, but was essentially a product designed and produced for professional use. Japanese firms acquired the technology and innovated new designs that were smaller and easier to use. Then, using the improved manufacturing technology developed earlier, these firms were able to offer the VCR at prices ordinary consumers could afford (Rosenberg and Cusumano, 1987). This particular event symbolizes not only the emergence of Japan into original product innovation as opposed to product improvement, but also shows that Japan continued to carry forward its previous strategic focus on production improvement.

The Japanese do not view product innovation as more important than process innovation. The two are viewed as having equal importance. This affects the way Japanese firms organize their innovation resources, particularly their engineering staff. Product and process innovation would originate from the same source, the factory engineering staff. What had occurred in the early 1970s was that Japan's industrial base had reached a point of development where truly original product innovation could begin to take place. The emergence of the audio compact disc, digital audio tape and high definition television is the fruit of product innovation project begun in the early 1970s. Along with the new products that are emerging is the ability to produce these with increasing efficiency and attention to quality.

In the two periods above, the emphasis was seen to shift from process to product innovation. Technological knowledge was still being acquired, mainly through license, from U.S. and Western European companies. The primary research focus was on applied an developmental research. Acquisition of and the quick diffusion of technological information for commercialization formed the backbone of Japan's research efforts during this period.

Some basic research was being done, but the creation of new scientific knowledge bases was not economical given the existence of such information in other countries. Confronted with the "make or buy" decision in basic research, it was simply more economical to buy the information. This situation began to change in the late 1970s. In many cases Japanese firms had come abreast of U.S. firms in certain technologies. As was seen in previous chapters, it was the Japanese who innovated the 64K DRAM in 1978, and every other DRAM generation since then. In other cases U.S. companies were becoming less willing to license technology to the Japanese.

Beginning in 1980, Japan declared its technological independence from the United States. Since that time, Japan has been attempting to build a basic research infrastructure that would be as good as that of the United States in generating new knowledge bases. This phenomenon will be explored in greater detail in the next chapter. What is important to recognize is that this phenomenon is real.

Organizationally, the Japanese government have a number of governmental and quasi-governmental agencies to help promote technological knowledge base generation activities and basic research activities. Operating directly with the Prime Minister's office is the Council for Science and Technology (CST) and the Science and Technology Agency (STA). Established in 1988 and operating with CST is the National Institute of Science and Technology Policy (NISTEP) to help develop science and technology policy. Each of the Ministries has a number of laboratories operating within them. The most important Ministries are the Ministry of Education (MOE), the Ministry of International Trade and Industry (MITI), and the Ministry of Posts and Telecommunications (MPT).

The Ministry of Education is responsible for the research carried out in the public universities in Japan. MITI, through its Agency of Industrial Science and Technology (AIST), administers a number of programs to aid the development of new technology. MPT operates a number of laboratories and in conjunction with MITI the Japan Key Technology Center (KTC). The Japan Key Technology Center was established to foster research into technologies for industries of the twenty-first century. One area of importance to the IC industry is the funding that KTC has given to SORTEC, a consortium of companies working on advanced x-ray lithography.

Another quasi-governmental organization, the Japan Research and Development Corporation (JRDC) established in 1961 by STA, has lead the push into basic research. The most significant program put in place by JRDC is the Exploratory Research of Advance Technology (ERATO). This program provides funds for researchers from universities and company laboratories to explore particularly challenging areas in the physical and biological sciences. Not directly aimed at fostering basic research, but still in the area of fostering greater creativity in the Japanese economy is the Venture Enterprise Center (VEC). VEC was set up to help entrepreneurial firms get established through guaranteed loans. These are but a few of the agencies and programs that have been established to move Japan into the area of knowledge generation. One question is whether Japan can accomplish this. Given the inherent time lags in conducting basic research, only time will tell. One indication of how results may turn out was recently observed in the area of high temperature superconductivity research.

A research team at the University of Tokyo under the guidance of Dr. Shoji Tanaka were the first to confirm the findings of the original research on high temperature superconductivity in IBM's Zurich Laboratory. They made their confirmation within months after the original finding and Japan has continued its momentum. While this team did not make the original breakthrough, the American lead in this technological knowledge base can no longer be measured in years. The race is on.

The U.S. approach is displayed in Figure 6.2. With the exception of the 1960s, there was no clearly formulated vision for American research. During the 1960s the vision of "placing a man on the moon and returning him safely, by the end of the decade" had given direction to much of the United States's research effort during those years. With the accomplishment of that goal, our research vision lapsed. Filling the vacuum was a growing need to perform technologically against the Soviet Union. Consequently, the de facto vision for U.S. research efforts was defined by the Cold War and the arms race.

This vision was reinforced by the lack of economic competition that existed until the 1970s and by the institutions of the military-industrial-scientific complex that had been set up to win the Second World War. This they had done and that success carried with it an air of legitimacy in helping to set and carry out the American national research agenda. The vision generated from this was essentially military. Commercial endeavors were best left up to the market.

With the competitive agenda being set in the world by American firms from the 1945 until the early 1970s, emphasis on improving production

Figure 6.2
U.S. Strategic Approach to Research

```
Production----------------/........................./-----------


Product---------------------------------/........../-----------


Technology--------------------------------------------------------

_____
    1945                  1970        1980        1995
```

efficiency and product quality began to fade by the late 1960s. With the exception of some industries such as chemicals and pharmaceuticals, the industrial base was not being renewed as fast as it was in Japan. Steel was slow to adopt the BOF (Lynn, 1982). The automobile industry was dominated by one firm which could act as a price leader, and pass on any inefficiencies in its manufacturing in higher prices without concern for loss of market or profit. The other automobile manufacturers were only too happy to follow suit (Halberstan, 1986). Producers of consumer electronics and other industries found it easier to retreat from Japanese competition rather than reinvest in the plant, equipment and personnel needed to meet the competition (Abernathy and Utterback, 1980).

It should also be noted that the savings rate in the United States was considerably lower than in Japan. This contributed to a smaller pool of available capital for use as financial resources in innovation and also contributed to the higher cost of capital that American firms confronted when investing in new technologies. America was also beginning to fall behind in education and training for its work force. Not only were managers and executives less knowledgeable of the technologies which underpinned the products that their companies produced, but remedial training had to be started at many companies to bring workers up to the level necessary to use the more sophisticated production equipment and service more sophisticated products.

By the mid-1980s, the United States was also falling behind in new product innovation. This has been chronicled above with the DRAM segment of the integrated circuit industry. In the automobile industry, Japanese companies were able to move from design to production in half the time that American automobile makers could. Japanese companies dominate the consumer electronics industry with a plethora of new products every year. Japanese companies are now gaining ground through new product introductions in the fastest growing segment of the personal computer industry, the laptop segment (Business Week, 1989). Although large sums of funds are being spent on applied and developmental research, a large portion of these are being siphoned into military research (NSF, 1987). The research needs of the military and civilian sectors are different and continuing to diverge. Hence, the spillover effect from military to civilian is beginning to slow, and in some cases has actually reversed (Mowery and Rosenberg, 1989).

American companies are responding, and progress in process innovation and product innovation is being made. More attention is being paid to investment in plant and equipment and to training of employees. The institution of quality control circles, just in time systems with multi-machine cell-based manufacturing, along with computer aided manufacturing has been done in many companies. The use of design for assembly/manufacturing is being implemented to improve product quality and reduce product development cycles. However, the Japanese, as described above, are not presenting a stationary target, but are also continuing to improve (Grayson and O'Dell, 1988). The race is on, as before. However, in many industries it is the Americans who must play catch-up.

One area where American research continues to lead is in the knowledge generation activities of basic research. The combination of government and some private funding, coupled with a strong university base for laboratories and researchers, has yielded a powerful team. The United States still dominates in the number of Nobel prize winning scientists it has each year. American companies are still making fundamental breakthroughs in fields such as biotechnology, superconductivity, supercomputing, and artificial intelligence. The question confronting American firms and the U.S. government is: how long will the lead last and in what areas? At this time the answers to these questions are by no means certain or final, but the decisions made by American policymakers in the coming few years will be crucial to determining them.

One last area concerning the approach taken by Japan and the United States towards innovation in industry needs to be examined. This is the matter of timing. In the United States, the approach is on again, off again. During the 1950s up until Sputnik, no real urgency was seen in the national research agenda. After Sputnik, that changed. The vision provided of putting a man on the moon only lasted ten years. With the 1970s and into the early 1980s no real discussion of a vision for American research was undertaken.

It has only been with the increasing challenge of international competition, especially from the Japanese, that talk of a research agenda for the United States has re-emerged. This stop-and-go timing does not mesh well with the flow of innovation and its impact on the growth and development of industries. Japanese timing in these matters seem to fit more closely the research done on innovations and the development and growth of industries.

JAPANESE GOVERNMENT POLICY AND THE LIFE CYCLE OF AN INDUSTRY

From the discussion of government interventions, it was evident that government policy has affected the diffusion of technological innovation in the Japanese economy. The extent of government influence on the diffusion process will now be discussed.

Several high-ranking U.S. embassy officials have commented to this author that the general approach of the Japanese government to the growth of a technology is in four stages. While names for the stages differ among the people interviewed, they can be categorized roughly as "embryonic," "take-off," "sustained growth," and "mature/declining." The Japanese queried have similar impressions, but break the government intervention along the lines of type of influence, such as information provision, research and development funding, gyosei shido (administrative guidance), cartelization and so forth. The common thread running through either description is the attempted matching of government actions to the stages of development of industries.

Embryonic Technologies

During the embryonic stage of a technology, the role of the government has in the past been limited. Much of the government effort was centered on information collection, usually from abroad, through agencies such as the Japan Information Center of Science and Technology (JICST). This information is then dispersed to companies. It is also usually during this stage that MITI issues its vision for the industry, and guidance councils made up of leading figures in government, education, and industry are formed to explore goals for the industry and establish broad frameworks for meeting those goals.

Several Japanese have commented that the real contribution of these efforts may be more psychological than real. Charting the course of an industry is extremely difficult, but the issuance of a vision of the importance of the industry and where it is going provides an insurance policy, or a "moral hazard" effect in reverse, for the companies involved. The government effectively bears some of the risk for entering a new technology.

An analyst for a Japanese securities research institute explained that the issuance of a MITI vision shifted the decision risk from managers in companies to the government. On the down side, if the market were to fail to materialize, or the company were to perform poorly, the government would receive the blame rather than the managers. On the up side, with the government pointing the direction, it would be easier to convince key managers to marshall the resources to support risky ventures. In addition to the information collection activities and the MITI visions, much of the current effort of the government is in fostering technology knowledge base generation and basic research in Japanese laboratories.

Growth Technologies

During the take-off stage, the type and level of government involvement becomes more focused on developing generic technology. An industry such as the opto-electric industry is currently in this stage. In the early part of the stage information on the state of the art in the commercialization of a technology is collected from every source imaginable. Many trade and industry tours go abroad. At home in Japan, the key companies in the new technology are identified. They become the "haves," as an analyst for a marketing/management consulting firm in Japan explained.

These are the companies which will pioneer the commercialization of the technology and will receive government subsidies, participate in government research and development projects, and receive government protection. These companies form a core around which enough experience will be built up to provide for unaided growth in the next stage. Examples of this type of activity was seen in the VLSI Research Cooperative and in the work done by the Japan Electronic Computer Company (JECC) to aid Japanese companies acquire computers. The JECC would buy computers from Japanese companies such as Fujitsu, and lease them to small and medium sized Japanese companies. These companies usually did not have the necessary capital to buy the computers outright. In this way, Japanese computer markers had an expanded market and the smaller and medium sized companies which leased the machines were able to use computers. A similar effort is now in the planning stages for commercializing HDTV. The only factor holding it up is a bureaucratic turf battle between MITI and MPT.

The other companies are divided into two further groups, the "intermediates" and the "have-nots." The "intermediates" receive some direct government aid, but rely on aid from quasi-governmental sources, engineering associations and the university system. The "have-nots" do not receive much aid either of the direct of indirect variety. During this study, in the integrated circuit industry the "haves" were NEC, Hitachi, Toshiba, Fujitsu, and Mitsubishi; the "intermediates" were Oki Electric and perhaps Matsushita and Sharp; and, the "have-nots" were companies such as Sony,

Pioneer, Tokyo Sanyo, Ricoh, and the like. These categories are not rigid, and may change based on the technology involved.

Sustained Growth

During the sustained growth stage, the influence of government weakens. This is where the integrated circuit industry is today. The market, both internal to Japan and the world market, plays the key role. In this stage, the companies may ignore or even go against the wishes of the government. Many executives of the integrated circuit firms interviewed expressed the notion that the government was too meddlesome, and that if they were left alone they could do better.

It is not that the government is seen as hostile, but it is seen as having "fat fingers," that is, not having the administrative dexterity and agility required to devise strategies for firms which would effectively compete in the open world market. Several government officials currently involved with the integrated circuit industry reported that the effect of administrative guidance is quite limited because the companies do not listen to it.

Thus, to the Japanese interviewed, the industry becomes less sensitive to the influence of the government. During this stage the market forces become predominant in technological innovation and diffusion. In the integrated circuit industry, the role of the private companies is strongest in this stage. They are the primary vessels of technological diffusion. As a result, many companies attempt to enter the market and there is fierce rivalry between them.

Findings from the previous chapters indicates that the Japanese government is not the only, or perhaps even the strongest element, in the diffusion process. It appears that a primary mechanism for learning is provided by the equipment firms. As noted in the discussion in chapters four and five, the equipment makers, because they are loosely coupled to the integrated circuit firms, act as a major disseminator of technological information. Thus, the entrance of firms into the 64K market could be explained by the role of the equipment firms described above.

Mature Technologies

In the mature/declining stage the influence of government increases. This is the stage the steel and textile industry is currently in. Cartelization and the gradual shifting of capital and human resources out of the industry and into growing industries is encouraged by the government. An example involving the integrated circuit industry concerns a firm in Kyushu which ground lenses for cameras. As the lens market declined, the firm was encouraged to shift to the polishing of silicon wafers. It now subcontracts for a large integrated circuit producer.

As mentioned in the beginning of this section, the perception of stages is a U.S. perception. It assumes a very proactive and well-informed Japanese government. The perception of the Japanese interviewed is that the government is not proactive but, with the exception of the visions, reactive. It cannot know when a technology or an industry is about to reach the take-off or sustained growth stages.

To the Japanese, the government is always exerting some influence and not always for reasons of technological promotion. What is important is the sensitivity of the industry to that influence. Some industries are more sensitive than others, and that is a direct result of the "health" of the rising or declining market. The government is perceived as reacting to the ebb and flow of market forces and smoothing the transition from declining markets to growing ones. It is not seen as directing the growth of markets or the development of technologies. It is also not seen as very effective in mapping out the details of surviving in a market. The government is seen as helping to set some broad goals and directions and letting the companies fill in the details of how best to accomplish those goals.

In the examination of government action, the VLSI Research Cooperative or Cho LSI Kenkyu Kumiai, as it is called in Japan, has often been referred to as an example of a successful intervention. Because the DRAM industry was well into its sustained growth stage, the inner workings of the project must be explored and evaluated.

DESCRIPTION OF GOVERNMENT INTERVENTIONS IN THE DRAM INDUSTRY

Differences between industries affect the innovation process. This inter-industry effect alters the impact of governmental policies irrespective of whether these policies were designed to enhance the innovation process or not. As is indicated below, for the period of this study no governmental policies were consciously designed by the U.S. government to enhance innovation in the DRAM industry. In spite of this, it is instructional to examine the instruments available to government and their respective effects on the innovation process.

Japanese DRAM Intervention

In the Japanese case, a policy existed which was designed to affect the DRAM market and both the financial and informational resources. This was the creation of the VLSI Cooperative Research Project, which ran from 1975 to 1979. This project brought together five private companies under the auspices of MITI to work on technologies relevant to very large

Table 6.2
Maximum Market Share Held by Japanese Firms in World DRAM Market

Device	Maximum Market Share Percent
1K	5.0
4K	17.3
16K	41.4
64K	71.7
256K	92.1
1Mb	96.3

Source: Dataquest, 1989.

scale integration. It is this policy which will be examined in this section. Through the use of three indicators, the effects of this policy will be assessed. First, the DRAM market share for the Japanese firms will be determined. Then the entry time of the firms participating will be compared across the device types. Finally, the sampling time of the participating firms will be compared across device types. If the market share of the Japanese firms increases substantially after the intervention, this would offer support to the proposition that the VLSI Cooperative was successful. Further, if the entry time and sampling time of firms participating in the intervention decreases relative to firms not participating, the intervention would appear to be successful.

In Japan, the initiation of the VLSI Cooperative Research Association in 1975 marked an attempt by MITI to influence the direction of the integrated circuit industry in Japan and to increase the competitive position of Japanese computer manufacturers.

The VLSI Cooperative was set up not only to increase the funding available to firms, but to increase the sharing of information. The amount spent by MITI was 300 million yen, while the amount spent by the participating companies was 400 million yen (Denshi Kiki Ka, 1983). The total amount of 700 million yen spread over the five years of the project from 1975 to 1979 is quite small, but does indicate that attention to the financial resource was considered. More important was the attention to the informational resources, which will be described below.

Informational Resource Provision and the Success of VLSI

The bringing together of five ferociously competitive companies—NEC, Hitachi, Toshiba, Fujitsu, and Mitsubishi—to work under one roof on

Table 6.3
Elapsed Entry Time for Japanese Firms Participating in VLSI Cooperative Research Project

Device	Entry Time (quarter year)
16K	7
64K	9
256K	3

Source: Dataquest, 1984.

research for as lucrative a market as the MOS DRAM market had not been attempted before. Each of the firms had ongoing research and production efforts in the DRAM market. Thus, firms were unwilling to share information vital to their own efforts. The necessity of doing so, because of the increasing competitiveness of U.S. computer firms, was clear to the Japanese. The VLSI Cooperative aimed at the development of generic production technology for the 256K DRAM (Tarui, 1981). From Table 6.2, it appears that the government intervention was successful.

The market share held by Japanese firms is quite large for the 256K DRAM market when compared to the 64K and 16K markets. These results must be considered tentative, however. The trend before the intervention was towards increasing Japanese market share, and the share figures for the 1K, 4K, and 16K are the maximum share held at any time by the Japanese, while the figure for the 256 K device market is based only on a couple of years of data. Since the 256 K device market is still young, the maximum market share of the Japanese firms may become larger.

To further test the effectiveness of the intervention, a comparison of the time difference between first firm and last firm entering is in order. Only the firms which participated in the VLSI project are compared. The results for the 16K, 64K, and 256K devices are presented in Table 6.3. The trend is downward with each device, and the difference between the 64K and 256K chip is quite large.

The VLSI Cooperative seems to have strengthened the individual performance of the firms that participated as evidenced by the decrease in time spent between the sampling and production phases. The difference is evidence in Table 6.4 and shows the effect on the provision of informational resources most clearly.

Table 6.4
Sampling Time for Japanese Firms Participating in VLSI Cooperative Research Project

Device	Sampling Time (quarter year)
64K	4.4
256K	2.2

Source: Dataquest, 1984.

These results tend to support the proposition in favor of the intervention and to argue against the strength of each firm's internal efforts in the research area. However, the success of the firm Oki Electric, which did not participate in the project, could argue in favor of the internal efforts of the firms and against the proposition. Questions are further raised by the entry of Matsushita, Sharp, Sanyo and especially the entrepreneurial startup NMB into the DRAM market. Like Oki Electric, these firms did not participate in the research cooperative. While not shown in Table 6.4, comparing the performance of Oki Electric with the VLSI project firms highlights the advantages to the project firms. Oki Electric took twice as long to reach the production stage as VLSI Cooperative firms.

A cautionary note should be interjected, however, because the performance of the United States is about the same as the Japanese firms. It is possible that the diffusion mechanisms which hastened learning in the 64K market were at work in the 256K market. Thus, the conclusion for the Japanese government intervention is that it did have some success, but not the overwhelming success that often is suggested in the popular press.

The results of the Japanese government's intervention has been reviewed. With this intervention, both the financial and informational resources were affected. The key resource was the informational resource. The results of that intervention support the proposition that the VLSI Cooperative was successful.

SYSTEMIC AND BEHAVIORAL ILLUSTRATION: VLSI RESEARCH COOPERATIVE

Because the VLSI Research Cooperative has served as a focal point for much debate in the United States and because it is often used as model for American efforts at enhancing innovation in the integrated circuit industry, it is important to examine its functioning in greater detail. Several executives of private companies who participated in the Cho LSI Kyodo Kenkyu Kumiai (VLSI Cooperative Research Association) as well as former members of MITI who helped establish and run the cooperative were interviewed and have noted that the primary reason for its inception was to give the Japanese computer manufacturers a chance against IBM.

This was and still is the vision which the Japanese electronic companies hold. It is held because computers are a central pillar to building a modern technological economy. It is also held because computers are at the highest end of the electronic value chain. Japanese computer manufacturers had tried to go head to head against IBM during the late 1960s and early 1970s, and even with government designed to develop new computers they were unsuccessful.

According to an analyst at a securities research institute, Japanese computer architecture is not considered as good as U.S. computer architecture. To compensate for this, the best quality ICs are used. With the advent of the IBM future system, and the impending liberalization of the Japanese computer market in the late 1970s, the computer manufacturers were worried that IBM would drive them out of business.

Providing an "Atmosphere" for Cooperation

To compensate for these trends, MITI offered the development of a research cooperative on integrated circuit technology, according to the computer manufacturers. According to former MITI officials, the computer manufacturers requested some sort of aid. Regardless of where the first glimmering for the project originated, MITI provided the umbrella for its establishment. It was recognized that the intense rivalry between Japanese firms would not permit cooperation. The proper "atmosphere" had to be generated and imposed on the market.

"Atmosphere" is a term used by Williamson (1975) to describe a variety of institutional elements not ordinarily found in standard neoclassical economic models. Cultural and sociological factors such as trust between individuals and group membership are examples of "non-economic" institutional elements. It has been noted in several studies of the Japanese culture that a strong "in-group" versus "out-group" orientation pervades many social interactions (Lebra and Lebra, 1974; Craig, 1979).

This particular group orientation puts strong barriers between two different groups and communication is limited. When this group orientation is combined with the lifetime employment existing among the major DRAM integrated circuit firms and the economic rivalry of oligopolists, horizontal communication between firms within the industry is difficult. Thus, the idea of a research cooperative which would bring together five of the most competitive firms to work on technology for one of the most lucrative markets was radical. It had not been attempted before, and there was much concern that it would not succeed. However, the company officials involved, as well as the former MITI people, argued that in order to compete in the integrated circuit market, some attempt had to be made to duplicate the "natural cross-fertilization" which occurs in silicon valley with the high turnover of engineers between companies. It was hoped that getting engineers from the various companies to work together would cut down on duplication of research efforts between firms and spark new approaches to the problems of VLSI process technologies.

Major Foci of the VLSI Project

In order for the project to work, it was decided that only process technologies of the 256K DRAM and beyond would be explored. Further, work would be in the "generic applied technology" side, that is, the work would be on developing prototype machines for producing 256K chips. Once this was accomplished, each individual firm could refine the original design to fit into its own unique process layout (Tarui, 1981). The three areas chosen for study were production process equipment, especially photolithographic technology of micron and less than micron level, silicon crystal technology, and silicon wafer size technology. These were chosen because they are crucial to the development of the 256K chip and beyond, and it was felt that IBM already had these technologies.

Since the project concerns process technology, why were the device manufacturers chosen and not the equipment and materials suppliers? The executive of a materials firm explained that because of the overall dominant position of the integrated circuit makers, the impetus for technical change resided with the device makers, not the equipment manufacturers. Also, some of the equipment firms noted above as having connections with the device makers did participate by sending engineers to the project (Nomura Research Institute, 1981).

Information Sharing in the Project

In total, about 100 engineers from the five companies participated. They were divided among the three main projects, or "research themes." While attempts were made to assign engineers to projects as evenly as possible, it appears that on the more important projects, one company attempted to dominate the research group. In a group researching production process equipment, one company had eight people on the team, two companies had two each, and two other companies had none. The materials development and wafer size groups were more evenly divided (Tarui, 1981, p. 36).

The reasons for the uneven proportions are unclear. Sources from the U.S. embassy state that the companies were afraid of losing technical secrets so they attempted to dominate an area that was important to them. Japanese sources state that companies with no expertise in an area had no engineers to send, thus they were not included on the teams. Whatever the reasons, certain important projects were dominated by certain firms. This would suggest that true "cooperation" may not have taken place. In examining the 400 patents that were granted, the proportions of these to single individuals, groups of individuals from one company, and groups of individuals from more than one company are fifty-nine percent, twenty-five percent, and sixteen percent respectively (Tarui, 1981, p. 37). While sixteen percent of 400 is not an insignificant number and does indicate some cooperation, it appears that individual company interests may have dominated.

Japanese executives whose companies had participated in the project and involved MITI officials felt that the project did generate cooperation, however, and was successful in advancing the state of the art in process technologies. Certainly, many activities were carried out to promote a sense of cooperation, such as sharing a common dining hall and "drinking parties" for all the participants. Whatever the actual state of affairs, based upon the empirical results, it appears that the research of the participating firms was more focused and they were able to enter the 256K target market much more rapidly than nonparticipants.

NTT AND INFORMATION SHARING IN THE INTEGRATED CIRCUIT INDUSTRY

Some U.S. embassy officials have called into question the efficacy of the VLSI project, arguing instead that Nippon Telephone and Telegraph (NTT) had contributed more to the development of integrated circuits during the period 1974 to 1980 and continues to do so. Less visible than the MITI-sponsored VLSI project, NTT did parallel it with its own project. From a former MITI official, it is known that meetings were held between members of the two projects about once every four months. The NTT efforts in the integrated circuit field are rated highly by U.S. embassy officials. In some respects, because they are still ongoing, they are more important than the VLSI Project. NTT, which is now a private company, in February of 1984 introduced the first prototype 1Mb DRAM, and has been working on the technology for a 4Mb DRAM since 1980. It was also the first to introduce a 4Mb DRAM device and has been working on various technologies for a 16Mb DRAM device since early 1983, subsequently introducing the first prototype 16Mb DRAM device in late 1986.

The relationship between NTT and the companies that comprise the "NTT family" is quite different than that which occurred during the VLSI Project. NTT has recently become a private company. However, for the period of the VLSI Research Cooperative, it was a quasi-public body regulated by the Ministry of Posts and Telecommunications, but deriving its revenues from its telephone and telegraph communications services. It has several research laboratories, but does not produce any equipment. It relies primarily on six firms to produce the telecommunications equipment it needs: NEC, Toshiba, Hitachi, Mitsubishi, Fujitsu, and Oki Electric.

Even when it was privatized in 1985, it continued to have relationships with supplier firms. First, it sets the specifications for all telecommunications equipment. Second, it is a buyer, and as such enjoys the privileges of a buyer. For example, it can send its engineers into any supplying company to inspect its facilities. Third, it has a very active and competent research program which usually leads the private company programs by several months to years. According to a senior vice president of a large communications firm, NTT would never directly tell his firm what other firms were doing. However, since NTT is privy to the work of other firms and since it has its own research facilities, it can tell the company's research department which research strategies are most promising and which are not. In this way, NTT can act as a coordinator for a specific field of research such as VLSI.

NTT is primarily concerned with telecommunications, and while this does not hamper it from actively participating in integrated circuit research, this research is generally oriented towards use in communications and not in some other field such as computers. NTT is not concerned with the production economics of development. The executive related that his engineers were surprised at NTT's lack of concern over problems of mass production of integrated circuits. NTT was primarily interested in the technical problems up to the prototype stage. After that, the problems of mass production are completely in the hands of the private companies. Even though it has become a private company, the relationships between it and its "family member" companies remain quite strong. The focus of its research still only continues up to the prototype stage, although that may change in time.

Recently, NTT has become a major player in developing x-ray lithography using synchrotron orbital radiation. NTT has been working on this technology for the past fifteen years and is expected to have IC devices made using this technology by 1993 (Liebowitz, November 27, 1989).

DESCRIPTION OF U.S. GOVERNMENT INTERVENTIONS IN THE DRAM INDUSTRY

Differences between industries affect the innovation process. This interindustry effect alters the impact of governmental policies irrespective of whether these policies were designed to enhance the innovation process or not. As is indicated below, during the period when the Japanese government actively intervened through the VLSI Research Cooperative, no governmental policies were consciously designed by the U.S. government to enhance innovation in the DRAM industry. In spite of this, it is instructional to examine the instruments available to government and their respective effects on the innovation process.

U.S. DRAM Intervention: The "Off Again" Period

In the United States case, no policy existed which was designed to directly affect innovation in the MOS DRAM market, or for that matter the integrated circuit market during the period 1974 to 1984. Most U.S. policy has been designed for some reason other than increasing innovation, as was shown above. This is not to say that U.S. government policies did not have an effect on the integrated circuit industry. Although not intended to have an effect on the innovation process, one policy which has been suggested as having an effect is the increase in the capital gains tax from twenty-eight percent to forty-nine percent which occurred in 1969. This policy was later reversed in 1978 when the tax level was decreased from the forty-nine percent level back to the twenty-eight percent level and was further decreased in 1980 to twenty percent. It went back up to twenty-eight percent in 1987. It has been suggested by several studies that these changes affected the entry of firms, and thus the innovativeness in the integrated circuit industry.

It is this tax policy which will be examined in this section. As discussed in chapter five, many U.S. firms have exited from the DRAM segment of the integrated circuit industry and have either entered or remained in the logic segment of the integrated circuit industry. Further, it was shown that it is in the logic segment, especially in the ASIC device category, that many entrepreneurial start-up firms have entered. These entrepreneurial firms are using either the most sophisticated CMOS process technology or ASIC product technology or often both these technologies. Conventional wisdom in economics suggests that by lowering the capital gains tax rate, the amount of venture capital available would increase. Although this increased pool of venture capital would be allocated among a number of competing investments, because of the growth in the integrated circuit industry throughout the 1970s and 1980s, and because of the future potential for continued growth, it would be expected, from this conventional wisdom, that as the amount of venture capital increased the number of firms entering the integrated circuit industry would also increase. Likewise, a decrease in the amount of venture capital would bring about a decrease in the number of firms entering. This view is not supported by the framework presented in chapter two, however. It is expected that only when both the financial and informational resources are affected will the number of entrepreneurial firms entering be affected. The U.S. government intervention is designed to affect only one, the financial resource. Further, it was not designed to directly affect the integrated circuit industry.

EMPIRICAL ANALYSIS OF UNITED STATES
GOVERNMENT INTERVENTION

With the decline of the military influence in the integrated circuit industry in the United States and the complementary increase in industrial and commercial factors, the direct role of the United States government has declined. The integrated circuit industry has become subject to market forces, among these the availability of capital resources. The development of new technologies in the integrated circuit industry has been associated with the emergence of new firms. These firms require a special type of capital because of the inherent riskiness of the new venture. This capital has, until recently, been available only through a select group of people and institutions who act as venture capitalists. Table 6.5 shows the amount of venture capital invested between the years 1969 and 1987.

While pre-1969 data is not available, the effects of the increase and then the decrease in the capital gains tax coincide with rather abrupt changes in the amount of venture capital. With a shrinking venture capital base, it is expected that the number of firms entering the integrated circuit industry would also decrease. As can be seen in Table 6.5, there does appear to be a close relationship between the capital gains tax rate and the amount of venture capital available to foster innovation. This tends to support the conventional wisdom of neoclassical economics. However, as can also be seen in Table 6.5, there appears to be no relationship between the increase in the capital gains tax and the number of firms entering the industry in silicon valley. The number of entrepreneurial firms entering does follow a pattern of ebb and flow, however. This pattern would seem to indicate that some other factor was playing a role at least equal to that of financial resource availability. These results would support the notion described in earlier chapters that some other factor related to informational resources should also be playing a role. It would be expected that this factor would be operative at approximately the same time as the government intervention. The opportunity provided by a technological breakthrough is a possibility. Figure 6.3 shows the date of capital gains tax changes, number of firms entering and the approximate date for commercialization of the negative MOS (NMOS) technology in the early 1970s and the improvement of the complementary MOS (CMOS) technology in the late 1970s. There is also a large number entering with the development of Application Specific Integrated Circuit (ASIC) technology in the mid-1980s.

Technological Opportunity and Informational Resources

From Figure 6.3, it appears that the existence of venture capital is a necessary, but not a sufficient condition, for the entry of a firm. The existence of a new technology and the movement of informational resources related

Table 6.5
Capital Gains Tax Rate, Venture Capital, and Number of Firms Entering Silicon Valley (by Year)

YEAR	TAX RATE (percent)	VENTURE CAPITAL (million $ in year noted)	# OF ENTERING FIRMS
1969	49	171	9
1970	49	97	4
1971	49	95	6
1972	49	62	9
1973	49	56	2
1974	49	57	2
1975	49	10	5
1976	49	50	3
1977	49	39	0
1978	28	570	6
1979	28	319	2
1980	28	900	3
1981	20	1250	6
1982	20	1425	2
1983	20	3408	9
1984	20	3185	6
1985	20	2327	11
1986	20	3332	1
1987	28	4017	na

Sources: Rogers and Larsen, p. 64, 1984; Genealogy Silicon Valley, chart, 1987.

to that opportunity can provide a niche from which the new firm will develop. This is also an ingredient in the entry equation. Further, the venture capital industry has not remained stationary over time.

In the early years, it was dominated by a small number of individuals who worked very closely with a few new ventures. In recent years, larger institutions have entered the industry with large amounts of capital. The decrease in the tax rate probably did occasion an increase in the amount of venture capital, but this increase could have been magnified by the

Figure 6.3
Capital Gains Tax Rate, Venture Capital, and Number of Firms Entering Silicon Valley (by Year)

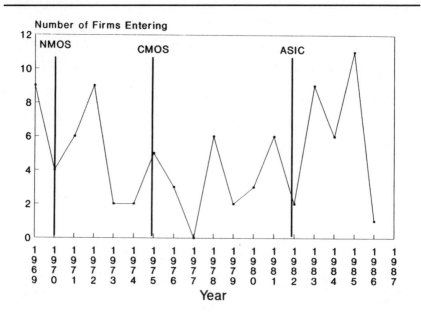

entrance of the larger financial institutions (Kotkin, 1984, p. 65). This is not to imply that changes in the tax rate do not affect the level of capital available. It is to suggest, however, that the situation is not as straightforward as first appeared when those tax changes were related to changes in innovativeness.

As noted earlier in this chapter, government policies designed to affect the macroeconomic environment, such as tax policy effects on financial resources or education policy effects on information resources, are necessary. These policies can set up the conditions for innovation, but these alone are not sufficient. Firms must, through the use of technological strategy, acquire, channel and focus these resources for best effect. The results also point to the crucial role played by the informational resource in combination with the financial resource.

THE ROLE OF GOVERNMENT IN THE UNITED STATES INTEGRATED CIRCUIT INDUSTRY: THE "ON AGAIN" PERIOD

Throughout most of the 1970s, the role of government declined. The major procurement contracts for the Minuteman missile and the NASA space program waned. Most of the government efforts had been directed at the environmental and labor aspects of the industry. The alternation of the capital gains tax and stock options rules have been noted by others as having effects at the fringe of the industry, but even these effects have been called into doubt by the results of the analysis conducted above. Consequently, the role of the U.S. government was negligible throughout most of the 1970s. As seen above, the major intervention was an attempt to alter the level of financial resources available by changing the capital gains tax rate. The motivation behind this attempt had little to do with innovation, however. The primary motivation was to redress perceived equity imbalances and to generate more revenue for the federal government (United States Congress, Joint Economic Committee, 1984, p. 8). Also, as determined by the analysis done above, the intervention did not slow the entrance of firms into the integrated circuit industry. The availability of new informational resources, provided by changes in processing technologies, created opportunities for firms to enter.

It was not until the advent of the Japanese challenge in the late 1970s that the integrated circuit industry began to look towards government again for aid. Aside from calls for changes in trade policy, the most striking changes that have occurred to date have been in the antitrust laws. The passage of the National Cooperative Research Act (NCRA) of 1984 loosened the antitrust constraints regarding firms collaborating on research projects. This new law came about partly because of the initiation of two research cooperatives begun in the early 1980s, the Semiconductor Research Cooperative (SRC) sponsored by members of the Semiconductor Industry Association, and the Microelectronics and Computer Consortium (MCC). Also currently under way and entering its second phase is a Pentagon-sponsored research and development project called the Very High Speed Integrated Circuit (VHSIC) Project. A number of new research cooperative projects have been started up since the passage of the NCRA law. Just recently started in fiscal year 1987 is another Pentagon-sponsored project called the Monolithic Microwave and Millimeter Wave Integrated Circuit (MIMIC) project. Two other miliary-related programs are the Microelectronics Manufacturing Science and Technology Program (MMST) and the building of a semiconductor facility for the National Security Agency at Fort Meade, Maryland. One final project is the Semiconductor Manufacturing Technology Initiative or Sematech, which is a consortium of U.S. integrated circuit firms and the U.S. government.

INFORMATION AND FINANCIAL RESOURCE CONSIDERATIONS

In the case of the research cooperatives, the motivation is to increase the financial resources available to the participating firms. The research cooperatives are also supposed to eliminate duplication of research efforts among the firms, thus increasing the informational resources available (Semiconductor Industry Association, 1983, p. 20). The primary concern among the participants are the intellectual property rights implications of the various research cooperatives (United States House Committee on Science and Technology, 1983). Several areas of concern are being raised by these projects. One area is that these projects, with the exception of SRC and MCC, are connected to varying degrees with the U.S. military. Another major area of concern involves the degree of sharing of the research findings with nonparticipating firms. These issues are directly related to the appropriability problem discussed in previous chapters.

The VHSIC and MIMIC Projects

Both the VHSIC and MIMIC projects are directly funded by the U.S. government and are designed to explore integrated circuit technologies that will enhance integrated circuit performance in hazardous environments. The VHSIC projects essentially is designed to develop integrated circuits that are able to analyze more information at a faster rate and in more harsh conditions than current integrated circuits. There is a concern for manufacturing in this project, but it is not designed to develop and test mass manufacturing techniques. It is administered by the Pentagon through the Defense Advanced Research Project Agency (DARPA), and is an ongoing project. The prime contractors in this project are IBM, Honeywell, TRW/Motorola, GE, Honeywell, TI, and Westinghouse.

Results from the first phase of the project are now beginning to emerge. Some of these results have been reported to have been used in nonmilitary applications. One example is that both Motorola and TI have both used VHSIC work in their ASIC and DRAM development work (McClean, 1988). While some results of phase I are now being used commercially, it is difficult to assess the impact of the project on the overall innovativeness of the integrated circuit industry. Even with some of the work being applied in the commercial area, the degree of diffusion of the developing technologies among other integrated circuit producers remains a question. These unresolved issues make it difficult to determine if this project will increase the international competitiveness of the U.S. integrated circuit industry.

The MIMIC project is also being administered through DARPA. It is designed to develop a gallium arsenide integrated circuit that will be the sensors, or "eyes and ears," for VHSIC chips. Currently in its first phase, it is too soon to determine if the project itself will be a success. However, MIMIC has very little to offer in the near term to strengthen the commercial competitiveness of its participants. The main contractors in the project, Hughes/GE, ITT/Marietta, Raytheon/TI, and TRW, are for the most part not mainline merchant integrated circuit producers. The one exception is TI. Further, the technologies that are envisioned for this project are rather esoteric and any commercial use for them would be several years off. The other projects, the MMST and the NSA semiconductor facility, are still being implemented and no real work has yet begun.

The focus of both the VHSIC and MIMIC projects appears to be on systems and systems interface rather than components. The prime contractors in both projects are systems houses and not integrated circuit producers. While each project will require the development of very sophisticated components, the systems houses are less concerned with manufacturing the integrated circuit than with interfacing it with others in various subsystems. Further, the level of sophistication being considered for these integrated circuits would be far beyond the needs of most commercial users. Finally, these projects not only must develop new technologies but must also disseminate them.

In the act of the new technologies, these projects will need to acquire the financial and informational resources that any other organization would require. Since these are government-funded, the main contribution from the firms are the researchers, the embodiment of the information resource. If part of the vision of these projects is to improve the commercial competitiveness of integrated circuit companies, a question arises in that these researchers may be more effectively and efficiently employed commercially rather than developing esoteric military integrated circuits. Once the new technology is developed, how the information will be transferred from the system houses to the integrated circuit producers is unresolved. While these projects may accomplish their goals of developing the integrated circuits that the military needs, it is doubtful that enough of a spillover into the civilian sector will occur to help American firms where they need it most; the ability to produce vast quantities of integrated circuits at costs lower than the Japanese.

MCC, SRC, and Sematech

These three organizations are different from the above in that they are true research cooperatives. Each is composed of a number of companies that contribute funds and/or personnel to the consortium. Some consortiums may hire permanent employees to conduct the research and these may be supplemented by member firms' researches. In any case, these resources are then divided among a number of projects. Projects may be chosen according to members needs or some form of mandate set forth when the research cooperative is established. The information derived from the projects is first shared with other members of the project, then with other members of the consortium, and finally with nonmembers on some type of restricted basis.

Each of the research cooperatives approaches these issues in a somewhat different manner. Both SRC and MCC have been existent since the early 1980s, 1982 for MCC and 1983 for SRC, and were set up with no time limit on their existence. Sematech, which began in 1987, has a minimum of five years, after which it may be renewed or not. The focus of the research also differs. SRC, which was established through the Semiconductor Industry Association (SIA), concentrates its research efforts on integrated circuit design and manufacturing technologies. Its members are primarily integrated circuit producers. MCC not only focuses on integrated circuit technology but also technology related to computer architecture and software. Its members come from a broader range of electronic and computer and precision instruments firms as well as integrated circuit firms. Sematech is focused essentially on integrated circuit manufacturing technology. Its members are primarily integrated circuit producers and computer firms.

Each of these consortium also organizes its research differently. MCC, which is made up of approximately fifteen to twenty firms, used to draw on its member firms for researchers as well as financial support. But because of problems with member firms exiting and mergers or acquisitions by nonmember firms, MCC began to hire its own personnel. The research is conducted at MCC. Member firms can choose to participate in a project, but they are entitled only to the information generated in projects they directly participate in. The original focus of the projects at MCC was to be on basic research. Knowledge areas that would not yield products for some time but were deemed as necessary for the long-term survival of member firms were chosen. While some of this fundamental knowledge base building research may still be conducted, MCC underwent a series of changes beginning in 1984 which has forced it to focus its research on projects that have more immediate commercial value to its members.

SRC has over thirty members. It acts in many ways as a broker between the member firms and universities to which it disperses funds to carry out its research projects. The member firms are able to send their own researchers to participate in the research and all members are allowed access to the research findings through seminars and training sessions. Since it is universities that carry out the research, SRC is more concerned with the dissemination of the information resource than with its actual creation. This is a major different between MCC and SRC. This may account for SRC's better track record in funding medium and long-term research projects, which are not aimed at immediate applications for member firms. SRC has largely avoided the problems that have affected MCC in terms of staffing and transfer of new knowledge.

Sematech is the newest member of research cooperatives. Its overall goal is to develop advance integrated circuit manufacturing technology. This is to be done so as to improve the competitiveness of American integrated circuit firms against the Japanese. Sematech is, in theory, to accomplish this goal by 1993. As such, this research cooperative is the most focused of the three. Its membership is limited only to U.S.-owned integrated circuit producers. Even American-based ASIC design companies that have foreign foundries are not allowed to participate. The integrated circuit members are assessed a fee of one percent of their integrated circuit sales. There is a minimum of one million dollars expected from each firm and the maximum amount that can be contributed is up to fifteen percent of the total private funding for Sematech. Semiconductor equipment firms can also participate through a specially organized chapter of the Semiconductor Equipment and Material Institute (SEMI). These firms must pay a fee ranging from $2,000 to $18,000 for membership. In addition, about $100 million is provided by the U.S. government to match the yearly contribution of the private members. These funds are administered through DARPA.

Sematech has both its own "research production" facility and contracts out its research to universities, national laboratories, and also to the SRC. The research findings contributed by itself and these other sources are to be tested in an actual fabrication facility. This facility is located in Austin, Texas. Each of the various subtechnologies necessary for manufacturing integrated circuits will be developed by semiconductor equipment firms. Further refinement of these subtechnologies will be done within Sematech's fabrication facility. Also designated to this facility will be the full testing of all the various subtechnologies as one unified manufacturing technology. This will be done using a particular integrated circuit device. Sematech has chosen the static random access memory (SRAM) device as its test bed model. The SRAM is similar to the DRAM in that it is also used as a process technology driver.

Sematech is working to achieve its goal of American superiority in integrated circuit manufacture by 1993 in a three-phase process. The first phase, completed in 1988, was to establish a fabrication facility and begin to produce the equivalent of a 1Mb SRAM using 0.8 micron line width with optical photolithographic equipment. By 1990, it is scheduled to produce the equivalent of a 4Mb SRAM using 0.5 micron linewidth with optical equipment. By 1993, Sematech is scheduled to produce the equivalent of a 16Mb SRAM with 0.35 micron linewidth with optical equipment and a 0.3 micron linewidth using X-ray lithography. In essence, Sematech hopes to have established the base for its efforts by the end of 1988, come abreast of the Japanese by the end of 1990 and surpass them by the end of 1993.

This is quite an ambitious project, especially when a 1Mb SRAM is equivalent to a 4Mb DRAM in its design and manufacturing complexity. The 4Mb DRAM is currently in the introductory stages of its life cycle. Once each goal has been met, the information is to be transferred back to the member firms through equipment and material transfer. Member firm engineers and researchers will also be able to receive training at the Sematech fabrication facility.

Sematech has been able to partially meet its first goal in 1988, because IBM donated its 4Mb DRAM production technology, which uses 0.7 micron linewidth. In the same year, AT&T also donated its 64K SRAM production technology which also uses a 0.7 micron linewidth. Sematech has also been able to select a number of universities to carry out basic research into integrated circuit manufacturing technology. The achievement of its remaining goals is far from certain.

Sematech combines some of both of the elements of MCC and SRC. It is quite focused in its endeavor. While it must develop generic production technologies, the aim is to develop specific semiconductor equipment and techniques which would be immediately applicable to integrated circuit firms. In this sense it is more like MCC than SRC. It is like MCC in another way in that it is responsible for both the generation and transfer of the new information. This is somewhat modified from the MCC case in that Sematech can contract out to universities, other laboratories, and even SRC. It must contract with the semiconductor equipment firms in order to modify or build the needed equipment. Still, issues of appropriability of the innovative effort are stronger than in the case of the SRC. In addition, as pointed out in chapter four, U.S. semiconductor equipment firms are exiting from a number of crucial subtechnology areas. It is likely that in some subtechnology areas, such as photolithography, only Japanese firms will be left supplying the necessary equipment. Given the close ties that exist between Japanese semiconductor equipment and integrated circuit firms, it is unlikely that new knowledge would advance to American hands.

It is also possible that the strategic alliances that were described in chapter five may also serve as a vehicle for the transfer of Sematech-generated knowledge to nonmember firms, whether Japanese or American. A similar issue exists between Sematech and the pattern of strategic alliances that was described previously. Many of the alliances that American firms entered into with Japanese firms were to gain process technology knowledge. The success of these alliances from the American side, as was pointed out, depended on the in-house capability of the American firms to absorb the information. If American firms use Sematech or the alliances as a substitute rather than a complement for their own research efforts, they are not as likely to gain the full benefit of the cooperative effort.

Are these research cooperatives worth the effort? To the extent that these efforts, whether of the VHSIC type or the Sematech type, increase the pool of financial or informational resources available to firms, or increase the productivity of these resources in the innovation process, then some benefit will accrue, at least to the economy as a whole. Likewise, if these cooperative research endeavors can increase the diffusion of new innovations to a wider group of firms than would occur under individual effort alone, then benefit will again accrue to the economy as a whole.

None of the research endeavors discussed above, even the purely military-oriented ones, will do much harm to the innovative initiative of American companies. Since these are likely to increase the pool of innovation resources available, they should at least be tried. But in saying this, it should be pointed out that each one should be carefully studied and evaluated. As with any strategic plan, the key to success is as much in the implementation as in the original design.

Each of the cooperative research endeavors above has stated goals and methods for meeting the necessary goals. Various organizational structures have been established, and can be evaluated as to how each has handled the issues of intellectual property rights and appropriability of research effort. The lessons learned from the evaluation of these current cooperative research efforts will go a long way toward guiding future cooperative research efforts. Irrespective of the lessons learned, one point is clear: these cooperative endeavors cannot be viewed as substitutes for individual initiative by the firms that participate. Each firm will have to make the necessary investment, not only to participate in the research cooperative, but also to utilize the information once it is received. Integrated circuit firms will still have to invest in the plant and equipment at the ever-increasing rates that are demanded by the innovation envelope. This investment will have to be in the form of qualified personnel and funds. If the firm does not wish to invest in these things or if the available pool is too small, then the research cooperatives may accomplish their goals only to see no result in the economic competitiveness of the firms. Consequently, the broader macroeconomic policies which increase savings, thereby increasing the pool of funds available for investment and lowering the cost of capital, and those policies which increase the number of highly educated and skilled engineers and workers involved, must also be brought into play. The various policy instruments for doing this are available. What is lacking is a vision which would guide their use.

The Japanese Since the VLSI Research Cooperative

The direct role of the Japanese government in guiding the integrated circuit firms, in particular MITI and the Ministry of Posts and Telecommunication (MPT), has waned since the days of the VLSI Research Cooperative. Recalling from earlier in the chapter, the integrated circuit industry is well into its growth stage and Japanese firms are quite profitable. Consequently, the ability of MITI or MPT to influence these firms has lessened from a purely financial resource perspective. The Japanese integrated circuit firms are also quite vigorous in terms of the information of resources necessary for innovation. Also, there are other technologies that are still embryonic and can more easily be influenced, such as biotechnology and high temperature superconductive materials. Consequently, the research effort among Japanese integrated circuit firms is even more strongly focused on in-house projects.

This is not to say that government-sponsored research projects are nonexistent in the integrated circuit area nor that the integrated circuit firms are not participating in them. Japanese firms and the Japanese government are acutely aware of how dynamic the innovation process has become. They recognize the need to continually innovate and the increased need for resources that results. The development of the Japan Key Technology Center is a clear indication the efforts to stay ahead in technological competitive arenas are alive. This center was established by MITI and MPT and has over two hundred research projects underway. While not all are in the integrated circuit industry, most touch some form of electronic technology and are of interest to the integrated circuit firms. What is being exhibited by the Japanese integrated circuit firms is more selectively as to the project and the degree of participation that is engaged in by the firm. This selectivity is more and more governed by the internal research agenda set by the firm. The direction of that research agenda and the implications of it will be discussed in the next chapter.

SUMMARY

In this chapter, the role of government in the innovation process has been examined. A number of the policy instruments available to governments and their intended and actual effects have been discussed. Most of the policy instruments used by governments, and in particular the U.S. government, are used without much forethought as to how they will affect the innovation process. The approach that the Japanese government has taken, on the other hand has paid careful attention to the innovation process. Efforts have been made by the Japanese to assess the needs that exist in the overall economy of Japan and to meet those needs. Careful attention has also been paid to the timing and type of intervention that should be applied in a particular segment of the economy or in a particular industry. This has been seen in the timing and execution of the VLSI Research Cooperative, a project aimed at developing the production technologies that would be used in the 256K and 1Mb DRAM devices. It enhanced the financial and informational resources available to integrated circuit firms and aided in the diffusion of the innovations that resulted. While it had its difficulties and may not have been a truly cooperative effort, it was nonetheless successful.

The U.S. government's approach to innovation has been more haphazard. Preoccupied with the political/military competition of the Cold War, what research agendas have been set were done so with those priorities in mind. Innovation in the commercial sector of the economy has been left up to market forces and the firms that operated in them. Changes in the capital gains tax rate in the late 1970s have had no impact on new integrated circuit firm entry unless a technological innovation existed that provided a vehicle for entry. With mounting competitive pressure from the Japanese, a number of research cooperatives have been initiated by the U.S. government in the early 1980s. It is too soon to fully evaluate these cooperative research efforts. However, since each differs in its scope of goals and organization it is possible to learn lessons from the various successes and failures of each to guide future endeavors. One lesson that is evident, even in the early stages of these cooperative research efforts, is that participating firms cannot use these efforts as substitutes for their own research efforts.

7

Policy and Strategy Implications for Competing in a Techno-Global Environment

INTRODUCTION

This chapter will present a summary of the major issues discussed in the previous chapters. Central to this discussion will be the conceptual framework introduced in chapter two. From this framework the technological and institutional factors that were dominant in the DRAM industry will be reviewed. Following this discussion the directions that Japanese competition will take in the integrated circuit industry in the future will be examined. Finally, the current responses that the United States is taking will be discussed, with recommendations for future actions.

Review of Chapter One

In this chapter, technology was defined as a stock of knowledge which creates capabilities for organizations to develop and produce products to meet market needs. Inventions were defined as resulting from improvements in the knowledge base. These improvements could be embodied in either products or processes. Commercialized inventions were defined as innovations. The processes by which an invention becomes an innovation was determined to be made up of a number of stages. These stages were related to the research and development activities of firms. Further, because the innovation process is closely intertwined with the product development process, a firm's strategy can have a strong influence on its use of the technological knowledge base.

Review of Chapter Two

Although the issues discussed in this chapter will be described in greater detail in the next section, a brief summary is provided here. In this chapter, the conceptual underpinnings were discussed. First, the work done in evolutionary economics provided the concept that technologies can progress along a trajectory of development. As a technology progresses along its trajectory, the conditions of that movement have a direct effect on an industry's development and the competitive state of the industry. The conditions of the movement along a technological trajectory are marked by both economic and technical signposts. Knowing these signposts can help a firm to establish a technological strategy.

In establishing this strategy, a firm must determine if it is to be first to market with a product or process improvement or if it is to lag behind the innovation leader. It must also determine its strategic technological area (STA). The firm's STA is determined by linking together various technological knowledge bases. This is done horizontally by determining the market breadth of products offered by the firm and vertically by linking into supplier or user technology bases. Determining the firm's STA has institutional consequences in that the firm must acquire the knowledge bases or the resources needed to develop them itself. From this the innovation envelope, a more useful concept for forming a firm's technological strategy, was presented.

The innovation envelope concept suggested that the technological trajectory of a focal product forms an envelope curve applicable to innovation in technologies necessary to design and produce that focal product. These necessary technologies were called subtechnologies. From this concept, various research lessons were derived which were used to guide the rest of this work.

Review of Chapter Three

The dynamic random access memory (DRAM) product within the integrated circuit industry was chosen as the focal product for operationalizing the concepts discussed in chapter two. The integrated circuit industry was chosen because of its importance to the electronics industry as an area of intense competition between U.S. and Japanese firms. It was shown that all integrated circuit devices share common technical and economic characteristics with the DRAM that can act as signposts for determining a technological trajectory. The most important technical signpost was determined to be circuit density. The technology of the DRAM was shown to follow a technological envelope.

As the technology progressed along that envelope through succeeding innovations, it increased in sophistication and required more of both financial and informational resources. This was seen in the increasing cost of equipment that embodied subtechnologies crucial to the DRAM and the increasing time needed to learn those subtechnologies. Movement along the DRAM's technological trajectory, coupled with the increasing need for financial and information resources from the innovation envelope, creates a technological innovation imperative. For firms to compete, they must innovate, but in order to innovate, firms must acquire the necessary resources. The firm's technological strategy was expected to influence this resource acquisition capability.

Review of Chapter Four

Firm strategies were examined in this chapter. This was done for both U.S. and Japanese firms that had participated in the DRAM industry. The innovation strategy for the firm was determined as being either a "first mover" innovating firm or a "fast second" imitative firm. The STA was determined for each firm. This was done horizontally, in terms of the breadth of other integrated circuit devices produced by the firm. Vertically, the STA was determined in terms of whether the firm producing the DRAM device has connections with either a downstream user of DRAMs or an upstream producer of equipment which embodied critical DRAM subtechnologies.

From the examination of firms that participated in the DRAM device industry, it was shown that firms which adopted an innovative rather than an imitative technology strategy were more likely to survive. More important was how a firm defined its STA. Broad-based producers of integrated circuit devices were more likely to acquire the financial resources necessary to survive as the DRAM moved over succeeding generations on its innovation envelope. More critical was how the firm determined its vertical STA. Firms which were forward-connected into DRAM users were better able to acquire the financial resources necessary for continued innovation. Firms which were backward-connected were better able to acquire the informational resources necessary for continued innovation in the DRAM device. This backward connection was the most crucial because the DRAM is a process/manufacturing driver for the entire integrated circuit industry.

Firms which had the strategic approaches of being innovative, broad-based integrated circuit producers which were forward- and backward-connected, were predominantly Japanese firms. The direction of forward and backward connection was found to differ between the U.S. and Japanese firms. U.S. firms were often forward-connected, but not as often backward-connected. Japanese firms were more often both forward- and backward-connected. Japanese firms were better able to acquire and focus the resources needed for innovation in the DRAM device technology.

These firms were better able to continue to innovate and now dominate the DRAM industry. In addition, Japanese equipment firms have also been able to dominate crucial subtechnology industries such as the lithography and silicon material industries.

Review of Chapter Five

Diffusion was singled out as an important aspect of the overall innovation process, since it is in the diffusion of a product based on improvements in the technology's knowledge base that competition between firms takes place. It is also in this stage of the innovation process that the ultimate success of failure of the innovation is determined. Diffusion for the DRAM was examined in terms of the product technology; whether the market was accepting 4K, 16K, 64K, 256K, or 1Mb DRAM devices. It was also examined in terms of process technology; whether the various DRAM devices were being produced using Bipolar, NMOS, or CMOS processes. In both the product and process technology cases, the diffusion of the innovations followed the classic S-curve shape.

Diffusion was also examined in terms of the number of firms that produced each generation of DRAM device. A small number of firms entered and exited the DRAM market with each product innovation. Continuity over the innovations was seen and this indicated that a core group of firms existed. Consequently, the diffusion process was not seen as following a classic S-curve. The pool of potential adopters appeared to be stabilizing. This trend was stronger for the U.S. segment of the market than for the Japanese segment. The mechanisms for this diffusion were also examined. The role of supplier firms and the government were seen as important in whether a firm would tend to enter the DRAM industry. The role of supplier firms in the diffusion process was in accord with the innovation envelope concept. Further, it was determined that firms that were exiting the DRAM segment of the integrated circuit industry were remaining in or entering the logic segment of the industry. Most of these firms were U.S. firms. Consequently, the integrated circuit industry appeared to be bifurcating into two competing and complementary camps.

Logic integrated circuits tended to be design subtechnology drivers, while memory integrated circuit devices tended to be process subtechnology drivers. The United States firms appeared to be dominant in logic integrated circuit devices such as microprocessors and application specific integrated circuits, while Japanese firms appeared to be dominant in the memory segment, such as DRAM devices. Because of the higher value added aspect of logic devices, Japanese firms are also entering this segment. One of the most important diffusion mechanisms through which this entrance is accomplished is by strategic alliances with U.S. firms. U.S. firms exchange information on design of logic devices for information from Japanese firms on memory device and process technology. One of the most important findings is that for firms to participate in these alliances and to gain from the participation, firms must not use the alliances as substitutes for their own in-house research efforts.

Review of Chapter Six

In this chapter, government policy effects on technological innovation were examined. Both the Japanese and U.S. government approaches were examined. It was determined that for the United States, there has been little coordination or consistency in the government's approach to the technological innovation in the integrated circuit industry. The Japanese government has taken a more consistent and coordinated approach to innovation in general, and in particular to innovation in the integration circuit industry. One of the important differences between the overall Japanese and U.S. policy approaches has been the mechanism that the Japanese government has used to give consistency to its policies. Japanese government policies are given a general direction through a broad "vision" of the future.

These two approaches were characterized in two specific policies. For the United States, changes in the capital gains tax rate were examined for their impact on new firm formation. For the Japanese, it was the initiation of the VLSI Research Cooperative. The U.S. policy was successful in opening up more funds for venture capital, but a stronger influence on the formation of firms in silicon valley was the technological opportunity presented by and innovation. Japan's policy was directed to influence innovation in the DRAM device technology. The VLSI Research Cooperative appeared to be successful for the firms that participated in it.

The differences in these two policies lay not only in that the Japanese policy was directly related to innovation, while the U.S. policy was not directly related, but also in the resources that were effected. In the U.S. case, only the financial resources were affected. In the Japanese case, both the financial and informational resources were affected. The apparent success of the VLSI Research Cooperative has spawned a number of research cooperatives in the United States. Three were examined, the Microelectronic Computer Corporation, the Semiconductor Research Cooperative, and Sematech. Assessments were made as to which would most likely be successful. Cooperative research associations which focus on the diffusion of new technological information as opposed to just generating this information would most likely have a greater positive impact on the technological progress of the industry.

Overview of Chapter Seven

This chapter examines the direction of future competition in the integrated circuit industry with particular attention to the role that Japan will play.

The central thrust of this chapter is that competition in the integrated circuit industry is evolving into a techno-global industry. The technological side of this competition emerges from the fact that competitive advantage in this industry will still depend on the ability of firms to generate new products quickly from technological bases. These bases will be changing from the technological base in silicon-based solid-state physics that currently powers innovation in the integrated circuit industry. It is yet to be determined what the configuration of the new knowledge base will be, but some of its aspects are beginning to emerge. Firms will need to compete not only in developing new products but also in mastering the new technological knowledge bases. The global aspect of this competition is that the competition in new product development and in the new technological knowledge bases will come from any country around the globe. Before examining these trends, the theoretical implications of the work presented will be reviewed.

IMPLICATIONS FOR THEORETICAL FRAMEWORK

In chapter two, a theoretical model was presented which was a combination of the previous work of both technological evolution economists, strategic management theorists, and institutional economists. A important aspect of this combined framework was the incorporation in the definition of technology and technological innovation of an information component. From this definition, technology was viewed as a process characterized by an array of potentials, or probable events; that is, innovations. It was also argued that the institutional and technological factors for industrial development coexist and need to be considered in a firm's technological strategy.

Technological factors are the primary reasons for industrial structure change and, as a consequence, changes in competitive conditions. As the technology changes with each innovation it becomes more sophisticated, requiring more financial and informational resources to continue to innovate. On the financial resource side, this has often been described in economic theory in terms of greater capitalization and economies of scale. On the information side, more than just increased information is needed. As the technology becomes more sophisticated, it becomes more team-embodied and hence there are strong institutional influences. These institutional influences have strategic ramifications, especially as a firm defines its Strategic Technological Areas (STAs).

What the firm decides to include as part of its STA, and how it relates institutionally to these technological areas, form its strategic technological core. Defining a firm's strategic core technologies also defines the boundaries of the firm itself. The firm must also decide how to institutionally link together its core technologies. This can be done in a very tight coupling, such as setting up captive suppliers, wholly owned subsidiaries, or mergers and acquisitions. This can also be done through loose coupling such as outsourcing, long-term purchasing agreements, or strategic alliances.

By defining its own boundaries, through its strategic core technologies, and by institutionally linking these technologies together, the firm can not only affect the structure of its own industry but those of other industries. This is explicitly recognized in the concept of the innovation envelope. From this concept, the firm can identify crucial technologies to include in its STA, and may even help in determining the degree of institutional linkage. How strong or weak the coupling that the firm decides on is important, but of greater importance is how the firm recognizes technological change as a dynamic process.

As a result, potential contributions of subtechnologies will change as a product improves through succeeding innovations. Some subtechnologies will become more important, that is, their potential contribution to innovation in the focal technology will increase, while others will wane in importance. This will necessitate changes in the institutional links relating the various technologies in the STA. Those firms exhibiting expertise in important subtechnologies become more centrally linked, while those in less important subtechnologies are less centrally linked. Consequently, technological innovation powers the changes in the institutional factors through the information component of a technology.

Each innovation increases the need for information, which becomes more "team-embodied," necessitating different institutional arrangements and more complex management structures and systems. As the technology matures, becoming more difficult to innovate along a given technological path, the technological impetus behind the changes wanes and the institutional factors assume a greater role. In an industry with a mature technology, other forces such as the demand side of the market will have a stronger effect on the factors for industrial change. Successful firms have adopted structures that are better able to monitor and react to institutional factors. The dominance of multidivisional, strategic business unit structures in industries with mature technologies is indicative of this phenomenon.

The conceptual framework represented by the innovation envelope was used to generate several research lessons. The implication of the empirical findings for the links in the conceptual model will be examined.

INNOVATION PROCESS/TECHNOLOGY LINK

The importance of both informational as well as financial resources has been established. Technological development occurs along a path marked by succeeding waves of innovation. It is fueled by increasing amounts of both types of resources. It has been shown, through the examination of governmental policies, that where one type of resource exists in abundance, another is in relative scarcity, the level and pace of innovation is low. Innovations alter the technology by increasing the sophistication level. This, in turn, results in increased requirements of financial and informational resources. The first research lesson is that as a technology becomes more sophisticated through succeeding innovation more of the financial and informational resources are required.

FIRM STRATEGY/INNOVATION/MARKET STRUCTURE LINK

Firm strategy plays an important role in acquiring the resources necessary for continued innovation. As shown, firms which follow certain strategic approaches are able to maintain the innovative momentum required to compete technologically. Firms which adopt an innovative approach and develop proprietary products are able to gain enough of a lead in time and market share to be able to acquire the financial and information resources to continue innovation. Firms which define their STAs broadly are able to take advantage of the "portfolio effect." The knowledge gained in producing DRAMs can be applied to other integrated circuit devices. Further, if there is a downturn in DRAMs, other integrated circuit devices may not as be as severely affected, thereby maintaining a more even flow of financial resources.

This "portfolio effect" is also active for firms that define their STA broadly; connecting forward, backward, or in both directions. The ability to diversify market risk over several industries helps to maintain a steady flow of financial resources to the firm. These resources can then be allocated to the product areas that would most enhance the innovation capabilities of the firm. There is also the ability to diversify the technological risk by linking both forward and backward.

Information about designs of products which will use DRAMs helps in the designing of the next generation of DRAM devices. Information about the design of the next generation of DRAM device assists in the development of the equipment that will be needed in producing the new device. Since the equipment can be developed more rapidly, the new DRAM device can be brought to market ahead of competitors who do not have this strategic advantage of deeply defined STAs. Adoption of these strategic approaches has enhanced the success of firms in the DRAM segment of the integrated circuit industry. The success of certain firms over others has altered the market structure of the DRAM segment and consequently the entire integrated circuit industry.

The influence has not been one way, however. We have shown that the level of resources needed affects the characteristics of the firms that exist in the market. Certain firms are better able to acquire and utilize these resources and thus survive. Market development and change is influenced by the changes in the firms as they alter their definitions of their strategic core technologies. This influence is tempered by other factors, however, such as the changes in demand for the products of the industry.

If the demand for a product is increasing, as is the case with the DRAM device, then firms utilizing a variety of strategic approaches may have equal chances of survival. Further, with increasing demand there still may exist enough of an incentive for firms to enter, even if resource needs are greater. The concentration level of the market may remain stable or even fall. Thus, the market structure is seen as affecting the innovation process and as being affected by innovation. The research lessons linking firm strategy, market structure, and innovation was also supported.

Firms that fail to take into account the effects that institutional factors can play in the diffusion of technology in their technology strategy may find that they have become isolated from the mainstream of technological development. Diffusion of technological innovations is a means by which the average practice of the industry is raised the level of the best practice. In the integrated circuits industry, the linking of integrated circuit producers with integrated circuit users and equipment makers is a way to continually provide for more efficient innovation. The impact of institutional factors on innovation and its diffusion were shown in the link between integrated circuit producers and equipment firms in firms in Japan.

In the DRAM market, where process technology is more important than design technology, the link between integrated circuit producers and equipment firms that exists in Japan is a key factor to understanding the current dominance by the Japanese in the DRAM market. This link has allowed for the flow of information between those engineers that have designed the integrated circuits and those engineers that built the equipment that would produce the integrated circuit. This efficient innovation process aids in the diffusion of the technology because the equipment firms are not complete captives of the integrated circuit producers. From a societal perspective, it is a more effective innovation process. Consequently, the research lessons concerning diffusion of technology and market structure are also supported.

PUBLIC POLICY/INNOVATION LINK

Government policy has also been shown to affect the innovation process through alteration in the level of resources available. Government intervention has achieved the expected results in the Japanese case and has failed to achieve the expected results in the U.S. case because the former has affected both types of resources, while the latter has affected only one type. Consequently, the link between public policy and innovation has been supported.

As noted in chapter six, a number of government policies can affect innovation. The link between public policy, market structure and technological innovation has not been tested in this research because no policy actions have been taken in either country which were designed to alter directly market structure in the integrated circuit industry. It can be argued that allowing research cooperatives indirectly alters market structure in the hope of encouraging innovation. While the VLSI Research Cooperative succeeded, it is still too early in the existence of the research cooperatives set up in the United States to offer a definitive conclusion on their success. The same is true with the link between public policy and technology. While the VHSIC and MIMIC programs have started to increase the technological knowledge base, it is too soon to determine if substantial commercial applications will result. Thus, this link also cannot today be examined.

KEY FINDINGS CONCERNING THE U.S. AND JAPANESE INTEGRATED CIRCUIT INDUSTRIES

In this section the key empirical findings that have been discussed in the earlier chapters will be summarized. The importance of these findings will be related to the conceptual framework. This will form the base for discussions of where the integrated circuit industry is evolving.

Firm Strategy, Innovation and Market Structure

We have seen Japanese and U.S. DRAM industries to be similar in a number of characteristics. The strategic approaches of successful firms are similar. The innovations in the DRAM technology open up market opportunities, thus increasing demand for DRAM devices. In both industries the opportunities are capitalized upon by large established firms. It appears that entry into the DRAM market, while not closed, requires some minimal level of capital and knowledge with each innovation. This level increases with each innovation. Both nation's industries maintain a high level of technological vigor, though the Japanese have been more successful in process technologies rather than design technologies. The U.S. firms have tended to emphasize design technologies over process technologies. The importance of process technologies in the development of the DRAM device, and other commodity devices such as SRAMs, ROMs, and EPROMs, therefore, aids the Japanese firms in the development, production and marketing of these devices.

This importance of processing technology lead to one of the major differences between Japan and the United States. By comparing the industrial structures and relationships in Japan and the United States, it has been determined that the equipment and materials suppliers have played an important role in the diffusion of technological innovation. This relationship between integrated circuit users and integrated circuit suppliers is important in simulating innovation. The Japanese have been able to introduce the major innovations of the 64K, 256K, 1Mb, and 4Mb devices before the U.S. firms did. This is remarkable since they lagged behind the U.S. firms by about one year for the 4K and 16K devices. The close connections between the integrated circuit firms and the equipment suppliers and integrated circuit users accounts for much of the gain of the Japanese.

The difference in diffusion is not the only difference that exists between the United States and Japan. The Japanese industry can be characterized as having very low transaction costs in vertical relationships, but high transaction costs in horizontal relationships. One of the prime reasons for the VLSI Cooperative Research Project has been to provide an environment where horizontal sharing could occur between firms of the same industry. The U.S. industry has had low transaction costs associated with its horizontal relationships, but high transaction costs in its vertical relationships. The primary reason for this lies in the fact that market forces have been stronger in the United States than in Japan. Firm forces, or the power of the firm over the market, have a key characteristic of the Japanese industry.

The U.S. industry is predominantly a fragmented industry, populated by many small- to medium-sized firms, while the Japanese industry is populated by a smaller number of large firms. The conditions of increasing technological opportunity and investment returns along with increasing resources needs that is occurring in both country's industries will have differing effects because of the initial industrial structure.

The Japanese firms have a greater opportunity to gain power over their market because there are fewer firms and the conditions of increased technological opportunity and increased resource need leads to a decrease in concentration. These conditions can result in a situation where relative market share is more evenly distributed among a smaller number of firms. This will increase strategic rivalry among the Japanese firms and make them even more aware of the actions of other firms, both inside of Japan and outside.

For the U.S. industry the similar conditions of increased technological opportunity and increased investment need has lead to a decline in concentration and is again interpreted as a more equal distribution of the market among the firms in the DRAM market and the other segments of the integrated circuit industry. The number of firms is larger in the U.S. segment, and their size is smaller, relative to the Japanese firms. The U.S. firms are at a strategic disadvantage because they react less to other firms' long-term actions and more to the immediate actions of the market. They are also at a disadvantage because of the smaller resource base form which they must generate the necessary resources to continue innovation.

In terms of overall integrated circuit technological opportunity, the

United States is still more vigorous. This is particularly true in the pioneering of new integrated circuit technologies. The U.S. firms still maintain the lead in the microprocessor and logic markets. They also hold the lead in the application specific technologies such as programmable logic array (PLA) devices and in the custom and semi-custom devices. These technologies usually require more design effort, the area where the U.S. firms have placed strategic emphasis.

As noted in chapter five, these devices are known collectively as application specific integrated circuits (ASICs). These devices are essentially logic devices because they carry out some control function. What makes these devices unique is that the control function can be designed to meet different needs from a common base of circuits or "cells." The importance of ASIC devices is that by designing a single device to carry out a specific function, the integrated circuit user does not have to acquire several standard logic and memory devices to accomplish the same task. Although ASIC-type devices have been in existence for some time, it is only with recent improvements in design technology, especially in the software to drive computer aided design techniques, that ASIC devices have gained market advantages over standard logic devices. Early ASIC type devices such as programmable read only memory (PROM) and erasable programmable read only memory (EPROM) are now available, but have taken much time to design. If the initial design was found to be flawed, redesign was difficult. Further, the logic pattern on the PROM could only be set once, and could not be altered. The logic pattern on the EPROM could be altered, but the process was time consuming and difficult.

In the mid-1980s a technological change in the ASIC market occurred. This is seen in the introduction of Static RAMs and EEPROMs or electronically erasable programmable read only memories as the process drivers for ASIC devices. The SRAM is a more complicated offshoot of DRAM technology, but is still more sensitive to changes in process rather than design innovation. The EEPROM requires more design technology, but is also sensitive to process technology. These devices are part of one of the fastest growing segments of the integrated circuit industry in that these devices are forming an important process technological base for the programmable logic device (PLD) segment of the ASIC industry. The outcome of the competition between U.S. and Japanese firms in this segment will shape the composition of not only the integrated circuit industry but also of the industries that utilize integrated circuits. While the Japanese have gained a lead in SRAM devices, the EEPROM technology has been developed by entrepreneurial firms in the United States.

CURRENT U.S. RESPONSE: COMPANIES

As noted above, the integrated circuit industry has divided into two segments. The memory segment is dominated by the DRAM device. The logic segment, which includes microprocessors, is becoming dominated by ASIC devices. Each of these segments has characteristics unique to it, but both are driven by the same technological forces. As has been noted, U.S. firms, primarily entrepreneurial start-ups, have been able to hold their own against the Japanese firms in the logic segment. This has not been true in the older memory segment. The question confronting these firms is can they compete in the current environment and prepare for the techno-global competition which is now emerging.

The "False Promise" of the Independent Entrepreneur

Entrepreneurial firms usually stand on the forefront of the new integrated circuit technologies. However, the United States must be cautious about placing too much hope in such activity. The promise of the independent entrepreneurial perspective is that a nation's industry can be continually renewed and compete effectively on a global scale through radical technology innovation. This innovation is most successfully conducted by independent entrepreneurs operating in a free and open market system. This particular perspective is most forcefully developed and espoused by George Gilder (1988).

In essence, this perspective assumes that all meaningful competition will be carried out only along one technological dimension; that is, innovation which creates whole new classes of products. Rather than compete through innovation in existing products, by pushing these along their technology trajectory, this perspective argues for the creation of new trajectories, as was seen with the invention of the DRAM and later with ASIC devices. In order to compete in the global integrated circuit industry, as has been shown in earlier chapters, U.S. firms had to compete along all the dimensions of technology, product and process, radical, major and incremental.

Another perspective has been put forward by Charles C. Ferguson (1988). He argues that given the financial mechanisms for rationing capital resources for innovation, it may be detrimental to the U.S. segment of the global integrated circuit industry to encourage the growth of small entrepreneurial firms which siphon away funds from the established firms which can better follow through on a technological innovation. Also, the continual bleeding of engineering talent, which is the primary receptacle for the informational resource, away from established firms and towards start-ups, may not allow for the necessary critical mass to congregate in one place. Firms in the U.S. segment suffer from a loss of continuity among both their engineering and production staff. These are the very personnel who are crucial for success in integrated circuit markets like the DRAM. The result of unbridled entrepreneurialism is further fragmentation of the industry and lessening ability to compete globally. Only large firms can survive in the global IC industry.

Evidence and arguments put forth by both Gilder and Ferguson appear to support their respective views. Likewise, as has been described in earlier chapters, the trend in the DRAM segment of the IC industry appears to support Ferguson's perspective, while the emergence of RISC-based MPUs and the ASIC segment appears to support Gilder's perspective. A paradox arises that must be resolved before any proper policy guidance can be given.

The Emerging ASIC Integrated Circuit Industry: the EEPROM

As a way of further illustrating the Gilder/Ferguson paradox and the dynamic interplay of technological and institutional factors in affecting the resources needed for innovation, let us examine an an emerging ASIC technology. The electronically erasable programmable read only memory (EEPROM) is appropriate. As noted above, the EEPROM has been pioneered by entrepreneurial firms. With the emergence of the ASIC device, the IC industry entered into a new era. A potential model for ASIC competition is most explicitly illustrated in the market battle between the EPROM and the EEPROM.

The EEPROM is a more sophisticated version of the older erasable programmable read only memory (EPROM) device. In true silicon valley fashion, the EEPROM was brought to market by entrepreneurial start-up firms. The Japanese, using the older EPROM technology coupled with their superior processing technology, have adopted a strategy of attrition with the EEPROM producers who are their most direct competitors. During the 1980s Japan has lowered the price on EPROMs to such an extent that the price-performance ratio has allowed for this older technology to compete favorably with the newer EEPROM technology. The entrepreneurial firms do not have the financial resources nor the market staying power to last long and many are consequently folding.

The EEPROM technology has greater technical potential than does the older EPROM and in time will dominate the market. Japanese firms have been developing the know-how to design and produce the EEPROM, both through internal R&D efforts and by strategically linking with U.S. entrepreneurial firms. The buyout of Excel by Exar and the increasing array of second-sourcing and cross-licensing agreements and other strategic alliances between Japanese firms and the U.S. start-up firms are examples of what will become an ever-increasing trend in the U.S. integrated circuit industry. While these arrangements have existed before, their implications have changed. Instead of being primarily tactical in gaining near-term market advantage, these arrangements have become means to acquiring long-term technological advantage. This is particularly true since, as was shown in chapter five, a number of these alliances are between small U.S. firms and large Japanese firms.

The U.S. integrated circuit industry is still driven by the entrepreneurial dream of single individual effort leading to success. However, the reality of competition in the techno-global integrated circuit industry requires that both the financial and informational resources be amassed in large quantities. This requires, more than ever, the effort of teams of entrepreneurial companies, not isolated entrepreneurs. During the 1950s, 1960s, and early 1970s the independent entrepreneur dominated technological innovation. This was because whole new technologies were developed that were technically and economically clearly superior to previous technologies, such as the transistor or the integrated circuit. The integrated circuit industry, especially in the advent of the ASIC segment, has entered a new era, where a new device derived from an innovation is in direct competition with other devices. The focus of competition shifts from products that did not exist before to one of close substitutes where the price performance of each device is the key. The technology has also become "team embodied." No single individual, no single firm for that matter, can produce integrated circuit devices today without important technical and economic links to other firms both in the integrated circuit industry and in related industries.

Industrial Teams and Technological Survival

An alternative to the Gilder/Ferguson paradox is the utilization of industrial teams. "Strategic alliances," first mentioned in chapter five, are leading to the development of de facto "industry teams." The need to cope with the more complex technological and marketing environment is becoming paramount and is forcing firms into cross-national and cross-industrial alliances. This is creating cross-national, cross-industrial teams. These new types of industrial structures will require different managerial skills and strategic outlooks. A crucial question is whether the U.S. can develop industrial teams with sufficient vitality to compete. It appears that Japanese integrated circuit firms have an inherent advantage. The strategic origin of that advantage is illustrated in comparing the starting points for the equipment industries in the respective countries.

In the United States, the equipment firms evolved out of the machine tool industry and the semiconductor industry. Because of this, the firms in the equipment industry are independent of the integrated circuit firms. There is a more "arm's length" relationship between the integrated circuit firms and the equipment firms, which erodes transactional efficiencies. U.S. firms are just now beginning to develop the loose connections between firms that may evolve into industrial teams.

In Japan, as was discussed earlier, the equipment industry developed out of the needs of the integrated circuit producers. Extant firms in already existing industrial keiretsu groups were chosen for special attention by the integrated circuit producers in Japan, and these firms are now the most vibrant in the equipment industry. Consequently, in many integrated circuit equipment technologies, the Japanese lead U.S. equipment firms by one to two years. In many cases U.S. firms have exited key subtechnology areas. As a result, in order to establish an industrial team in the United States, many of the firms will have to be Japanese. This has been illustrated by the rapid decline of a number of U.S. semiconductor equipment manufacturers and the fact that Sematech has had difficulty in putting together and maintaining in "all-U.S. team."

The industry is reaching a shakeout, but it will be a shakeout initiated not by a decline in demand alone, but also by the ever-increasing sophistication of the technology of integrated circuits and the requisite need for more financial and informational resources to keep pace and compete globally. Thus, strategies which work in the well known demand/marketing shakeout will not work for the ASIC industry in particular and the integrated circuit industry in general. The strategic stance calls for both attention to the market and marketing strategies and also attention to the technological and institutional aspects of production and innovation.

In order for firms to survive in this type of environment, they must adopt strategic stances which allow them to keep the critical mass in resources necessary for both product and process innovation. They must not only secure access to financial capital, but to engineering talent and production worker talent. Once acquired, these resources must be maintained and improved. This strategic stance also calls for attention to the market and a closer relationship with customers and suppliers. The two strategies, innovation and marketing, are complementary and require a team approach. To emphasize one to the exclusion of the other will ultimately lead to the firm's demise.

In order for start-up companies to succeed in this, however, they must not only be on the cutting edge of technology, but also have the production and marketing systems in place as well. As has been shown in the earlier chapters, this is not often possible because of the cost. Further, the traditional mode of handling start-ups in the integrated circuit industry complicates matters more. The traditional mode has been for the established company to look at the start-up as a threat and to take whatever legal or market actions are necessary to counter it. The start-ups, for their part, siphon off valuable engineering and managerial talent. This mode of operating has been tolerable only when small- to medium-sized U.S. firms dominated the industry. With the emergence of a techno-global environment, this mode needs to change.

An alternative mode has emerged which potentially can give the U.S. integrated circuit industry the industrial teams it needs to survive. Beginning in 1983, a number of new firms have been "spun off" in a cooperative manner as opposed to "spun out" forcefully and often acrimoniously. These new firms have been internally funded by already established integrated circuit firms and have remained linked to these firms (Lineback, 1988). This is not the dominant mode yet, but it offers an alternative to the current mode of management where the parent company expels the would-be entrepreneur and threatens the newly formed company with lawsuits over proprietary technology.

By spinning off firms through internal funding, companies such as Cypress Semiconductor Corporation, Analog Devices, and Quantum Corporation are beginning to develop industrial teams. If careful attention can be paid to the continuing development of ties with these neighboring firms as the new venture grows, an industrial structure capable of competing with the keiretsu may emerge. The advantage of such an arrangement is that it will help to foster the entrepreneurial spirit, while keeping a critical mass of technical and managerial talent available to compete in the technoglobal environment, thus combining the essential truths in both of Gilder's and Ferguson's arguments. Establishing this new mode has been difficult, not only because of the traditional silicon valley way of handling new startups, but also because of the legal and tax difficulties of internal funding that currently exist (Lineback, 1988; Rayner, April 30, 1990).

CURRENT U.S. RESPONSE: GOVERNMENT

An important role that government can play is to encourage the development of industrial teams. It is recognized that government policy may do much to establish a climate that fosters and supports innovation and favors the development of certain institutional arrangements to carry out this innovation. The role of the VLSI Cooperative Research Association in Japan and its American counterparts such as MCC, SRC, and Sematech are attempts to foster cooperation among competitors. Much of the current policy initiatives, such as Sematech, are modeled on the success of the Japanese VLSI Cooperative Research Association.

However, it should be noted that the role of the Japanese government was found to be far from the omnipotent and omniscient position that is often characterized in the U.S. popular press. The previous chapters have shown that the government can be characterized as playing a sometimes important, but not crucial role in the facilitation of the development of technology in Japan. It altered the pace of the trend, but it could not, at least in the case of VLSI technology development, start and control the trend. That trend was started and continued by the firms in the integrated circuit industry.

This book supports the view that actions taken in the private sector have been more relevant than actions taken in the public sector in describing the current state of Japanese technological development in the DRAM market. It should be noted, however, that the role of other Japanese government policies with broader effects, such as tax and trade policies, were beyond the scope of this book, and their effects on DRAM technological development were not assessed. Further, the Japanese governmental interventions came at a time which was late in the development of DRAM technology. The impact on the technology at an early stage would be expected to be greater. Timing is crucial, but of greater importance is the necessity that any governmental initiative be part of a coherent vision of what direction the U.S. economy is to take and what type of industrial structure would provide the best vehicle to negotiate the challenges emerging in the competitive environment of the 1990s and beyond.

FUTURE DIRECTION FOR THE JAPANESE: MOVEMENT TOWARDS A TECHNO-GLOBAL WORLD

As discussed in chapter six, the focus of the Japanese government and Japanese companies has shifted over time. Initially, in the period following the Second World War until the 1960s, the focus was on mastering production technology. While not all government policies nor all company strategies were focused on production technology, judging from results it was the production-based strategies which succeeded. The increased production efficiency, productivity of the labor force, and product quality of Japanese products is still recognized as the standard to match. Beginning in the late in the late 1960s and early 1970s, Japanese companies began to focus on product development. By the early 1980s, Japanese companies began to experience success in these strategies. Success in developing the VCR, and in other areas such as pioneering work in digital audio tape products is indicative of the success of these strategies. The emerging focus of Japanese companies is now on technological knowledge base development. This new focus emerged in 1980 and is still developing. The importance of this new focus is that it is beginning to alter the competitive ground for all companies. As will be discussed throughout the next few sections of this chapter, competition between U.S. and Japanese companies will occur not only on the production technology and product development dimensions but also in the development of new technological knowledge bases.

A number of studies have reported on the relative balance between the United States and Japan in a number of technological knowledge base areas. The strength of Japanese companies is clearly recognized in the production technology area (Grayson and O'Dell, 1988). The strength of Japanese companies is just now beginning to be recognized in the product development area (Abegglen and Stalk, 1985; Bower and Hout, 1988). Studies of Japan's basic research abilities are also just now being done. One of the most recent was a study done by the National Science Foundation and reported in summary form in a special section of the Wall Street

Journal on technology. For more detailed information, the reader should consult *The Science and Technology Resources of Japan: A comparison with the United States*, published by the National Science Foundation in June of 1988.

The report provided the results of the study which evaluated the relative position of the United States and Japan in twelve technological areas in terms of basic research, advanced development of products based on the technology, and the production and engineering abilities. These technological areas included artificial intelligence, automated factory assembly, biotechnology, compact disk technology, computer design, computer integrated manufacturing (CIM), computer software, fiber optics, high-strength construction plastics, integrated circuits, mobile radio systems, and telecommunication networks (*Wall Street Journal*, November 14, 1988).

Several of the results are of interest. The relative strength of the Japanese was strongest in the production and engineering area. In seven of the twelve technological areas noted above, Japan was clearly ahead. In only three areas, artificial intelligence, high-strength construction plastics and telecommunication networks, was Japan judged to be behind, and in one area, mobile radio systems, Japan and the United States were even. One area, biotechnology, was determined not to have any production technology (*Wall Street Journal*, November 14, 1988). In the area of advance development of products, Japan was determined to be ahead in four areas, automated factory assembly, compact disk technology, fiber optics, and integrated circuits. Japan was even but gaining in the three areas of biotechnology, computer design, and mobile radio systems, and behind in the other five areas. In these five areas, Japan was gaining in two, computer integrated manufacturing and high-strength construction plastics. It was holding even in two, telecommunications networks and artificial intelligence, and losing ground only in computer software.

According to the study, only in the area of basic research does the United States have a clear lead. Only in three technological areas does Japan lead, one of them integrated circuits, the other two fiber optics and mobile radio systems. In each of these three areas, Japan is continuing to gain ground. Japan's position is even in automated factory assembly and is holding constant. In all the other technological areas, Japan is behind. Of those areas, Japan is gaining ground in two areas, CIM and high-strength construction plastics. It is holding its position in two, biotechnology and compact disk technology. Japan losing ground in four areas, artificial intelligence, computer design, computer software, and telecommunications networks. It is clear that the one area of weakness for the Japanese is in the basic science and basic research area. As noted earlier in this book, the strategic orientation of Japanese companies is towards self-sufficiency.

In addition, the Japanese are now reaching a point in their development where their strategic approach toward the acquisition of knowledge must change.

During the 1950s, 1960s, and early 1970s, the choice for Japan of either developing the technological knowledge bases needed to compete or acquiring these from abroad was clear. The balance of technological trade for those decades between Japan and the United States clearly indicated that Japan imported more technological knowledge than it exported. During this period, Japanese engineers and scientists were quite capable of knowing what technological information to acquire, how to most effectively assimilate it and where to improve it so as to create products that would be competitive in world markets. During the mid- to late-1970s, much more technological knowledge was being generated through internal sources in Japan. It was not until the early 1980s, however, that factors truly began to push Japan into stronger internal development of technological knowledge bases.

As was described above, the areas of knowledge where the Japanese lag the United States are decreasing. In terms of production and product development from existing technological knowledge bases the Japanese have come abreast of the United States in a number of crucial areas and are gaining in a number of others. The case of high definition television (HDTV) is illustrative. Japanese researchers at NHK and a number of company laboratories began to explore this technological area in the late 1960s and early 1970s. While some of the initial technological knowledge base was imported, the Japanese were able to improve upon it and surpass it. Currently, Japan leads the United States in this technological knowledge area by some three to five years (Iversen, 1989).

Another example is in developing machines which use "fuzzy logic." Although pioneering work on the mathematical foundations of fuzzy logic was done in the mid-1960s in the United States, it is Japanese companies which have put the theory to work. Hitachi has utilized fuzzy logic computers in subway trains operating in the city of Sendai. Hitachi, Sanyo and Matsushita are using fuzzy logic controllers in their camcorders. Matsushita has also installed these devices in products as diverse as vacuum cleaners, washing machines and kerosene heaters. Mitsubishi Electric, Hitachi, and Toshiba have used fuzzy logic in elevators (Mitsusada, June 16, 1990). Only one small U.S. entrepreneurial start-up, Togai Infralogic, is making fuzzy logic controllers.

The one area where Japan clearly lags the United States is in the basic research necessary to develop new technological knowledge bases. Consequently, the Japanese are now beginning to ask more and more of the type of questions that would be considered "basic science questions." The role that Japanese researchers are playing in developing the high temperature superconductive field is a case in point. The Cho Den Do Kogaku

Kenkyu Jo or Superconductivity Laboratory was established in 1988 as a jointly funded laboratory. The funding members are the Ministry of International Trade and Industry (MITI) and participating members of the laboratory. The laboratory is open to any company, including U.S. and Western European companies which are willing to pay the membership fee. Currently, there are 110 ordinary member companies. These companies, some of which are American, are allowed access to the results of the laboratory's research and can be licensed to use the patents developed by the laboratory. Another category of member exists, special member companies. By paying a higher fee, these companies can send up to two researchers to the laboratory to work on the various research projects. There are forty-six such companies. Although American companies can join this group as well, none have chosen as yet to do so.

These forty-six companies represent in sales about fifteen percent of the GNP of Japan and about thirty percent of the manufacturing-based GNP of Japan. This is a powerful group of companies who are also working on superconductivity in their own company laboratories. The Cho Den Do laboratory has currently about 100 researchers working on various aspects of high temperature superconductive research. It should be remembered that it was the Japanese researchers at the University of Tokyo who confirmed the original findings of the IBM European researchers. The team that did this was headed by Professor Shoji Tanaka, who is now one of the researchers directing the efforts of the Cho Den Do laboratory.

Because of these efforts and others, MITI has recently published a report entitled *Sangyo Gijutsu no Doko to Kadai.* This was a report on the status of Japanese industrial technology which was published in December of 1988. The report examined where Japanese industry was acquiring its technological knowledge and what were the future directions for Japanese companies with respect to research. One major conclusions from this report was that the majority of technological knowledge now utilized by Japanese companies was generated in Japan. Domestically generated technological knowledge averaged about seventy-five percent of the technology base for Japanese high technology products while that from non-Japanese sources was twenty-five percent. The second major conclusion was that Japanese companies needed to spend more on basic research in order to generate the technological knowledge bases necessary to compete in the twenty-first century.

Japanese companies are also receiving another set of signals stimulating them to increase their basic research efforts. These are coming from the United States and Western Europe. There is a growing movement among both private companies and governments to establish greater control over research findings generated in-house. These activities come under the rubric of "intellectual property rights" laws. The Japanese view these activities as the beginning of an effort to freeze them out of the technological mainstream. Consequently, Japanese companies are placing more efforts in the basic research area. These efforts will be examined next.

Japan's Basic Research Focus

Competition in the world's industries is becoming increasingly technological. The traditional focus of companies on manufacturing efficiency and product development is still important. The key competitive challenge, however, will be the ability of companies to generate new technological knowledge bases and quickly translate that new technological knowledge into a wide variety of efficiently produced products. The "superconductivity race" is just one example. This emerging "techno-competition" requires that firms explicitly explicitly incorporate knowledge of the innovation process into their technology strategy.

Recalling the discussion of the innovation process from chapter one, the key focus of the competitive situation during the 1970s and 1980s has been on the latter portion of the process. This is the part of designing and producing products. The research focus has been on applied and developmental research. During the 1990s and into the twenty-first century, the importance of this section of the innovation process will continue, but the focus of technological strategy will need to consider sources of innovation, in particular knowledge generation. The research focus will be increasingly on basic research and the rapid translation of the information generated by such research into products and processes.

Further, recalling from chapter one, the definition of basic research is the one used by the National Science Foundation. In this definition, the essence of basic research is that it is not directed towards any commercial end. This is a goal-oriented definition and emphasizes less the process of the research and the type of questions that the researcher must ask. There is no difference between an academic laboratory or a corporate laboratory in researching how a neuron functions in terms of the process of the research. Since both researchers are on the cutting edge of the knowledge frontier, the types of questions asked will be the same and the methodologies used to answer the questions will not differ significantly. What will differ is what is done with the results. Issues related to the output of the results will be discussed in a later section of this chapter. For now the key issue is to understand that there are no significant differences between academic-based and corporate-based "basic research."

The importance of understanding this distinction is evident when asking the question of whether the Japanese are performing basic research and whether they can overcome the U.S. lead in this area. The answer to the first question is fairly evident, although somewhat controversial. The second question is far more difficult to assess. In terms of the first question, many Japanese companies and research institution claim to be doing basic research. There is a basic research boom occurring in Japan. Japanese managers can be just as prone to succumbing to fads as can their counterparts in the United States. Further, Japanese companies realize that in order to attract the best young minds graduating from college, having a basic research laboratory can help in recruiting.

Having said this, it is clear from conversations with the research heads of a number of the larger Japanese companies that efforts are being made to do basic research in the corporate setting. To begin, the definition of basic research varies. There is the recognition among Japanese researchers of the concept of pure basic research; that is, developing knowledge for its own sake. There is also another type of basic research that is being performed. This type is called "mission oriented basic research," "fundamental research," or "generic technology research." This type of research has a commercial goal as an outcome, but that outcome may not materialize for ten to twenty years. Examples include work being done on x-ray lithography, synchrotron orbital radiation technology, Josephson junctions, and high temperature superconductive materials.

While the percentage of the total research budget that is devoted to either pure basic research or the mission-oriented basic research is small, usually ranging from one percent to four percent, the total amount is still large. This is because the amount of funds devoted to research by companies is large. In total R&D expenditures, Fujitsu spent $1,870,500,000 in 1989, while Toshiba spent $1,738,488,000 in 1988, and NEC spent $1,677,960,000 in 1988, with Hitachi spending $2,591,208,000 in 1988 (Company Annual Reports). The amount that these and other companies is spending have been increasing each year.

In some cases it has been reported that spending on research and development has, in aggregate, become greater than spending for capitalization. According to a survey of sixty-eight companies done by the Nomura Research Institute, the amount spent on capital investment was Y1,949.3 billion in 1987. The amount spent on research and development was Y2,138.8 billion (Kodama, June 4, 1988). The corresponding amounts for 1986 were Y2.1 trillion for capital investment and Y2 trillion for research and development. For 1985, the amounts were Y2.4 trillion for capital investment and Y1.8 trillion for research and development (Kodama, June 4, 1988). The trend of spending more on research and development is recent and sharp, but for the firms mentioned above, and others in the electronics industry, the trend continued in 1988 and 1989. This trend is indicative of the shift towards a competitive strategy based on the development of new technology and its rapid insertion into products and processes.

This trend is also being reflected organizationally. Japanese companies are currently using a two-pronged approach in conducting the research portion of their technology strategy. First, the largest Japanese companies in the electronics industry have established central research laboratories to conduct basic research in Japan. Second, many Japanese firms are establishing research facilities in the United States and Western Europe. This second approach will be discussed later in this chapter.

Most recently, Japanese firms that have been associated primarily with consumer electronics have begun to establish basic research facilities. Sony, Matsushita, and Sanyo all established such centers in 1988 (Kitamatsu, December 24, 1988). This is in addition to NEC, Hitachi, Mitsubishi Electric, Toshiba, and Fujitsu, electronics firms which have already established such facilities or programs for basic research. Personnel is also a key issue in moving to a technology-based strategy. The movement towards greater use of internally generated research knowledge in products is seen in the increasing number of researchers at Japanese companies. The number of researchers per 1,000 employees in Japanese corporations was twenty-four in 1978. That number has increased each year until it reached forty-four researchers per 1,000 employees in 1988 (Technology Research and Information Division, 1989). In addition the number of researchers employed in private corporations as a percentage of total researchers in Japan has increased from 55.7 percent in 1979 to 63.2 percent in 1988 (Technology Research and Information Division, 1989). It should be noted here that the greatest threat to Japan's success in this strategy is having enough qualified researchers. This issue will be discussed below. Further, the differences in organizational settings such as private corporation, university, and government for carrying out research will be discussed in a later section. The important point to realize is that Japanese corporations are shifting their emphasis to a more technologically-based competitive strategy.

What direction will this technologically-based competitive strategy take? A number of strategic directions have been indicated by Japanese companies. In tying basic research to the area of production, many Japanese companies are adding increased flexibility to their manufacturing systems through technology. The strategic thrust is towards shoryo takeshu or small quantities/many varieties. The development of CAD/CAM and computer integrated manufacturing (CIM) is the process by which the companies are attempting to do this. This area is heavily dependent upon software to control the various robotic systems needed for true computer integrated manufacturing. Although the Japanese are lagging in software development, they are currently using the development of CIM as the catalyst to improve their software capabilities. The Japanese movement into ASIC devices is also indicative of another strategic thrust.

This strategic thrust into more basic research is related to product development approaches. As noted in previous chapters, Japanese companies are moving towards producing products that have higher value-added or fukakatchi. In order to create fukakatchi, Japanese firms are focusing on greater systematization or fukugoka. Perhaps the best presentation of this is concept was the adoption by NEC of the "C&C" strategy, as formulated by Koji Kobayashi, former Chairman of the Board of NEC. The C&C concept stands for computers and communications. Computer technology and telecommunication technology were seen as merging because of the increasing use of integrated circuits by both. These technological knowledge bases were beginning to fuse into one technology base. The driving force behind this fusion has been the increasing sophistication of integrated circuits (Kobayashi, 1986).

One example that has recently emerged is HDTV. In discussions with Japanese executives of a number of Japanese firms in the electronic industry, HDTV was described as the computer and telecommunication center of the electronic home of the future. The HDTV set is no longer seen as a stand-alone television set used only for entertainment. It will hold the vital role of system integration component for individual workstations at home.

Another important trend in basic research as being conducted by Japanese companies is the fusion of seemingly different knowledge bases into entirely new technologies. This is illustrated by the number of major Japanese electronics firms, such as Hitachi, NEC, and Mitsubishi Electric, which have laboratories devoted to biotechnological research. These firms are carrying out a variety of research projects in biotechnology. Part of the rationale for electronics firms to be doing research in biotech offered by Japanese executive in charge of this research is that products based on the biotechnological knowledge base will become highly important in the twenty-first century. The other part of the rationale for doing such research is that as integrated circuit density increases, circuit size is moving towards the molecular level. Developing a "biochip" and from that a "biocomputer" is on the agenda of a number of Japanese companies (McClean, 1986). Although the biochip and biocomputer is a number of years away, work begun ten years ago by Professor Karube while at Tokyo Institute of Technology has already yielded a number of biosensors ready for commercial use. In addition, the continued work on Josephson junctions being done by Japanese firms is being fused with the work just starting up on high-temperature superconductive materials. While the work of these Japanese researchers has been featured in such popular business press as *Business Week* and the *L.A. Times*, what is often overlooked in such articles is the extended commitment to the research both in terms of time, money, and researchers.

This work is being done because the Japanese companies feel that the knowledge base that powered the integrated circuit industry up to now is reaching its limits. By exploring other technological knowledge bases, along with doing research in the traditional integrated circuit technologies such as x-ray and electron beam lithography, Japanese firms are developing the capabilities to create new breakthroughs. This is clearly seen in the area of material science. Japanese electronic firms are not only exploring ways to extend silicon as a substrate but are also working on improving gallium arsenide as a substrate. This work is being done at the same time as the work on the so-called "123 materials" used in high temperature superconductivity. The work on silicon has immediate returns. The work on gallium arsenide may not yield a return for five years and the work on superconductive material far beyond that.

This work is being done predominantly by companies. In the United States, most of the basic research done is performed in universities and government institutions. In Japan, it is in companies that have the financial and research personnel to conduct this research effectively. The share of research and development expenditures held by private companies has been above seventy percent since 1983 (Technology Research and Information Division, 1989). Further, while the percentage of total research that is devoted to basic research has held at about fourteen percent, the percentage of basic research performed by private companies was at about thirty-four percent in the period 1985 through 1987. The research personnel figures were discussed above.

The institutional history of Japanese universities also makes them less likely to carry out the same role as U.S. universities. The mission of Japanese universities is primarily knowledge disseminator more than knowledge generator. Government institutes have also traditionally played a small role. Consequently, the technological breakthroughs most likely occur in private corporate laboratories.

The importance of this consequence is in the outputs of the research findings. In the United States, the results of university basic research are often viewed as belonging to the public. Research conducted by universities and funded by the Department of Defense or private companies may have restrictions, but the majority of university research is open. In Japan, if the institutions which are most able to carry out basic research are private corporations, how the findings of that research will be disseminated is more problematic. These problems also exist when corporations in the United States and Western Europe conduct this type of research. The decision rule on whether to release the results depends on the size of the potential profits and the immediacy of realizing those profits, rather than on benefiting an abstract ideal such as knowledge advancement. Consequently, intellectual property rights issues will play an increasingly important role in the emerging technologically-based competition.

As noted above, the decreasing pool of qualified university graduates to do research is perhaps the most serious problem confronting Japanese companies (Oguchi, July 28, 1990). This is partly due to the fact that Japan is aging, as a society, faster than the United States. As a result the total number of qualified new graduates entering the research pool is decreasing.

In addition, a number of technically trained university graduates are opting for careers in banks, stock brokerage houses and other financial investment institutions. The primary reason for this is the opportunity for larger salaries and greater career freedom (Agency of Industrial Science and Technology, 1989). Consequently, Japanese companies have shifted their recruiting focus for researchers from Japan to the world.

The Emergence of Techno-Global Competition

The second approach adopted by Japanese companies towards increasing the research content of their technology strategy has been to link with university laboratories and more importantly to establish R&D facilities in the United States and Western Europe and hire researchers from those countries. For a number of reasons in addition to a shortage of researchers, Japanese companies have begun to establish these overseas research facilities. Since Japanese research facilities have not traditionally been set up to do basic research, there is a lag between when an strategy is started and when it will begin to yield results. Because of the longer tradition of performing such research in the United States and Western Europe, many Japanese companies have established research facilities in these countries. A survey of 177 companies done by the Nihon Keizai Shimbun in 1988 showed increased research activity abroad (Inoue, September 24, 1988). Most of this activity began in 1987. Fifty-eight Japanese companies have established sixty-six research centers in other countries. Of these, the survey found, twenty-three were established in 1987 or 1988 (Inoue, September 24, 1988). Further, thirty-seven firms had plans for establishing research centers in countries other than Japan and fifty-three were looking into the possibility of such plans (Inoue, September 24, 1988).

Another reason for establishing these facilities is that while a number of them will be set up to do basic research, others will be devoted to applied and developmental research (Kitamatsu, December 24, 1988). Setting up such facilities not only allows the Japanese companies to tap the talent of U.S. and Western European researchers, but also allows the companies to be closer to the customer. This will provide an advantage in translating new technological knowledge into products. Further, by locating abroad, Japanese firms will be able to circumvent any intellectual property restrictions placed on the movement of technological knowledge out of a country. It should be noted that a number of U.S. and Western European companies are establishing research facilities in Japan. Since 1986 about twenty U.S. and Western European firms have either established or announced plans to establish research facilities in Japan (Inoue, September 24, 1988). This is in addition to the firms which have longstanding research facilities in Japan, bring the total to 137.

More indicative of the competitive forces emerging in the techno-global environment is the type of research U.S. facilities in Japan are now conducting. The research facilities of such firms as Du Pont, Dow Chemical, IBM, Eastman Kodak, and Fuji-Xerox are doing more sophisticated applied research, and are often taking the research lead away from their American parents in developing products. As a result of this cross-national research facility development, the technological competition noted above is becoming global. Companies are not only in a race to constantly improve production efficiency or to develop new products from existing technology, but also to develop new technologies to incorporate into both products and processes.

Characteristics of Techno-Global Competition

Several strategic factors are now emerging and will come to characterize the techno-global competitive environment of the next ten to twenty years. First, focus on competitive conditions will replace the locus of where competition occurs as the major determinants of strategy. Competition in the United States or Western Europe or Asia will be characterized by the same need to develop technology and quickly translate these developments into commercially viable products and processes. No longer will the United States be considered advanced or high tech and the others not so. Companies will not be able to offer their technologically less sophisticated products in one region while saving their most sophisticated products for their home markets. Competition will require the best products incorporating the most advanced technology and manufactured by the most efficient methods in all regions, simultaneously.

Second, breakthroughs in technology will occur on any point on the globe. This was illustrated most clearly by development of new high-temperature superconductive materials. The original breakthrough occurred in the IBM laboratory in Zurich, Switzerland. Within a few months it was confirmed by a University of Tokyo laboratory, and improvements in these materials have been emanating from laboratories around the world. This strategic factor demonstrates the speed at which the information needed for technological innovation can appear throughout the world. A key to participation in this aspect of techno-global competition will be the availability of receptor sites, that is, laboratories that have adequately trained personnel who can acquire, interpret, and improve upon the original breakthrough.

As more companies in various parts of the world begin to produce products that are at the cutting edge of technology, breakthroughs will increasingly occur outside the United States. Laboratories, both public and private, in Europe, Japan, and throughout Asia are increasingly becoming cites for potential breakthroughs in electronics, biotechnology, software, and other technological areas that will power the industries of the next century. Companies in South Korea and Taiwan, countries that were considered not so long ago as developing nations, are producing products at the leading edge of their respective technologies. In the not so distant future, laboratories in South America and Africa will offer the potential of fundamental breakthroughs in technology. One of the consequences of techno-global competition is that innovation can occur any place in the world.

A third factor which will characterize the techno-global environment is the continuing acceleration of the pace of innovation. This pace will be occurring across all levels of the innovation spectrum from incremental to radical. Much of the innovation will remain hidden to view in the proprietary recesses of a company's manufacturing facility. However, as more companies engage in research, the increasing innovation will manifest itself in the number and type of new products being introduced and the number of patents being issued. Japanese dominance in manufacturing is well known. Their presence in product development and major product innovation is now recognized (Abegglen and Stalk, 1985). Movement into the basic research area will also increase the pace of radical innovations. In addition to the company efforts, Japan's government has created the Exploratory Research for Advanced Technology Office (ERATO). The purpose of this agency is specifically to fund high-risk basic research projects. The consequence of this increasing pace of innovation will be to compress the cycle from idea generation to commercial product. Although much of the basic research done will result in discoveries that will not have any commercial value, as more of the products and the processes used to make those products become dependent on knowledge of the fundamental aspects of materials and the atomic make-up those materials, the commercial value of basic research will increase. Consequently, rapid product development will increasingly need to incorporate basic research.

A fourth strategic factor which will characterize techno-global competition is the increasing importance of "fusion technologies" as discussed with the development of bioelectronics, biochips, and biocomputers. The inexorable drive towards products with more features and increasing efficiency in manufacturing will widen the search for solutions. The fusion of technology knowledge bases is a natural extension of viewing technology as a process exhibiting probable events, or innovations, and the innovation envelop concept. Technology knowledge bases outside the mainstream for a product can be utilized if their potential for solving a problem is greater than existing subtechnologies. The development of mechatronics and bioelectronics are only two examples of this trend. As a result, companies must become more open to all types of technology knowledge bases.

Fifth, control over these knowledge bases and over the human resources needed to utilize these will become a dominant form of competition. Intellectual property rights issues, concern over the training of scientists and engineers and type and amount of research that should be conducted by various organizations, come to the fore when cast against the backdrop of the growing number of strategic alliances. The recent attempt by Hitachi to block Motorola from producing its 68030 MPU because of patent infringement is one example of the direction of this competition. Both Hitachi and Motorola accused each other of patent infringement, but unlike earlier battles, the U.S. firm was not in the clearly superior position. Consequently, Hitachi was almost able to stop Motorola from producing its top-of-the-line thirty-two bit MPU. The results would not only have severely damaged Motorola, but also Apple Computer, Hewlett Packard, and some seventy other companies dependent on the 68030 chip. Another example was the recent announcement of the purchase of International Computer Ltd. (ICL) by Fujitsu. Control of several key technologies by Fujitsu, rather than strict financial or market gains, led ICL into this merger situation.

RECOMMENDATIONS

Strategic Technology Perspective: Competing in a Techno-Global Environment

The consensus among U.S. policy makers, both in private enterprise and government, is that America has lost its production advantage (Grayson and O'Dell, 1988) and is losing its edge in product development (Dertouzos, Lester, Solow, 1989), but still has a lead in basic research, albeit a narrowing one. Policy initiatives have been being aimed at production or product development. In the integrated circuit industry this has been seen in the establishment of Sematech and the relaxing of the antitrust laws to allow for research cooperatives such as MCC. Each of these areas is important and efforts must be made to reverse the decline in production technology and to improve product development capabilities. To be successful, these efforts must be tied together in a framework of policies which reflects a clear and coherent understanding of the competitive pressures which are now emerging.

Competition in the techo-global environment will be occurring on several technological dimensions simultaneously. This competition will not be a simple case of product versus process. Both of these areas will be active. Consequently, all the areas of research, basic, applied, and developmental, in both product and process must be emphasized by companies. The firms which will emerge as top competitors will be those that can balance the resource demands that will occur from carrying out research at all three levels and can most effectively link together these levels to maximize their combined innovative potential. This requires a reexamination of the fundamental relationship that exists between the primary players in research activity, government, business, and universities. The view that the United

States is sufficiently ahead in basic research skills and new technology development that only universities and government need to focus in this area is untenable.

This is not to argue that those at work on the next radical innovation, equivalent to the transistor in its time, cannot be encouraged. This type of work must be continued, for from it spring the forces for economic growth. The conditions necessary for this endeavor are not the same in all respects to those conditions necessary for the commercial honing of the technology to compete in global markets. The necessary conditions for and the market circumstances which permit radical innovation to occur are not well understood and therefore not predictable. What is, however, understood is the consequences of such events. Economic relationships are altered to such an extent that entire industries disappear and are replaced by new industries based on the new technology.

Since the occurrence of a radical changes in technology, such as the invention of the transistor or recombinant DNA, does not follow a predictable and regular timetable, it would be highly risky to wager the fate of the nation's economy on such events. As this study has shown, the mere invention of a radical technology does not ensure dominance in the marketplace. At this study also indicates, the conditions necessary for commercial development of innovations are becoming known. There is the need for follow-through in the supporting technologies, especially the processing technologies, if economic success is to occur. Speed in translating the radical breakthrough into commercial products and processes is more likely to be maximized by companies that are conducting basic research and have personnel capable of understanding the innovation. Consequently, it is recommended that more firms carry out basic research in their own laboratories or become more closely linked with institutions that are carrying out such research. Recommendations as to the kind of basic research to be done must be left up to the individual firm.

Likewise, the view that only the market should be involved in the commercialization of new technologies, and that government should stay out completely, is untenable. This view is most prominently represented by the current approach taken by the United States to the development of HDTV technology. Funding from the government is only available for basic research, with commercialization left entirely up to the market. Unfortunately few U.S. firms are left to commercialize the technology. All but one electronics firm has exited television production, and computer firms need greater incentives to enter HDTV. Even firms such as IBM and Apple Computer may have difficulty in selling and making a profit in this consumer-based market. As with so many emerging technological areas, it is expected that commercialization will be carried out by unassisted, independent entrepreneurs. Lessons from the integrated circuit industry would argue differently.

The U.S. segment of the global integrated circuit industry invented the DRAM, and within three product generations lost its dominance in the market and the economic rewards that accompanied that dominance. The strategic shift from design to production technology in that industry and the need for greater team efforts were not accommodated by the market structure and industrial practices of the U.S. firms. This misreading of the technological comparative advantage contributed to the loss of dominance. A similar fate could be in store for the ASIC and RISC MPU segments of the integrated circuit industry. The implications of this, however, would be far more telling. Loss of U.S. dominance in these segments would mean loss of the entire integrated circuit industry and, in time, all industries which use integrated circuits. In both the DRAM and ASIC technologies, U.S. entrepreneurs initially had a lead in understanding both the market and the technology. This has not prevented their decline. How much less likely are the HDTV entrepreneurs to be successful in commercialization attempts when they are starting out with a deficit? Government needs to recognize that even the most technologically advanced U.S. entrepreneurial company is competing in a global world where its lead may be quite small over larger international competitors. Consequently, it is recommended that government become involved in aiding the commercialization of new technologies.

The need for follow-through in exploiting a technological breakthrough will require proper attention to the development of product and processing technologies. This, in turn must be linked to the need for continuity among the engineering and production staffs of technology-intensive industries. Many of the advances that occur in the process end of new product technologies is incremental and local. This is especially true of production innovation.

In order to exploit the learning curve, both government and industry must be aware of the need for stability in the production and engineering staff. Intercommunication between design and production engineers is a necessary condition for movement along the curve. High turnover among the production staff will lead to continual relearning of tasks. Poor communication between design engineers and production engineers or a rapid turnover in the participants in the relationship will also result in a decrease in learning.

With the emergence of techno-global competition, what is true at the intra-firm level is also true at the inter-firm level. The pressure for faster exploitation of technological inventions is driving the product development process outside the traditional boundaries of the firm and into cross-industry relationships. This phenomenon was seen in the relationship between integrated circuit firms and firms which make the production equipment for integrated circuits. Any advantage which is gained through the major innovation of a new product is eventually lost if this technological breakthrough is not followed up with continued attention to the processing technologies needed to manufacture the new design. This attention to production subtechnologies is increasingly occurring outside the firm and even outside the industry's traditional technology base, as was seen with the IC industry and the emergence of bioelectronics and superconductivity. Consequently, it is recommended that both government and private industry recognize the need to foster the development of industrial/technological teams, that can at the same time maintain the large number of personnel and capital needed to compete in established markets and encourage the entrepreneurial drive which creates new markets.

Furthermore, as the products become more technologically intensive, the information component of these products increases, and the comparative advantage wrought from radical or major innovations becomes more ephemeral. Again, as shown in this book, information has public good characteristics which make the exclusion of other consumers difficult. Thus, new technologies pioneered in one country's industry will eventually diffuse to another country's industry. This is because the communication of new ideas through journals, trade publications, and word-of-mouth cannot be limited to the geopolitical boundaries of one nation. The rapidity of the diffusion will also be enhanced by the telecommunications advances of the last decade. Consequently, there is a new strategic phenomena confronting firms which is found in the confluence between three previously separate strategic dimensions: technological innovation, production efficiency, and techno-global competition. It is quickly becoming the case that to compete successfully in one of the dimensions, a firm must also compete successfully in the others. Failure to recognize and adapt to this change in the strategic environment will result in the demise of the firm.

FIRM STRATEGY

In order for firms to compete in the techno-global environment, they must explicitly recognize the importance of a technology strategy, especially as it relates to defining their STA. This technology strategy should provide the firm with a vision of where it is going. This strategy should be open to ways of acquiring more of the resources needed for innovation and of maintaining those already in-house. This is particularly important with the human resource. In the integrated circuit industry, defining a firm's STA both horizontally and vertically was shown to be decisive in helping the firm compete. In the not-too-distant future, integrated circuit firms will have to define their STAs to include high temperature superconductivity, fuzzy logic, and biotechnology. For U.S. firms to compete in such an environment, careful attention must be paid to how they organize for innovation.

Internally, firms must be aware that organizational configurations will have an effect on their ability to acquire and keep the critical mass of financial and informational resources necessary to compete in global industries. Of primary concern is whether an organization can be designed to maximize the objective function of competition through product and process innovation. The design of such an organization must take into account the changes in the underlying technology knowledge bases which go into the product and process. These changes alter the kind as well as the level and combination of financial and informational resources needed to bring about the next innovation in the technology. Extended networks of firms operating in a number of industrial-technological settings will be more capable of acquiring and assimilating the necessary resources for innovation. Although careful attention must be paid to both the financial/ machine and information/human resources, it is the latter that is most sensitive in the techno-global environment.

Competing through continual innovation will also require a reframing of the social contract for innovation which more explicitly recognizes the interdependencies between the organization and the creative individual. Without the creative individual or team of individuals, the organization will increasingly be left with products based on obsolete technologies. Without the organization, the creative individual or team would most likely starve before their work could bear fruit in the marketplace. One area where this revised social contract must be put into place concerns intellectual property rights.

Currently, the company retains complete control over the creative work of its researchers. The economic rents of breakthroughs accrue to the company, not the individual. In order to keep talented individuals and teams, these economic rents should be more equitably shared. Some percentage of the profits accruing from the innovation should be paid back to the individual inventors. If a patent is granted and later licensed, some percentage of the royalty payments should also be paid to the individual inventors. A variety of schemes for such payments could be devised which would create the incentive to stay, rather than to leave with some breakthrough and set up an independent company. If the individual does decide to become an entrepreneur, rather than spin-out the individual and sever all ties, every attempt should be made to establish a symbiotic network of firms which can develop into an industrial team.

This book has shown that as the technology becomes more sophisticated, the ability of a single small firms to generate the required financial and informational resources becomes strained. Firms have compensated by becoming larger and integrating with other firms. What is of importance is the variety of the relationships and which type of organizational configuration is successful.

The merger of two firms in order to acquire financial resources has often spelled the end of innovation. Access to informational resources is often closed off through imposed managerial systems. The processing capacity for the informational resource is often lost as the best engineering and production talent leave the acquired firm because of the imposition of a different managerial style and organizational culture. Different organizational cultures may maximize different aspects of the technology. A less inclusive relationship, such as a partial equity acquisition or the symbiotic network relationship discussed above, may actually increased innovation and the diffusion of innovation, and allow for the necessary production and marketing follow through which will increase the firm's survival chances in the techno-global market.

GOVERNMENT POLICY

In this new strategic environment, the government's primary responsibility will be to foster the type of conditions which increase the supply of both types of resources for innovation. In order to do this governmental leaders must develop some vision of where they wish to move the American economy and nation in the next twenty years. This vision must be a civilian one. One of the central foci of this should be on encouraging the development of industrial/technological teams. An example of such teams now exists because of the internal funding activities of firms such as Cypress Semiconductor and others. Encouraging this type of activity, along with the other activities of research cooperatives, may provide the best change for U.S. business.

This will require close scrutiny of the financial and banking industries, however, to ensure that capital is available at low and predictable interest rates. It will also require that equity markets reflect the true potential of emerging industries and therefore provide another source for adequate financial resources. This is not an easy task and specific recommendations are beyond the scope of this book. However, several guidelines are forthcoming.

First, policies which are not specifically designed to effect innovation may still have effects on the development of industries. Therefore, the effects that all policies have on innovation, especially in the emerging industries such as composite materials/ceramics, biotechnology, integrated circuits, and opto-electrical devices should become a matter of course in all deliberations. Wherever possible, regulations which hinder the ability of firms to bring new products to market should be examined. Except in cases where possible harm could result to the public or the environment, all emphasis should be given to encouraging new ventures, both internally and externally funded.

Second, the world economy has entered an era where dominance in the older machine technologies does not guarantee dominance in the newer electronic, biological, and material science technologies. Therefore, policies which specifically affect innovation and help protect these infant technologies/industries should be developed. This may include positive incentives for further growth, such as tax credits. It may also include restrictions on the degree of foreign penetration into these new industrial/technological combinations. Policies which encourage the development of industrial teams, such as tax credits for internal funding, will be necessary.

Third, if these policies effect the financial resources in isolation of the informational resources, the impact on innovation will be muted. Finally, policies which are designed to foster radical or major innovations in technology may not be helpful to the follow through on the commercialization of these technologies. Therefore, policy makers must be attuned to the different set of conditions necessary for the invention of a radically new technology and its ultimate commercialization through the use of the learning curve.

Consequently, government policy must be aware of the role that the engineering and production worker play, especially as it relates to informational resource utilization. Human resource policies must encourage the development of talent and the stable and steady supply of it. Education and training policies will play an important role over the long term. However, careful attention must be paid so that a repeat of a fiasco such as the sudden surplus of aeronautical engineers following the decline of the space program is not repeated. The global environment for integrated circuits and other technology-intensive industries is less forgiving in the 1990s than was the aerospace environment in the 1970s. Hence, the government must rethink its policies with respect to the emerging industries such as integrated circuits, biotechnology, composite materials and ceramics, opto-electric devices, and artificial intelligence, on both the tax and financial end as well as the human resource end. There needs to be careful attention to the balance between supply and demand for highly trained workers and retraining when necessary.

As a technology emerges as a useful commercial venture, a primary need is for well-trained engineers. The development of centers for excellence in technology housed in educational institutions is one manner of assuring a ready supply of such talent. These centers should not be limited to the design end of the technology, nor to producing research confined to the frontiers of knowledge. The funding of centers which are concerned with the production and process technologies and the applied dimension of technology must occur. Otherwise, the fate of the DRAM will be repeated.

This vision should also recognize that traditional organizational structures and institutional arrangements will not be enough to carry out the continued innovation that is part of the techno-global environment. Consequently, new forms must be tied. Business, government, labor, educators, and the general public must take part in the defining these new forms, since all are stakeholders in them. It is only through the recognition that all of us have a stake in the outcome that we can influence that outcome to the betterment of all.

Bibliography

Abegglen, James C., and George Stalk, Jr. *Kaisha: The Japanese Corporation*. New York: Basic Books, 1985.

Abernathy, William J., Kim B. Clark, and Alan M. Kantrow. *Industrial Renaissance: Producing a Competitive Future for America*. New York: Basic Books, 1983.

Abernathy William J., and James M. Utterback. "Patterns of Industrial Innovation." In Tushman and Moore, eds., *Readings in the Management of Innovation*. 1982: 97–108.

Abernathy, William J., and Kenneth Wayne. "Limits of the Learning Curve." In Tushman and Moore, eds., *Readings in The Management of Innovation*. 1982: 109–121.

Allen, G. C. *The Japanese Economy*. New York: St. Martin's, 1981.

Armour, Henry Ogden, and David J. Teece. "Organizational Structure and Economic Performance: A Test of the Multidivisional Hypothesis." *Bell Journal of Economics*, Vol. 9, No. 1, Spring 1978: 106–122.

Arrow, Kenneth. *Essays in the Theory of Risk Bearing*. Chicago: Markham, 1971.

Arthur D. Little, Inc. *Barriers to Innovation in Industry: Opportunities for Public Change*. Washington, D.C.: National Science Foundation, 1973.

Axelrod, Robert. *The Evolution of Cooperation*. New York: Basic Books, 1984.

Ayers, Robert U. *The Next Industrial Revolution: Reviving Industry Through Innovation*. Cambridge: Ballinger, 1984.

B. A. Asia Consulting Group. *The Japanese Semiconductor Industry 1981/1982*. Hong Kong: B. A. Asia, 1982.

Baba, Marietta L. "The Local Knowledge Content of Technology-Based Firms: Re-Thinking Informal Organization." Conference on Managing the High Technology Firm, Boulder, Colorado, January 13–15, 1988.

Barney, Clifford. "Winds of Change Sweep the Industry." *Electronics*, Vol. 60, No. 7, April 2, 1987: 62–67.

Barny, Jay B. "The Relationship Between A Firm and Its Primary Investors: An Application of the Agency Costs and Efficiency Models." Unpublished manuscript, UCLA, July, 1982.

Berk, Richard A., Donnie M. Hoffman, Judith E. Maki, David Rauma, and Hurbert Wong. "Estimation Procedures for Pooled Cross-Sectional and Time Series Data." *Evaluation Quarterly*, Vol. 3, No. 3, August, 1979: 385–410.

Betz, Frederick. *Managing Technology: Competing Through New Ventures, Innovation and Corporate Research*. Englewood Cliffs: Prentice-Hall, 1987.

Borrus, Michael G. *Competing for Control: America's Stake in Microelectronics*. Cambridge: Ballinger, 1988.

Bruno, Albert V., and Arnold C. Cooper. "Patterns of Development and Acquisition for Silicon Valley Startups." *Technovation*, Vol. 1, 1982: 275–290.

Business Week. "Computers: Japan comes on strong." October 23, 1989: 104–112.

Butler, John E. "Theories of Technological Innovation as Useful Tools for Corporate Strategy." *Strategic Management Journal*, Vol. 9, No. 1, January–February 1988: 15–29.

Bylinski, Gene. "The Comeback of the Chip of the Future." *Fortune*, Vol. 108, No. 8, October 17, 1983: 85–86, 88, 90, 92.

Caves, Richard E., and Masu Uekusa. *Industrial Organization in Japan*. The Brookings Institution, Washington, D.C.: 1976.

Chou, Ya-lun. *Statistical Analysis*. New York: Holt, Rinehart and Winston, 1975.

Clark, Kim B. "The Interaction of Design Hierarchies and Market Concepts in Technological Evolution." *Research Policy*, Vol. 14, 1985: 235–251.

Clark, Rodney. *The Japanese Company*. New Haven: Yale University Press, 1979.

Cohen, Stephen S., and John Zysman. "Why Manufacturing Matters: The Myth of the Post-Industrial Economy." *California Management Review*, Vol. XXIX, No. 3, Spring 1987: 9–26.

Comptroller General of the United States. *Industrial Policy: Japan's Flexible Approach*. Washington, D.C.: U.S. General Accounting Office, June 23, 1982.

Congressional Budget Office. *The Industrial Policy Debate*. Washington, D.C.: U.S. Government Printing Office, December, 1983.

Corrigan, Richard. "Choosing Winners and Losers: Business, Labor and Political Leaders Are Searching for a U.S. Industrial Policy." *National Journal*, Vol. 15, No. 9, February 26, 1983: 416–452.

Dataquest, Inc. *Japanese Semiconductor Alliances: Memories and Microprocessors Dominate*. San Jose: Dataquest, Inc. October, 1989.

Dataquest, Inc. *MOS static and dynamic RAM shipments, second half 1983—year-end-review*. San Jose: Dataquest, Inc., May 15, 1984.

Dataquest, Inc. *MOS static and dynamic RAM shipments, second half 1989—year-end review*. San Jose: Dataquest, Inc., May 15, 1989.

Davies, Howard. "Technology Transfer Through Commercial Transactions." *The Journal of Industrial Economics*, Vol. XXVI, No. 2, December, 1977: 161–175.

Davies, Stephan. *The Diffusion of Process Innovation*. New York: Cambridge University Press, 1979.

Davis, Dwight B. "U.S. semi equipment makers must move the earth to survive." *Electronic Business*, May 14, 1990: 44–49.

Defense Science Board, "Report of the Defense Science Board Task Force on Semiconductor Dependency." Office of the Undersecretary of Defense for Acquisition, Washington, D.C., February 1987.

Dempa Publications. *Japan Fact Book '74: Complete Guide to Japanese Manufacturers in the Electric and Electronic Industries*. Tokyo: Dempa Publications, 1974.

Dempa Publications. *Japan Fact Book '79: Comprehension Guide to Japan's Electronic Industry and Manufacturers*. Tokyo: Dempa Publications, 1979.

Dempa Publications. *Japan Fact Book '80: Comprehension Guide to Japan's Electronic Industry and Manufacturers*. Tokyo: Dempa Publications, 1980.

Dempa Publications. *Japan Electronics Almanac 1981: Japan's Electronic Industry and Leading Firms*. Tokyo: Dempa Publications, 1981.

Dempa Publications. *Japan Electronics Almanac 1982: Japan's Electronic Industry and Leading Firms*. Tokyo: Dempa Publications, 1982.

Dempa Publications. *Japan Electronics Almanac 1983: Japan's Electronic Industry and Leading Firms*. Tokyo: Dempa Publications, 1983.

Denshi Kiki Ka, Tsu San Sangyo Sho. *Handotai Sangyo to Wa Ga Kuni no Seisaku*. MITI, June 1983.

Denki Kiki Shijo Chosa Kaihen. *Denshi Shijo Yoran 1971*. Tokyo: Kagaku Shinbun Sha, 1971.

Denki Kiki Shijo Chosa Kaihen. *Denshi Shijo Yoran 1972–1973*. Tokyo: Kagaku Shinbun Sha, 1973.

Denki Kiki Shijo Chosa Kaihen. *Denshi Shijo Yoran 1974*. Tokyo: Kagaku Shinbun Sha, 1974.

Denki Kiki Shijo Chosa Kaihen. *Denshi Shijo Yoran 1975*. Tokyo: Kagaku Shinbun Sha, 1975.

Denki Kiki Shijo Chosa Kaihen. *Denshi Shijo Yoran 1976*. Tokyo: Kagaku Shinbun Sha, 1976.

Denki Kiki Shijo Chosa Kaihen. *Denshi Shijo Yoran 1977*. Tokyo: Kagaku Shinbun Sha, 1977.

Denki Kiki Shijo Chosa Kaihen. *Denshi Shijo Yoran 1978*. Tokyo: Kagaku Shinbun Sha, 1978.

Denki Kiki Shijo Chosa Kaihen. *Denshi Shijo Yoran 1979*. Tokyo: Kagaku Shinbun Sha, 1979.

Denki Kiki Shijo Chosa Kaihen. *Denshi Shijo Yoran 1980*. Tokyo: Kagaku Shinbun Sha, 1980.

Dertouzos, Michael L., Richard K. Lester, and Robert M. Solow. *Made in America: Regaining the Productive Edge*. Cambridge: MIT Press, 1989.

DeYoung, H. Garrett. "Reinforcing the Composites Market," *High Technology*, Vol. 7, No. 2, February, 1987: 12.

Dodwell Marketing Consultants. *Industrial Groupings in Japan 1982/1983*. Tokyo: Dodwell Marketing Consultants, 1982.

Dodwell Marketing Consultants. *Industrial Groups in Japan 1986/1987*. Tokyo: Dodwell Marketing Consultants, 1986.

Dosci, Giovanni. *Technical Change and Industrial Transformation: Theory and an Application to the Semiconductor Industry*. London: The MacMillian Press, 1984.

Editor. "Electrical Communication Laboratory of NTT." *Science and Technology in Japan*, Vol. 3, No. 9, January 1, 1984: 42–44.

Editor. "Electrotechnical Laboratory (ETL)." *Science and Technology in Japan*, Vol. 3, No. 9, January 1, 1984: 42–44.

Eklund, M. H., and W. I. Strauss, eds. *Status 1982: A Report on the Integrated Circuit Industry*. Scottsdale: Integrated Circuit Engineering Corporation, 1982.

Eklund, M. H. and W. I. Strauss, eds. *Status 1983: A Report on the Integrated Circuit Industry*. Scottsdale: Integrated Circuit Engineering Corporation, 1983.

Evenson R. E. "Agriculture." In Nelson, ed., *Government and Technical Progress: A Cross-Industry Analysis*. 1982: 233–282.

Ferguson, Charles H. "From the People Who Brought You Voodoo Economics," *Harvard Business Review*, May–June, 1988: 55–62.

Flaherty, Therese, M. "Market Share, Technology Leadership and Competition in International Semiconductor Markets." in Richard S. Rosenbloom, ed., *Research on Technological Innovation, Management and Policy*. Volume 1. London: JAI Press, 1983.

Friedman, Philip, Sanford V. Berg, and Jerome Duncan. "External vs. internal knowledge acquisition: joint venture activity and R&D intensity," *Journal of Economic and Business*, Vol. 31, No. 2, Winter, 1979: 103–110.

Futia, Carl A. "Schumpeterian Competition." *Quarterly Journal of Economics*, Vol. 94, No. 4, June, 1980: 675–695.

Gerstenfeld, Arthur and Brainard, Robert, eds. *Technological Innovation: Government/Industry Cooperation*. New York: John Wiley & Sons, 1979.

Gilder, George. "The Revitalization of Everything: The Law of the Microcosm." *Harvard Business Review*, March–April, 1988: 49–61.

Gold, Bela, Gerhard Rosegger, and Myles G. Boylan, Jr. *Evaluating Technological Innovations*. Lexington: D.C. Heath, 1980.

Grabowski, Henry G., and Vernon, John M. "The Pharmaceutical Industry." in Nelson, ed., *Government and Technical Progress: A Cross-Industry Analysis*. 1982: 283–360.

Gramlich, Edward M. *The Benefits and Risks of Federal Funding for Sematech*. The Congress of the United States, Congressional Budget Office, September 1987.

Grayson, Jr., C. Jackson, and Carla O'Dell. *American Business: A Two-Minute Warning*. New York: The Free Press, 1988.

Hadley, Eleanor, M. *Antitrust in Japan*. Princeton: Princeton University Press, 1970.

Halberstam, David. *The Reckoning*. New York: William Morrow, 1986.

Hanson, Dirk. *The New Alchemists: Silicon Valley and the Microelectronics Revolution*. Boston: Little, Brown, 1982.

Hardin, Russel. "Collective Action as an Agreeable n-Prisoner's Dilemma." in Brian Bary and Russell Hradin, eds., *Rational Man and Irrational Society?* Beverly Hills: 1982.

Hause, John C. "The Measurement of Concentrated Industrial Structure and the Size Distribution of Firms." *Annals of Economic and Social Measurement*, Vol. 6, No. 1, 1977: 73–107.

Hays, Robert H., and William J. Abernathy. "Managing Our Way to Decline." in Michael L. Tushman and William L. Moore, eds., *Readings in the Management of Innovation*. 1982: 11–25.

Hazewindus, Nico, with John Tooker, *The U.S. Microelectronics Industry: Technical Change, Industry Growth and Social Impact*. New York: Pergamon Press, 1982.

Henkel, Robert W. "Is this the ultimate technology alliance?" *Electronics*, Vol. 60, No. 11, May 26, 1988: 3.

Hiraoka, Leslie S. "U.S.-Japanese Competition in High Technology Fields." *Technological Forecasting and Social Change*, Vol. 26, No. 1, August 1984: 1–10.

Hirshleifer, Jack. "The Private and Social Value of Information and the Reward to Inventive Activity." *American Economic Review*, Vol. 61, No. 4, September 1971: 561–574.

Hoefler, Don. "And the band plays on." *Microelectronic News*, May 17, 1975: 3.

Hoefler, Don C. "See you later, litigator." *Microelectronic News*, February 23, 1974: 2.

Hollerman, Leon, ed. *Japan and the United States: Economic and Political Adversaries*. Boulder: Westview, 1980.

ICE. *Status 1970: A Report on the Integrated Circuit Industry*. Scottsdale: Integrated Circuit Engineering Corporation, 1970.

ICE. *Status 1971: A Report on the Integrated Circuit Industry*. Scottsdale: Integrated Circuit Engineering Corporation, 1971.

ICE. *Status 1972: A Report on the Integrated Circuit Industry*. Scottsdale: Integrated Circuit Engineering Corporation, 1972.

ICE. *Status 1973: A Report on the Integrated Circuit Industry*. Scottsdale: Integrated Circuit Engineering Corporation, 1973.

ICE. *Status 1974: A Report on the Integrated Circuit Industry*. Scottsdale: Integrated Circuit Engineering Corporation, 1974.

ICE. *Status 1975: A Report on the Integrated Circuit Industry*. Scottsdale: Integrated Circuit Engineering Corporation, 1975.

ICE. *Status 1976: A Report on the Integrated Circuit Industry*. Scottsdale: Integrated Circuit Engineering Corporation, 1976.

ICE. *Status 1977: A Report on the Integrated Circuit Industry*. Scottsdale: Integrated Circuit Engineering Corporation, 1977.

ICE. *Status 1978: A Report on the Integrated Circuit Industry*. Scottsdale: Integrated Circuit Engineering Corporation, 1978.

ICE. *Status 1979: A Report on the Integrated Circuit Industry*. Scottsdale: Integrated Circuit Engineering Corporation, 1979.

ICE. *Status 1980: A Report on the Integrated Circuit Industry*. Scottsdale: Integrated Circuit Engineering Corporation, 1980.

ICE. *Status 1981: A Report on the Integrated Circuit Industry*. Scottsdale: Integrated Circuit Engineering Corporation, 1981.

Imai, Kenichi, and Akimitsu Sakuma. "An Analysis of Japan-U.S. Semiconductor Friction." *Economic Eye* Vol. 4, No. 2, June, 1983: 14–18.

Imai, Kenichi, and Akimitsu Sakuma. "An Industrial Organization Analysis of the Semiconductor Industry: A U.S. Japan Comparison." Discussion Paper No.

113, Institute of Business Research, Hitotsubashi University, Tokyo, Japan, December, 1983.

Inaba, Minoru. "For 64M DRAMs NEC Develops ECR Plasma Etching." *Electronic News*, June 11, 1990: 24.

Inaba, Minoru. "Japan Funds Synchrotron R&D for X-ray Litho: Target 0.2-Microns for Future DRAMs." *Electronic News*, May 21, 1990: 36–37.

Inoue, Yuko. "Japanese firms rapidly increase global research and development." *The Japan Economic Journal*. September 24, 1988: 6.

Japan Electronics Industry Association. *Shuseki Kairo Guido Bukku*. Japan Electronics Industry Association, 1984.

Jensen, M. C., and Meckling, W. H. "Theory of the Firm: Managerial Behavior, Agency Costs and Ownership Structure." *Journal of Financial Economics*, Vol. 3, No. 4, October, 1976: 305–360.

Johnson, Chalmers A. *Japan's Public Policy Companies*. Washington, D.C.: American Enterprise Institute for Public Policy Research, 1978.

Johnson, Chalmers A. *MITI and the Japanese Miracle: The Growth of Industrial Policy, 1925–1975*. Stanford: Stanford University Press, Ca., 1982.

Kagawa, Masato. "32-bit chip gives NEC processor lead." *The Japan Economic Journal*. November 18, 1989: 25.

Kamien, Morton I., and Nancy L. Schwartz. *Market Structure and Innovation*. Cambridge, U.K.: Cambridge University Press, 1982.

Kamien, Morton I., and Nancy L. Schwartz. *Market Structure and Innovation: A Survey*. June, 1971.

Katz, Barbara Goody, and Phillips Almarin. "The Computer Industry." in Nelson, ed., *Government and Technical Progress: A Cross-Industry Analysis*. 1982: 162–232.

Kerlinger, Fred N. *Foundations of Behavioral Research*, 2nd ed. New York: Holt, Rinehart and Winston, 1973.

Kitamatsu, Katsuro. "Firms add horsepower to high-tech R&D race." *The Japan Economic Journal*, December, 1988: 4.

Kitamatsu, Katsuro. "MITI fights to hold influence as Japanese firms go global." *The Japan Economic Journal*, April 1, 1989.

Kitti, Carole, and Trozzo, Charles L. *The Effect of Patent and Antitrust Laws, Regulations and Practices on Innovation*. Vol. II. Arlington: Institute for Defense Analysis, February, 1976.

Kobayashi, Koji. *Computers and Communications: A Vision of C&C*. Cambridge: MIT Press, 1986.

Kodama, Fumio. "Technological innovation drives structural changes in corporations." *The Japan Economic Journal*, June 4, 1988: 26.

Kodama, Fumio. " 'Technology Fusion' yields innovations from breakthroughs." *The Japan Economic Journal*, August 13, 1988: 22.

Kuznets, Simon. *Growth, Population, and Income Distribution*. New York: W. W. Norton & Company, 1979.

Levin, Richard C. "The Semiconductor Industry." in Nelson, ed., *Government and Technical Progress: A Cross-Industry Analysis*. 1982: 9–100.

Lewis, Jordan D. "Technology, Enterprise and American Economic Growth." *Science*. Vol. 215, No. 5, March 1982: 1204–1211.

Liebowitz, Michael R. "X-ray lithography: Wave of the future?" *Electronic Business*, November 27, 1989: 26–35.

Link, Albert N., and Gregory Tassey. *Strategies for Technology-based Competition*, Lexington, Mass.: Lexington Books, 1987.

Lowry, Glenn C. "Market Structure and Innovation." *Quarterly Journal of Economics*, Vol. 93, No. 3, August, 1979: 395–410.

Lundstedt, Sven B., and E. William Colglazier, Jr. *Managing Innovation: The Social Dimension of Creativity, Invention and Technology*. New York: Pergamon Press, 1982.

Lynn, Leonard H. *How Japan Innovates*. Boulder: Westview Press, 1982.

Magaziner, Ira C. and Thomas M. Hout. *Japanese Industrial Policy*. Berkeley: Policy Studies Institute, 1980.

Mansfield, Edwin. *Technical Change*. New York: W. W. Norton & Company, 1971.

Mansfield, Edwin. "Technical Change and the Rate of Imitation." *Econometrica*, Vol. 29, No. 4, October, 1961: 741–766.

Mansfield, Edwin, John Rapaport, Anthony Romeo, Samuel Wagner, and George Beardsley. "Social and Private Rates of Return From Industrial Innovations." *Quarterly Journal of Economics*, Vol. 91, No. 2, May, 1977: 221–240.

McClean, William J., ed. *Status 1985: A Report on the Integrated Circuit Industry*. Scottsdale, Az.: Integrated Circuit Engineering Corp., 1985.

McClean, William J., ed. *Status 1986: A Report on the Integrated Circuit Industry*. Scottsdale, Az.: Integrated Circuit Engineering Corp., 1986.

McClean, William J., ed. *Status 1987: A Report on the Integrated Circuit Industry*. Scottsdale, Az.: Integrated Circuit Engineering Corp., 1987.

McClean, William J., ed. *Status 1988: A Report on the Integrated Circuit Industry*. Scottsdale, Az.: Integrated Circuit Engineering Corp., 1988.

McClean, William J., ed. *Status 1989: A Report on the Integrated Circuit Industry*. Scottsdale, Az.: Integrated Circuit Engineering Corp., 1989.

McGreivy, Denis J., and Kenneth A. Pickar. *VLSI Technologies Through the 80's and Beyond*. New York: Institute of Electrical and Electronic Engineers, Inc., 1982.

McLean, Mick, ed. The Japanese Electronic Challenge. London: Frances Pinter Publishers, 1982.

Mensch, Gerhard. *Stalemate in Technology: Innovation Overcomes Depression*. Cambridge, Mass.: Ballinger, 1979.

Methé, David T. *Technology, Transaction Costs, and the Diffusion of Innovation: The Evolution of the United States and Japanese DRAM Integrated Circuit Industries*. University of California, Irvine, unpublished dissertation, 1985.

Methé, David T. "Innovation, Institutions and Strategies: The Evolution of United States and Japanese Firms in the DRAM Industry." Presented at the Strategic Management Society Sixth Annual Conference, Singapore, October 1986.

Methé, David T. "The Influence of Technology and Demand Factors on Firm Size and Industrial Structure." *Reseach Policy*, forthcoming, 1991.

Methé, David T., and James L. Perry. "Incremental Approaches to Strategic Management." In *Handbook of Strategic Management*, ed. Jack Rabin,

Gerald J. Miller, and W. Bartley Hildreth. New York: Marcel Dekker, Inc., 1989.

Mitsusada, Hisayuki. "Fuzzy logic moving smoothly into the home." The Japan Economic Journal, June 16, 1990: 14.

Mowery, David C., and Nathan Rosenberg. "The Commercial Aircraft Industry." in Nelson, ed., Government and Technical Progress: A Cross-Industry Analysis. 1982: 101–161.

Mowery, David C., and Nathan Rosenberg. Technology and the Pursuit of Economic Growth. Cambridge: Cambridge University Press, 1989.

Mueller, D. C., and Tilton, J. E. "Research and Development Costs as Barriers to Entry." Canadian Journal of Economics, Vol. 2, No. 4, November, 1969: 570–579.

Musgrave, Richard A., and Peggy B. Musgrave. Public Finance in Theory and Practice. Second Edition. New York: McGraw-Hill, 1976.

Myers, Sumner, and Eldon E. Sweezy. "Why Innovations Fail." Technology Review, Vol. 80, No. 5, March/April 1978.

Nagata, Kiyoshi. "The Culture Gap: Does It Limit Trade?" Mitsubishi Research Institute's Inside Japan Seminar Part II, Honolulu, Hawaii, September 15, 1983.

Nakao, Takeo. "Profit Rates and Market Shares of Leading Industrial Firms in Japan." The Journal of Industrial Economics, Vol. 27, No. 4, June, 1979: 371–383.

Nasbeth, L., and G. F. Ray. The Diffusion of New Industrial Processes: An International Study. Cambridge University Press, 1974.

Nelson, Richard R., ed. Government and Technical Progress: A Cross-Industry Analysis. New York: Pergamon Press, 1982.

Nelson, Richard R., and Sidney G. Winter. An Evolutionary Theory of Economic Change. Cambridge, Mass.: The Belknap Press of the Harvard University Press, 1982.

Nelson, Richard R., and Sidney G. Winter. "Forces Generating and Limiting Concentration Under Schumpeterian Competition." Bell Journal of Economics, Vol. 9, No. 2, Autumn, 1978: 524–548.

Nelson, Richard R., and Sidney G. Winter. "In Search of Useful Theory of Innovation." Research Policy Vol. 6, 1977: 36–76.

Nihon Kaihatsu Ginko, and Chosa Bu. "IC Sangyo '80 Nendai No Tembo." Chosa, January, 1984.

Nishimura, Yoshio. "Joho Purosesu No Bun Kyoku Ga Shinkoku Ka." Nikkei Electronics, October 24, 1983: 88–92.

Noll, Roger G., et. al. Government Policies and Technological Innovation. Vol. 1. Washington, D.C.: National Science Foundation, May, 1975.

Nomura Research Institute. SEMI Japanese Semiconductor Industry Report. Mountain View, California: Semiconductor Equipment and Materials Institute, 1983.

Nonaka, Ikujiro, Tadao Kagono, and Shiori Sakamoto. "Evolutionary Strategy and Structure: A New Perspective on Japanese Management." Discussion Paper No. 111, Institute of Business Research, Hitotsubashi University, March, 1983.

Okuda, Kenji. "The Role of Engineers in Japanese Industry and Education: An

Industrial Sociologist's View." *Journal of Japanese Trade and Industry*. Vol. 2. No. 5, September/October, 1983: 23–26.

Olson, Mancur. *The Logic of Collective Action*. Cambridge, Mass.: Harvard University Press, 1965.

Omichi, Yasunori. *Handotai Denshi Buhin Gyokai*. Tokyo: Kyoiku Sha, 1982.

Ouchi, William G. "Markets, Bureaucracies and Clans." *Administrative Science Quarterly*, Vol. 25, 1980: 129–141.

Peck, Merton, J., and Akira Groto. "Technological and Economic Growth: The Case of Japan." in Michael L. Tushman and William L. Moore, eds., *Readings in the Management of Innovation*. 1982: 626–641.

Phillips, Almain. *Technology and Market Structure: A Study of the Aircraft Industry*. Lexington, Mass.: D.C. Heath and Company, 1971.

Prindl, Andreas R. *Japanese Finance: A Guide to Banking in Japan*. New York: John Wiley & Sons, 1981.

Rao, Potluri, and Roger LeRoy Miller. *Applied Econometrics*. Belmont, California: Wadsworth Publishing Co., 1971.

Rayner, Bruce C. P. "For Cypress, growing fast means thinking small." *Electronic Business*, April 30, 1990: 35–38.

Robertson, Jack. "To Regain Consumer Market: Semicon Group Urges Private Capital Firm." *Electronic News*, November 27, 1989: 8.

Rogers, Everett M. *Diffusion of Innovations*. Third Edition. New York: The Free Press, 1983.

Rogers, Everett M., and Judith K. Larsen. *Silicon Valley Fever: Growth of High-Technology Culture*. New York: Basic Books, 1984.

Rosenbloom, Richard S., ed. *Research on Technological Innovation, Management, and Policy*. Volume 1. London: JAI Press, 1983.

Rosenbloom, Richard S., and Robert A. Burgelman, eds. *Research on Technological Innovation, Management and Policy*. Vol. 4, Greenwich, Conn.: JAI Press Inc., 1989.

Rosenbloom, Richard S., and Michael A. Cusumano. "Technological Pioneering and Competitive Advantage: The Birth of the VCR Industry." *California Management Review*, Vol. 29, No. 4, Summer 1987: 51–76.

Ruttan, Vernon W. "Usher and Schumpeter on Invention, Innovation and Technological Change." *Quarterly Journal of Economics*, Vol. 73, No. 4, November 1959: 599–606.

Sahal, Devendra. *Patterns of Technological Innovation*. Reading, Mass.: Addison-Wesley, 1981.

Sahal, Devendra. "A Theory of Evolution of Technology." *International Journal of Systems Science*, Vol. 10, No. 3, 1979: 259–274.

Saito, Masaru. "Internal Transfer and Technology Transfer From Abroad: Japanese Experience." Workshop on Technology Transfer and Plan, Kuala Lumpur, December, 1983.

Samuelson, Paul A. "The Pure Theory of Public Expenditure." *Review of Economics and Statistics*, Vol. 36, 1954: 387–389.

Sanger, David E. "Trying to Regain the Market in Chips." *The New York Times*, March 8, 1987, E 7.

Schlender, Brenton R. "Apple, Digital Equipment Outline Pact to Devise Ways to Link Their Computers." *The Wall Street Journal*. January 18, 1988: 6.

Schlender, Brenton R., and Stephen Kreider Yoder. "Falling Chips: U.S.-Japanese Accord on Semiconductors Has an Impact, but Not the One That Was Hoped For." *The Wall Street Journal*. February 12, 1987: 10.

Schumpeter, Joseph, A. *Business Cycles: A Theoretical, Historical and Statistical Analysis of the Capitalist Process*. New York: McGraw-Hill, 1939.

Semiconductor Industry Association. *SIA 1980–1981 Yearbook and Directory*. San Jose: Semiconductor Industry Association, 1981.

Semiconductor Industry Association. *SIA 1983–84 Yearbook and Directory*. San Jose: Semiconductor Industry Association, 1983.

Semiconductor Industry Association. *SIA 1985–86 Yearbook and Directory* San Jose: Semiconductor Industry Association, 1983.

Semiconductor Industry Association. *SIA 1988 Yearbook and Directory*. San Jose: Semiconductor Industry Association, 1988.

Scherer, F. M. *Industrial Market Structure and Economic Performance*. Boston: Houghton Mifflin, 1980.

Schnee, Jerome R. "Government Programs and the Growth of High-Technology Industries." In Tushman and Moore, eds., *Readings in the Management of Innovation*. 1982.

Science and Technology Agency, *White Paper on Science and Technology 1988: Towards the Establishment of a New Creative Research Environment*. Tokyo: Science and Technology, December, 1988.

Science and Technology Agency. *STA: Its Roles and Activities 1987*. Tokyo: Science and Technology Agency, 1988.

Science and Technology Agency. *STA Today*, Vol. 2, No. 4, April, 1990.

Science and Technology Agency. *STA Today*, Vol. 2, No. 5, May, 1990.

Science and Technology Agency. *STA Today*, Vol. 2, No. 6, June, 1990.

Science and Technology Agency. *STA Today*, Vol. 2, No. 7, June, 1990.

Shimura, Yukio. *IC Sangyo Dai Senso*. Tokyo: Daimond Sha, 1981.

Shimura, Yukio. *IC Sangyo Saizen Sen*. Tokyo: Daimond Sha, 1980.

Spence, A. Michael. "The Learning Curve and Competition." *Bell Journal of Economics*, Vol. 12, No. 1, Spring, 1981: 49–70.

Spital, Francis C. "Gaining Market Share Advantage in the Semiconductor Industry by Lead Time in Innovation." In Richard S. Rosenbloom, ed., *Research on Technological Innovation, Management and Policy*, Volume 1. London: JAI Press, 1983.

Solow, Robert M. "Technical Change and the Aggregate Production Function." *Review of Economics and Statistics*. Vol. 36, 1957: 312–320.

Strauss, William I. ed. *Status 1984: A Report on the Integrated Circuit Industry*. Scottsdale, Arizona: Integrated Circuit Engineering Corporation, 1984.

Sugano, Takuo. "Preparation of New Electronic Professionals in Japan." Paper presented at The Japan Society Meeting, Palo Alto, California, May 1, 1981.

Sunohara, Tsuyoshi. "Japan firms aim for 32-bit MPUs: Makers pin hope on RISC, non-computer markets." *The Japan Economic Journal*, June 2, 1990: 15.

Takai, Toshio. "Setting the Record Straight on Semiconductors." *Journal of Japanese Trade and Industry*, Vol. 2, No. 4, July/August 1983: 24–30.

Tarui, Yasuo. "Basic Technology for VLSI (Part II)." *IEEE Transactions on Electron Devices*, Vol. 27, No. 8, August, 1980: 1321–1331.

Tarui, Yasuo. "Cho LSI Kyodo Kenkyu Jo No Kiroku." *Shizen*, September 1981: 34–41.

Tatsuno, Sheridan. "Matchmaking Japanese Style: The Surge in Japanese Strategic Alliances Continues." *Japanese Research Newsletter*. San Jose, Ca.: Dataquest, January, 1986.

Technology Research and Information Division. "Outline of Science and Technology Activities in Japan." Tokyo: National Institute of Science and Technology Policy, May 1989.

Teece, David J. "Economics of Scope and the Scope of the Enterprise." *Journal of Economic Behavior and Organization*, Vol. 1, 1980: 223–247.

Teece, David J. "Internal Organization and Economic Performance: An Empirical Analysis of the Profitability of Principal Firms." *The Journal of Industrial Economics*, Vol. 30, No. 2, December, 1981: 173–200.

Teece, David J. "Technology Transfer by Multinational Firms: The Resource Cost of Transferring Technological Know-How." *The Economic Journal*, Vol. 87, June, 1977: 242–261.

Thorelli, Hans B. "Networks: Between Markets and Hierarchies." *Strategic Management Journal*, January–February, 1986: 37–51.

Tilton, John E. *International Diffusion of Technology: The Case of Semiconductors.* Washington, D.C.: The Brookings Institution, 1971.

Tornatzky, Louis G., and Mitchell Fleischer, *The Process of Technological Innovation.* Lexington, Mass.: Lexington Books, 1990.

Toyo, Keizai. *Japan Company Handbook*. Tokyo: Toyo Keizai, 1989.

Tsu San Sho. *Sangyo Gijutsu no Doko to Kadai*. Tokyo, 1988.

Tushman, Michael L., and William L. Moore. *Readings in the Management of Innovation*. Marshfield: Pitman Publishing, 1982.

U.S. Congress, Joint Economic Committee. *Policies for Industrial Growth in a Competitive World*. Washington, D.C.: U.S. Government Printing Office, April 27, 1984.

U.S. House of Representatives, Committee on Science and Technology. *Research and Development Joint Ventures*. Washington, D.C. U.S. Government Printing Office, July 12, 1983.

U.S. House of Representatives, Subcommittee on Trade of the Committee on Ways and Means. *High Technology and Japanese Industrial Policy: A Strategy for U.S. Policymakers*. Washington, D.C.: U.S. Government Printing Office, October 1, 1980.

U.S. National Science Foundation. *Research and Development in Industry 1972*. Washington, D.C.: National Science Foundation, NSF 74–312, 1972.

U.S. National Science Foundation. *The Science and Technology Resources of Japan: A Comparison with the United States*. Washington, D.C.: National Science Foundation, NSF 88–318, 1988.

U.S. Senate, Committee on the Judicary. *The Patent Term Restoration Act of 1983*. Washington, D.C.: U.S. Government Printing Office, June 22, 1983.

Utterback, James M. "Innovation in Industry and the Diffusion of Technology." in Michael L. Tushman and William L. Moore, eds., *Readings in the Management of Innovation*. 1982: 29–41.

Verner, Liipfert, Bernhard and McPherson. *The Effect of Government Targeting on World Semiconductor Competition*. Cupertino, California: Semiconductor Industry Association, 1983.

von Hippel, Eric. "The Dominant Role of Users in the Scientific Instrument Innovation Process." *Research Policy*, Vol. 5, 1976: 212–239.

White, Lawrence J. "The Motor Vehical Industry." in Nelson, ed., *Government and Technical Progress: A Cross-Industry Analysis*. 1982: 411–450.

Williamson, Oliver E. *Markets and Hierarchies: Analysis and Antitrust Implications*. New York: The Free Press, 1975.

Wilson, Robert W., Peter K. Ashton Thomas P. Egan. *Innovation, Competition, and Government Policy in the Semiconductor Industry*. Lexington, Mass.: D.C. Heath and Company, 1980.

Yano, Keizai Kenkyu Jo. *1982–83 Denshi Buhin Sangyo Nenkan*. Tokyo: Yano Keizai Kenkyu Jo, 1983.

Yano, Keizai Kenkyu J. *1984 Handotai Sangy no Chuki Juyo Tembo*. Tokyo: Yano Keizai Kenkyu Jo, 1984.

Yano Keizai Kenkyu J. *1984 Handotai Sangy no Chuki Yosoko*. Tokyo: Yano Keizai Kenkyu Jo, 1984.

Zipper, Stuart. "See 256K Dynamic RAM Market Segmenting As Suppliers Field Variety of Bit Protocols." *Electronic News*, Vol. 30, No. 1509, August 6, 1984: 1, 82–83, 89.

Index